CALLED TO BE THE CHILDREN OF GOD

CALLED TO BE THE CHILDREN OF GOD

The Catholic Theology of Human Deification

Edited by

DAVID VINCENT MECONI, S.J.

CARL E. OLSON

IGNATIUS PRESS SAN FRANCISCO

All citations from official Church documents, unless otherwise indicated, have been taken from the Vatican website (http://w2.vatican.va/content/vatican/en.html).

Cover art:
The Transfiguration
By Theophanes the Greek
15th century icon
Tretyakov Gallery, Moscow, Russia
Wikimedia Commons

Cover design by Carl E. Olson

ISBN 978-1-58617-947-2
Library of Congress Control Number 2014944006
Printed in the United States of America ♾

CONTENTS

FOREWORD

Scott Hahn

Christianity is about salvation. Jesus made that clear, and the New Testament is about nothing else. "For the Son of man came to seek and to save the lost" (Lk 19:10). "I did not come to judge the world but to save the world" (Jn 12:47). Believers have always looked to Jesus as "Savior". All who profess the Christian religion—or even simply study it from afar—can agree upon that one simple fact. The most ancient sources agree with the most recent tracts left behind on the subway, the claims of viral emails, and the scrawl of roadside graffiti ("Jesus Saves!"). "The saying is sure and worthy of full acceptance, that Christ Jesus came into the world to save sinners" (1 Tim 1:15).

But what do we mean when we speak of salvation? Ask a hundred Christians today, and you will hear many answers, but most come down to this: Jesus saves us from sin and death. Rescue from sin and death is indeed a wonderful thing—but the salvation won for us by Jesus Christ is incomparably greater. And *that* is the subject of this book.

Salvation is much more than most people believe and hope it could be. For we are not merely saved *from* sin; we are saved *for* sonship, to be divinely adopted sons and daughters of God. Forgiveness is the precondition for God's greater gift, the gift that will last beyond our death: the gift of divine life.

God adopts us as children, so that we can share the life of the eternal Son, Jesus Christ. He can only adopt us, however, when we have come to share his nature. Adoption and fatherhood imply a certain commonality, a degree of sameness. I can be a father to any living human being by means of adoption; but I cannot adopt my pets, no matter how much affection I feel toward them. Adoption requires a sharing of life; and so God gives us by grace what the eternal Son possesses from all eternity. God gives us a created share of his uncreated nature. When we are saved, we participate in Jesus' divinity. We become "partakers of the divine nature" (2 Pet 1:4).

The early Church Fathers were so bold as to call this process "divinization" and "deification", because it is the means by which we enter the life of the Trinity, the eternal family of God. Salvation could not get any better than this. We are God's children now. This is our primary identity (see 1 Jn 3:1–2), and this is the primary reason why the Word became flesh. God stooped down to become man in order to raise us up as his children. Thus we are made divine. Saint Basil the Great put it boldly, in A.D. 375 in his *De Spiritu Sancto*, when he enumerated the gifts of the Spirit: "abiding in God, being made like God—and, highest of all, being made God" (9.23).

This is classic Christianity. In recent centuries, however, this primal language of salvation has fallen into disuse in the Western Church. Its decline began in the late Middle Ages, with the nominalist corruption of philosophy and then theology. It is still present, though faintly, in the works of the Protestant reformer Martin Luther. It is identifiable, but barely, in Luther's later contemporary, John Calvin; but it vanishes entirely in subsequent generations of Protestantism. Even in the Catholic Church, the idea of divinization got lost amid all the post-Reformation disputes over the relationship of faith, works, and justification. For four centuries, Catholic and Protestant theologians alike focused so narrowly on these controversies that they obscured the central fact of Christian salvation.

By the late nineteenth century, the Protestant historian of dogma Adolf von Harnack (1851–1930) dismissed divinization as a pagan corruption of the Bible's pristine and primitive message, which he reduced to "the Fatherhood of God and the brotherhood of man". His assertion itself, however, *requires the classic doctrine*, which (as the contributors to this book ably demonstrate) is explicit anyway in the biblical texts. Mankind cannot know God as "Father" unless we come to share the nature of the only begotten Son. We cannot know one another as brothers until we are saved—until we have become brothers in Christ and heirs with him, sharing his divine nature as he has shared our human nature.

Christ is the only begotten Son of God. So our sonship is not the same as his, but it is a participation in his. We are not God; but Jesus himself described our sonship by saying, "[Y]ou are gods" (Jn 10:34). His Sonship is uncreated and eternal. Ours is a grace; it is created and adoptive. But it is real. In the supernatural order as in the natural order, adoptive children are real children who enjoy the real paternity of their adoptive fathers.

What we have received by grace, however, is greater still than the gift we received from our parents. Through baptism, we are more truly God's children than we are children of our earthly parents. Through baptism, we are more truly at home in heaven than in the place where we grew up. Saint Maximus Confessor said that we "become completely whatever God is, save at the level of being", and we receive for ourselves "the whole of God himself", in all his infinity, in all his eternity.

This seems paradoxical: the finite contains the infinite. But it is almighty God who made it possible, by assuming human flesh in Jesus Christ. In doing so, he humanized his divinity, but he also divinized humanity; and thus he sanctified—made holy—everything that fills up a human life. This book in all its parts, like Christianity in all its parts, is about salvation. But that means it's about everything that fills our lives, on earth and in heaven.

INTRODUCTION

The apostolic and Catholic faith is the continuation, imitation, and appropriation of Christ's own life. As important as ethical growth in virtue is, Christianity can never be a religion of law and moral bookkeeping. Rather, the new way of life in Christ is ultimately the essence of love: for the lover is never content simply gazing upon the beloved but longs to be mutually transformed into the other, thereby becoming no longer two but one. This is the heart of love, to find one's own eternal welfare in another. While it is commonplace for all Christians to stress God's becoming human—what theologians have named the "Incarnation"—this book wants to show what happens when such love is returned, when we humans become God—what is referred to as "deification", "divinization", or the Greek term "theosis".

This collection of essays arose out of our mutual interest in the ancient Christian teaching that, as so many of the great Church Fathers expressed it, in Christ God becomes human so we humans can become divine. What this entails and why it is the absolute fulfillment of our unique humanity and not its absorption or annihilation, how this "becoming God" is realized through prayer and sacramental worship, and how the greatest thinkers of the Church have expressed this is the purpose of the pages before you. Here you will find some of the Church's top scholars bringing their area of theological specialization to bear on the beauty of our call to become God's own divinely adopted sons and daughters, to see our Christian life as the glory of Christ's now dwelling in and as each of his baptized members.

When the Church at Galatia found freedom too demanding and too indefinite, they sought to return to the Old Law. They found in the externals of the law control and safety—there was no need for humility or vulnerability. Furthermore, the freedom found in charity was too ambiguous and bereft of the kind of certitude every religion before Christianity promised its adherents. The members of the Galatian Church were nostalgic for that day when they remained relatively in charge of their relationship with God; that is, by keeping the law they knew where they stood with God and could determine their own status as members of his sacred bond. The Torah prescribed 613 precepts (*mitzvot*) that the chosen people dutifully fulfilled so as to keep their covenant with God. It must have been quite shocking to learn from one of their own, Paul of Tarsus, that the law in fact no longer had the ability to save.

Once God had become human, there was no other way back to God except through the human. No longer was the law the measure of one's relationship with God. Love of neighbor thus became the new measure by which one understood his relationship with God. Paul therefore writes that salvation is now a matter of allowing the God-Man Jesus Christ to grow within one's soul, to inform all we think and say and do, so that we may become other Christs as he has become one of us:

> For I through the law died to the law, that I might live for God. I have been crucified with Christ; it is no longer I who live, but Christ lives in me; and the life I now live in the flesh, I live by faith in the Son of God who loved me and gave himself up for me. (Gal 2:19–20)

By giving himself up for all who have fallen short of the law, Christ has come into this world not to reestablish a law-based religion but to offer his children the freedom of allowing him to live their lives. Through our Lady's *fiat*, God has come not only to us and for us, but he has come *as* one of us, sanctifying and thus offering us his very own divine life.

This is what the earliest Christian thinkers called the "great exchange". In the Incarnation the Son lowers himself to humanity so as to elevate humans to divinity. In his kenosis is our theosis. To explain this, could the Church enroll any more foundational theologians than Saint Peter, Saint Irenaeus of Lyons, Saint Athanasius, and Saint Thomas Aquinas? This is precisely what the *Catechism of the Catholic Church* has done; it points us to the heart of the faith by teaching that

> the Word became flesh to make us "*partakers of the divine nature*" (2 Pet 1:4): "For this is why the Word became man, and the Son of

> God became the Son of man: so that man, by entering into communion with the Word and thus receiving divine sonship, might become a son of God" (St. Irenaeus, *Adv. haeres.* 3, 19, 1: PG 7/1, 939). "For the Son of God became man so that we might become God" (St. Athanasius, *De inc.*, 54, 3: PG 25, 192B). "The only-begotten Son of God, wanting to make us sharers in his divinity, assumed our nature, so that he, made man, might make men gods" (St. Thomas Aquinas, *Opusc.* 57:1–4).[1]

Notice that the Christian understanding of deification is one of participating, of becoming a *partaker*, never the possessor, of divinity—that is, Christian deification is never an autonomous sovereignty but one of humble reliance on God to inform us of all we are, to fulfill that divine image and likeness originally implanted deep within every human soul. Christian deification is not a matter of autonomy as in Mormonism, but a matter of eternally *receiving* the divine attributes that Christ longs to give his saints: charity, true wisdom, unalloyed joy, incorruptibility, and immortality.

While this phrase of our "becoming God" is ancient, this is just the message we need to place at the center of today's call for a "New Evangelization". As Pope Saint John Paul II exhorted all of us today, the Church in the twenty-first century is to help others *duc in altum*, to "[p]ut out into the deep" (Lk 5:4), by seeing how the divine longings of their hearts will be satisfied only by the God for whom we are all made.[2] We must present to the world a Christ who rushes past our own sinfulness and shortfalls in order not only to heal and embrace us, but to transform us into himself. He sends us his own Holy Spirit and thereby adopts us into his own life, making us divinely adopted sons and daughters, children of the same heavenly Father.

Accordingly, John Paul II rightly rooted the New Evangelization in the "Trinitarian shape" of the Christian life. He called us all to learn "this Trinitarian shape of Christian prayer and [to live] it fully, above all in the liturgy, the summit and source of the Church's life, but also

[1] *Catechism of the Catholic Church*, 2nd ed. (Washington, D.C.: Libreria Editrice Vaticana—United States Conference of Catholic Bishops, 2000), no. 460, emphasis in original. Hereafter all citations from the *Catechism* will be referenced in the main text as "*CCC*" with the paragraph numbers following.

[2] See Pope John Paul II, Apostolic Letter *Novo millennio ineunte*, January 6, 2001, no. 1.

in personal experience". This, John Paul argued, "is the secret of a truly vital Christianity, which has no reason to fear the future, because it returns continually to the sources and finds in them new life."[3] Eternally, the "Trinitarian shape" of the Christian life is the Father's begetting of the Son in the Spirit; economically, it is the Spirit's uniting us as adopted children in Christ before the same loving Father. As Maximus the Confessor once imagined this movement, "Because God has become human, humans can become God. He rises by divine steps corresponding to those by which God humbled himself out of love for us."[4] The steps out of which the Son descends from heaven are the very means by which we ascend: love of God and love of neighbor. This is the new life promised by the ancient faith, the new life to be preached in the New Evangelization—life in Christ. Nothing else ultimately matters.

The fifteen essays that follow take the reader through the various figures and the varying ways the Christian theology of deification has been stressed in our tradition. We begin by offering our own insights into how humanity's glorious transformation in Christ is expressed in both Sacred Scripture as well as in the first generation of Christian thinkers, the Apostolic Fathers. Daniel Keating (Sacred Heart Major Seminary) next shows how theosis was the central metaphor by which the Greek Fathers presented the Christian life, Jared Ortiz (Hope College) concentrates on the Latin Fathers, while David Meconi, S.J. (Saint Louis University) provides the towering Church Father Saint Augustine of Hippo with his own chapter. Next come the beginnings of medieval religious life with essays on divinization in Saint Thomas Aquinas and the Dominican tradition by Andrew Hofer, O.P. (the Pontifical Faculty at the Dominican House of Studies in Washington, D.C.) and in Saint Francis, Saint Clare, and the Franciscans by Sister M. Regina van den Berg, F.S.G.M. (Rome, Italy).

With the Council of Trent (1545–1563), the Church began to synthesize and formulate doctrine anew; thus, in the next chapter, Chris Burgwald (Diocese of Sioux Falls) treats the Church's theology of deification during this time of the Counter-Reformation. From

[3] Ibid., no. 32.

[4] Maximus the Confessor, *Theological and Economic Chapters* (*Patrologia Graeca* 90.1165).

there, Michon Matthiesen (Providence College) introduces us to the unique strains of divinization as taught by the French School of Spirituality, where the familiar voices of Saint Francis de Sales, Saint Thérèse of Lisieux, and others come alive in a new way as we hear how they spoke of God's deifying grace. Oxford's eminent John Saward then takes us through the "neo-Thomistic" revival of the nineteenth century. Two very important figures from that same century are given their own chapters, with Timothy Kelly (International Theological Institute) focusing on Matthias Scheeben and Daniel Lattier (Intellectual Takeout Institute) concentrating primarily on John Henry Cardinal Newman.

How divinization was being used to present the Catholic life in Christ between the end of Vatican I (1870) and the opening of the Second Vatican Council (1963) is examined by Adam Cooper (University of Melbourne), while Tracey Rowland (John Paul II Institute for Marriage and the Family) treats Vatican II and the beautiful writings of Pope Saint John Paul II. Carl Olson (Ignatius Press) next shows how the theology of deification runs throughout the *Catechism of the Catholic Church*, and David Fagerberg (University of Notre Dame) rounds things off rightly with an examination of how Catholic liturgy is the means by which we today continue to receive and thus become Christ. Finally, we would like to thank Andrew Chronister of Saint Louis University's Department of Theology for his constant laboring in editing. His careful attention and intelligent suggestions are to be found on every page.

David Meconi, S.J.
Carl E. Olson
January 25, 2016
The Conversion of Saint Paul the Apostle

Chapter One

THE SCRIPTURAL ROOTS OF CHRISTIAN DEIFICATION

David Vincent Meconi, S.J. and Carl E. Olson

This collection of essays begins where every Christian mind goes to discover the mystery and the truths of God: his sacred Word and the embodiment of this Word in the life of God's people. Accordingly, we open by examining how Christian deification is foreshadowed in the Old Testament and, then, how it receives fuller expression thereafter in the Gospels and in Saint Paul. For the human desire to be godlike is found in the opening story of our Sacred Scriptures. Adam and Eve are created for God, made in his divine image and likeness, and as the story of Israel's history unfolds, we catch deeper and deeper glimpses into what God is preparing to do fully in Christ. Yahweh initiates and enters into a transformative covenant with the chosen people he has created to become particularly his own. In that graced union, he slowly reveals the fullness of his life and how he longs to communicate it to all those made in his image.

Deification in the Old Testament

The first part of this chapter accordingly examines how deification is suggested in the Old Testament. Since the true deification of the human person is essentially a Christian doctrine, the Jewish people of God's original covenant could only foreshadow and hint at such a reality. But two fundamental principles of Christian deification find their foundation in the Old Testament. The first is God's creating Adam as a divine image and toward the divine likeness. Here we shall look at how the human person was established so as to become like God, the model in whose image he was created. The second is how God longs to unite his people to himself so as to share his otherwise unapproachable attributes. Yahweh labors so as to forge a special bond with Israel, and in this covenant the Jewish people receive a new understanding of themselves as the children of God, the bride of a new lover, and other images of intimacy. While neither of these characteristics of Judaism captures fully what occurs in God's becoming human, they do prepare the way in showing how God longs to share his life and his love, thereby making other persons ever more like him.

The anthropological bedrock of deification is found in Scripture's opening: we are made in the image and likeness of a God who brings mankind into existence in order to share his life and to rule over all other creatures:

> Then God said, "Let us make man in our image, after our likeness; and let them have dominion over the fish of the sea, and over the birds of the air, and over the cattle, and over all the earth, and over every creeping thing that creeps upon the earth." So God created man in his own image; in the image of God he created them; male and female he created them. (Gen 1:26–27)

While Christians see in the Genesis narrative here a Creator who looks at his own life of triune love and perfect self-gift ("Let us"), the first Jews heard in this command a God ruling over an assembly of other heavenly beings. Whether the "us" here is a dialogue within the Trinity or among God and a court of celestial creatures, two things are nonetheless clear. First, God creates other persons like himself, beings made for communion. In fact, in the whole of the Genesis story, we are the only creatures made for relationship, fashioned in the image and likeness of one outside ourselves. Second, the fulfillment that that need for relationship points to will not be found in the created order, as it is in the *divine* similitude, in which we have been brought into being. God alone can therefore satiate. Genesis' account of the creation of humanity thus maintains that we are brought into existence not to find eternal satisfaction in either ourselves or in the created order, but in the one in whose image and likeness we have been fashioned.

Furthermore, it would appear that fulfilling such a divine call involves not just God but two other parties. It is highly significant that the human person is the only creature whose dual gender is scripturally regarded ("male and female he created them"). Of course the author of Genesis knew how other animals are likewise created sexually "male and female", but there must be something salvific about this human covenant, this invitation to fulfill the divine image within each of us in communion with and through another. Here we also learn that the individual person is established as God's appointed steward over the rest of his good creation. Our responsibility as divine images somehow includes our care of God's creation, our role as intermediaries between the spiritual and the material orders.

But if all things are good and the divine has imprinted himself in his other selves on earth, how could sin and destruction ever be found here? This too is a matter of deification for the Jewish people. How did the enemy tempt the first humans? What did Satan hold out as the one possible allurement in order to entice Adam and Eve away from the God with whom they are eternally meant for communion?

> And the woman said to the serpent, "We may eat of the fruit of the trees of the garden; but God said, 'You shall not eat of the fruit of the tree which is in the midst of the garden, neither shall you touch it, lest you die.'" But the serpent said to the woman, "You will not die. For God knows that when you eat of it your eyes will be opened, and you will be like God, knowing good and evil." (Gen 3:2–5)

The enemy of our human nature realized that he could not tempt paradisiacal creatures like Adam and Eve with anything they already possessed perfectly. The one thing for which they were created that they still lacked was that deifying union which would transform their mere human nature into something even more glorious; that is the thing Satan knew he could use to bring humanity from God to himself: "and you will be like gods."

The groundbreaking German Old Testament scholar and orientalist Julius Wellhausen (1844–1918) famously characterized Judaism more as a monolatrism than a monotheism: more the worship (*latria* in Greek) of one God seen as dwelling over many other divine beings, than a strict recognition that one and only one deity exists—that is, the Old Testament does not hesitate to refer to God's people as gods. Satan knew this and exploited this one lack in our first parents to his own nefarious gain. In the Old Testament, there is of course one God by nature, but there are many other "gods" mentioned. The tendency in later Judaism was to understand these (lowercase) gods as either those created beings God has graciously brought into his company (for example, Ps 29:1; 89:6), or those nefarious demons who wander the world seeking the ruin of God's faithful ones (for example, Job 1:6; 2:1). It is a matter of either divinization or demonization.

Take, for example, the term "Elohim", one of the more frequent names for God in the Old Testament. This name is actually a plural noun (as are other common Hebraisms used in English today—for example, cherubim, seraphim, and the anawim). The Jewish people understood that while God's name is holy, he longs to share it by bringing his chosen people into everlasting union. For example, the divine name Elohim is used for both God himself as well as those who come close to God in Psalm 82:6 (used again by Christ in Jn 10:34): "I say, 'You are gods, sons of the Most High, all of you." God's people thus understood that as they grew in union with God, they would come to share his own heavenly life.

This is how God sends Moses to Pharaoh, as one now made like the Almighty and, therefore, one to whom human obedience is owed: "And the Lord said to Moses, 'See, I make you as God to Pharaoh; and Aaron your brother shall be your prophet'" (Ex 7:1). Having drawn close to the Unapproachable, Moses has now received a portion of God's own life and power, transforming him into one "above" those who remain fallen. Moses of course never ceases to be human, but his humanity has now been so elevated that he himself becomes a model of godliness for others. Such transformation is not, however, reserved for individuals but is for all of God's people. In his covenant God wills to bring not just Israel's leaders to himself but all peoples.

Old Testament filiation is one of the first direct precursors to Christian adoption: "And you shall say to Pharaoh, 'Thus says the Lord, Israel is my first-born son'" (Ex 4:22). In Hosea we hear an even more caring metaphor come to life: "When Israel was a child, I loved him, and out of Egypt I called my son" (Hos 11:1; cf. 2 Sam 7:14). As we make our way through Israel's story of salvation, we see more amplified imagery for those brought into a transformative communion with God. In this progression the metaphors used for not only Israel's patriarchs but the people as a whole open up—all of Israel is now God's people, his children, his bride, his beloved: "And I will walk among you, and will be your God, and you shall be my people" (Lev 26:12). This act is a sign of God's making Israel his own, showing his love and care for them in a way unique and unmatchable. Such a union is also expressed in erotic and nuptial imagery. "For your Maker is your husband.... For the Lord has called you like a wife forsaken and grieved in spirit" (Is 54:5–6). "I will greatly rejoice in the Lord, my soul shall exult in my God; for he has clothed me with the garments of salvation, he has covered me with a robe of righteousness, as a bridegroom decks himself with a garland, and as a bride adorns herself with her jewels" (Is 61:10). The prophet Hosea is thus able to depict God wooing Israel by promising, "I will allure her, and bring her into the wilderness, and speak tenderly to her.... [Y]ou will call me, 'My husband,' and no longer will you call me, 'My Baal'.... I will espouse you for ever; I will espouse you in righteousness and in justice, in steadfast love, and in mercy; I will espouse you in faithfulness; and you shall know the LORD" (Hos 2:14, 18, 21–22). Israel does not remain simply a consecrated populace, as glorious as that would be, but becomes even more one with God as the two grow in communion and thereby begin to share the attributes of the other.

In this divine embrace, Yahweh spousally unites himself to his people and gives her his own name, "give[s] them an everlasting name" (Is 56:5). With her he likewise shares his life, enabling the virtuous not only to approach and draw near to him, but even to receive his otherwise unobtainable blessings (cf. Ps 24). To these chosen ones, God sends his own refulgent wisdom, "passes into holy souls and makes them friends of God, and prophets" (Wis 7:27). From this relationship comes a new grace to participate in God's own attributes of holiness and perfection. God gives them his own breath and consequent ability to understand as he understands (cf. Job 32:8), and the eternal effect of thus drawing near to God will be "quietness and trust forever" and the grace to "abide in a peaceful habitation, in secure dwellings, and in quiet resting places" (Is 32:17–18).

As central as these Jewish ideas of the divine *imago Dei* and the willingness of God to share his own life with those with whom he establishes a covenant may be, there is nothing in the Old Testament that is tantamount to theosis. Being made in God's own image and entering into a transformative and progressive covenant with him definitely prepare what the Father aims to do in Christ, but they are not synonymous. It is only by breaking into history and into the human condition that God can bring our broken images and faltering likenesses to himself. By uniting divinity and humanity perfectly and personally within himself, God chooses to deify us as one of us. Only in the perfect mediator Jesus Christ are God and humanity able to meet; only here can God become human and humans become ever more like God. Accordingly, let us now turn to the reality of human deification as expressed throughout the New Testament.

Deification in the New Testament

The Benedictine monk and spiritual writer Dom Idesbald Ryelandt, O.S.B., wrote, "When we move on from the books of the Old Testament to the Gospels we feel transported into an atmosphere of which the perspectives are on quite another plane."[1] While the seeds of theosis, or what Ryelandt usually calls "adoption" or "divinization", are foreshadowed in the Old Testament, as we have seen, they blossom forth in the New Testament in forms both diverse and unified. So much so, insists Ryelandt, that the "outstanding message of the Evangelists was the revelation of the mystery of God's love willing to raise man to an entirely new sonship.... This, then was the mission of Jesus: to establish this new relation of sonship between man and God."[2]

In its 2012 document "Theology Today: Perspectives, Principles, and Criteria", the International Theological Commission, established by Pope Paul VI to study specific theological issues and questions, noted the centrality of divine revelation in Christian theology and stated that the "obligatory reference point is the life, death and resurrection of Jesus Christ". It then made a statement that summarizes, in many ways, the theme of this chapter and entire book:

[1] Dom I. Ryelandt, O.S.B., *The Life of Grace* (London: Burns and Oates, 1964), 32.
[2] Ibid., 32–33.

> The Mystery of God revealed in Jesus Christ by the power of the Holy Spirit is a mystery of *ekstasis*, love, communion and mutual indwelling among the three divine persons; a mystery of *kenosis*, the relinquishing of the form of God by Jesus in his incarnation, so as to take the form of a slave (cf. Phil 2:5–11); and a mystery of *theosis*, human beings are called to participate in the life of God and to share in "the divine nature" (2 Pet 1:4) through Christ, in the Spirit.[3]

The two essential mysteries of the Christian faith are the Trinity and the Incarnation, and any study of theosis—man's participation in the divine life of God—must begin and end with them. First, the Trinity is "the central mystery of the Christian faith and life"; it is the "mystery of God in himself" and is "therefore the source of all the other mysteries of faith, the light that enlightens them" (*CCC* 234). The triune nature of God, who is Father, Son, and Holy Spirit, was revealed first at the baptism of Christ (Mt 3:13–17; Mk 1:9–11; Lk 3:21–22; Jn 1:29–34) and is directly or indirectly expressed in the Gospels and the New Testament. Second, "belief in the true Incarnation of the Son of God is the distinctive sign of Christian faith" (*CCC* 463): the belief that the second Person of the Trinity, the Word, "became flesh and dwelt among us, full of grace and truth" (Jn 1:14). The same God who created man out of love has called man back to communion with himself, a communion that is given expression in several different, yet interrelated, ways in the New Testament. These various expressions can be broken down into four basic groups: the Synoptic Gospels (the Gospels of Matthew, Mark, and Luke); the Gospel of John and Johannine writings; the Pauline writings; and Second Peter.

The Synoptic Gospels

The Synoptics contain three key themes relating to theosis: the Fatherhood of God, believers described as "sons of God", and mankind's participation in the Kingdom of God (or Kingdom of heaven).[4]

[3] International Theological Commission, "Theology Today: Perspectives, Principles, and Criteria", March 8, 2012, no. 98.

[4] See Petro B. T. Bilaniuk, "The Mystery of *Theosis* or Divinization", in *Studies in Eastern Christianity*, vol. 1 (Munich/Toronto: Ukrainian Free University, 1977), 53, and Matthew Vellanickal, *The Divine Sonship of Christians in the Johannine Writings*, Analecta Biblica, vol. 72 (Rome: Biblical Institute Press, 1977), 53–68.

All three are found in the Sermon on the Mount (Mt 5–7), where Jesus is revealed as the new Moses who ascends a mountain in order to deliver the new Law and so "broadens the Covenant to all nations",[5] pointing to the founding and formation of a new Israel, the Church. "Blessed are the peacemakers," Jesus stated, "for they shall be called sons of God" (Mt 5:9). The Son, the Prince of Peace, restored peace between the Father and mankind by becoming man; this peace refers to the life-giving relationship between the Creator and those he has created, a relationship now expressed in the intimate language of filial love: the "Law in the New Kingdom is the law of love".[6]

The connection is made even more explicitly a bit later: "But I say to you, Love your enemies and pray for those who persecute you, so that you may be sons of your Father who is in heaven" (Mt 5:44–45). This love is exemplified not by mere absence of discord or hatred, but by communion, acts of goodness, and prayer. "We are to love without qualification because the Son of the Father has, through the power of his word, made us children of this same Father."[7] The goal of this *agape* love is perfection: "You, therefore, must be perfect, as your heavenly Father is perfect" (Mt 5:48). This is also made evident in Matthew 19, the only other place the word *teleioi* appears (in Jesus' statement to the rich young ruler): "If you would be perfect [*teleioi*], go, sell what you possess and give to the poor, and you will have treasure in heaven; and come, follow me" (Mt 19:21; cf. Lk 6:35). This perfection of divine sonship is found in following the perfect example of Christ, the Son of God, who reveals the radical nature of divine love on the Cross. Those who enter into and pursue this love, as Benedict XVI pointed out in his first encyclical, *Deus caritas est*, embark on

> an ongoing exodus out of the closed inward-looking self towards its liberation through self-giving, and thus towards authentic self-discovery and indeed the discovery of God: "Whoever seeks to gain his life will lose it, but whoever loses his life will preserve it" (Lk 17:33),

[5] Pope Benedict XVI, *Jesus of Nazareth: From the Baptism in the Jordan to the Transfiguration* (New York: Doubleday, 2007), 66.

[6] Vellanickal, *Divine Sonship of Christians*, 56.

[7] Erasmo Leiva-Merikakis, *Fire of Mercy, Heart of the Word: Meditations on the Gospel according to St. Matthew*, vol. 1 (San Francisco: Ignatius Press, 1996), 238.

> as Jesus says throughout the Gospels (cf. Mt 10:39; 16:25; Mk 8:35; Lk 9:24; Jn 12:25). In these words, Jesus portrays his own path, which leads through the Cross to the Resurrection: the path of the grain of wheat that falls to the ground and dies, and in this way bears much fruit. Starting from the depths of his own sacrifice and of the love that reaches fulfilment therein, he also portrays in these words the essence of love and indeed of human life itself.[8]

The eschatological character of sons—that is, their inherent orientation to eternal life—can be seen in the Gospel of Luke, where Jesus contrasts the "sons of this age" with the "sons of the resurrection", saying of the latter that those who "are accounted worthy to attain to that age and to the resurrection from the dead neither marry nor are given in marriage, for they cannot die any more, because they are equal to angels and are sons of God, being sons of the resurrection" (Lk 20:35–36). Matthew Vellanickal notes how central is the resurrection "as an eschatological good" in the Lukan theology (cf. Lk 7:22; 14:14; Acts 13:30–34; 25:8) and states, "It is only here that the divine sonship is explicitly connected with the resurrection in the whole [New Testament]."[9]

In the Sermon on the Mount, there is an emphasis on the fact that God the Father is not only a Father in relation to God the Son, but also to those who answer the divine invitation to be sons in and through the Son. Thus, the good works of Christ's disciples, done in love and in humility, are meant to bring glory "to your Father who is in heaven" (Mt 5:16; cf. Mt 5:45; 6:1–4). The great prayer given by Christ to his disciples and to the Church is directed to "Our Father". The adjective, "Our", as the *Catechism* notes, does not express a possession of God, "but an entirely new relationship with God" (*CCC* 2786).[10] This relationship is not merely poetic

[8] Pope Benedict XVI, Encyclical Letter *Deus caritas est*, December 25, 2005, no. 6.

[9] Vellanickal, *Divine Sonship of Christians*, 63. The word "explicitly" is important since, as we will note, the apostle Paul also indicates connections between divine sonship and resurrection.

[10] Of the "Our Father", Leiva-Merikakis writes: "God's fatherhood of us is the deepest mystery of faith and the heart of scriptural revelation. The praying of the Our Father in the eucharistic liturgy is surrounded by the Church with the utmost solemnity, impressing upon us the metaphysical miracle involved in our being able and entitled to utter the words 'Our Father', addressing them to the Lord of eternity and Creator of the universe.... For God to

or metaphorical, but speaks to the astonishing depths and riches of God's love, which has made it possible for creatures to be called and truly be "sons of God". Those who are children of God pray that the Father's will "be done"; those who are filled with divine life reveal it in their actions, which reveal in turn the orientation to God's will. "Not every one who says to me, 'Lord, Lord,' shall enter the kingdom of heaven," warned Jesus, "but he who does the will of my Father who is in heaven" (Mt 7:21).[11]

The ecclesial dimension is highlighted in Mark's Gospel, where Jesus insists, "Whoever does the will of God is my brother, and sister, and mother" (Mk 3:35). Benedict XVI, in commenting on this passage, writes, "Communion with [Jesus] is filial communion with the Father—it is a yes to the fourth commandment on a new level, the highest level. It is entry into the family of those who call God Father who can do so because they belong to a 'we'—formed of those who are united with Jesus and, by listening to him, united with the will of the Father, thereby attaining to the heart of the obedience intended by the Torah."[12]

The Gospel of John and Johannine Writings

"The teaching of *theosis* enters into a new phase of development through the writings of St. John," notes Bilaniuk, "where it received a very special mystical Johannine trait."[13] The Carmelite Scripture scholar Father Paul-Marie de la Croix, O.C.D., gave the fourth Gospel the title "The Gospel of Filial Adoption", writing, "St. John desires to

---

be holy means to beget, to love, and to adopt other children in his one Child. 'Abba!' is the sweetest word in God's ear. The present prayer, then, implies the Christian's love and gratitude for having been adopted in Christ, and these acts of the heart tend to expand and include all other men in the grace of adoption" (*Fire of Mercy*, 1:255, 257).

[11] "In the new kingdom of God proclaimed by Jesus, all his followers will share in his kingship, which means sharing in his sonship. The gift of divine sonship fulfills the deepest longings of human beings who were originally created in grace. To be a son of God means to have the fourfold harmony of rightly loving God, one's neighbor, oneself, and the whole created order" (Michael Dauphinais and Matthew Levering, *Holy People, Holy Land: A Theological Introduction to the Bible* [Grand Rapids, Mich.: Brazos Press, 2005], 146).

[12] Pope Benedict XVI, *Jesus of Nazareth*, 117. In *Deus caritas est*, Benedict XVI wrote, "Love grows through love. Love is 'divine' because it comes from God and unites us to God; through this unifying process it makes us a 'we' which transcends our divisions and makes us one, until in the end God is 'all in all' (1 Cor 15:28)" (no. 18).

[13] Bilaniuk, "Mystery of *Theosis*", 53.

point out from the beginning of his Gospel the close bond that exists between the coming of the Word into the world and the revelation He makes of His Father and our adoption as sons of God."[14]

The Incarnation is the starting point in the Gospel of John, the Prologue asserting in overture-like fashion the divinity of the Logos, who has always existed, who is God, and whose power and Person were integral to the act of creation and the sustaining of all that has been created (Jn 1:1–3). The first verse of the Gospel presents a new creation, a purposeful re-presentation of Genesis 1:1—"In the beginning ..."—in the light of the incarnate Word, and this "new creation is a communion in the Trinity's superabundant life of wisdom and love".[15] A key descriptive used by Saint John is *tekna theou*—"children of God"—which first appears in John 1:12: "But to all who received him, who believed in his name, he gave power to become children of God." John clearly distinguishes, of course, between the only begotten Son, Jesus Christ, and those who become children through baptism and grace.[16] For example, while the word *pater* (Father) is used nearly 140 times in the Gospel of John, the term "Our Father" does not appear and "your Father" appears just once (in contrast to the Synoptics), and then only after the Resurrection when Jesus addressed the grieving Mary Magdalene (Jn 20:17). John, in short, emphasizes the reality of the "children of God" while strongly distinguishing between the filial adoption given by grace to mankind, and the unique Sonship of the incarnate Word, who is God by his very nature.[17]

The apostle John tightly connects theosis, the divine sonship of men, with faith and belief in Jesus Christ. This sonship, or divinization, involves the reception of grace from the One who is full of grace: "And from his fulness have we all received, grace upon grace"

[14] Paul-Marie de la Croix, O.C.D., *The Biblical Spirituality of St. John* (Staten Island, N.Y.: Alba House, 1966), 175. He adds: "This is the ultimate purpose of the Incarnation, viz., the revelation of a Father to whose love His children have been restored (1 John 3:1)."

[15] Dauphinais and Levering, *Holy People, Holy Land*, 170.

[16] See Vellanickal, *Divine Sonship of Christians*, 92, for an examination of the different terms used in the Greek text to describe the Sonship of the second Person of the Trinity and the sonship of men and women.

[17] See Raymond E. Brown, *The Gospel according to John I-XII: The Anchor Bible Commentary* (Garden City, N.Y.: Doubleday, 1966), 11, and Louis Bouyer, *The Christian Mystery: From Pagan Myth to Christian Mysticism* (London: T&T Clark International, 1990, 2004), 117.

(Jn 1:16; cf. 1:14). What, then, is the fullness of the only begotten Son's grace? His sonship, in which men are called to share through active faith. Another example of this is found later in John's Gospel, following Jesus' triumphal entry into Jerusalem, when he tells the disciples, "The light is with you for a little longer.... While you have the light, believe in the light, that you may become sons of light" (Jn 12:35, 36). Both "light" and "life" are key words in the Prologue, used to describe the incarnate Word (Jn 1:4–5, 9). In sum, "it was the fullness of the divine sonship that made Jesus possess the fullness of the Grace of Truth (Revelation). Hence 'to receive from His fullness' means to accept the Revelation in Christ and consequently to share in his sonship."[18]

The new birth given in and through Christ is not natural, not of human origin, and not of "the will of man", but "of God" (Jn 1:13). Having been introduced in the Prologue, this birth is the focus of Jesus' conversation with Nicodemus (Jn 3:1ff.), where the word "born" appears seven times. Verses 3–5 comprise the core of the passage:

> Jesus answered him, "Truly, truly, I say to you, unless one is born anew, he cannot see the kingdom of God." Nicodemus said to him, "How can a man be born when he is old? Can he enter a second time into his mother's womb and be born?" Jesus answered, "Truly, truly, I say to you, unless one is born of water and the Spirit, he cannot enter the kingdom of God." (Jn 3:3–5)

As is often the case in John's Gospel, Jesus uses natural images or objects (water, bread, light, etc.) as the basis for revealing a supernatural truth. John does not argue for the reality of the sacraments, but assumes it as part of the tapestry of his theological vision. "From chapter 3 to chapter 5," Father Louis Bouyer observes about the Gospel of John, "there is always water about"—in the talk with Nicodemus (chapter 3), the "living water" revealed to the Samaritan woman (chapter 4), and the water of the pool of Bethseda (chapter 5).[19] In Scripture, water is closely involved in creation, salvation, and death. Genesis relates that while the earth was "without form and void ... the Spirit of God was moving over the face of the waters" (Gen 1:2).

[18] Vellanickal, *Divine Sonship of Christians*, 161.

[19] Bouyer, *Christian Mystery*, 121.

"In the beginning" there already existed an intrinsic relationship between the Holy Spirit and water. In Genesis (the first creation) this resulted in physical, natural creation; in John's Gospel (the new creation) it resulted in spiritual rebirth, or regeneration. Saint Peter writes that God created by his word and "means of water" (2 Pet 3:5). Jesus speaks to Nicodemus of being "born again", "born of water and Spirit", "born of the Spirit", and "born again" in rapid succession (Jn 3:3, 5, 6, 7). And Saint Paul, as we will see in more detail below, explains that "if any one is in Christ, he is a new creation; the old one has passed away, behold, the new has come" (2 Cor 5:17). Thus baptism "is birth into the new life in Christ" (*CCC* 1277) and the ordinary means by which we are filled with divine life—that is, divinized. For, as Jesus states, "That which is born of the flesh is flesh, and that which is born of the Spirit is spirit" (Jn 3:6).[20]

The First Letter of John states that those who are born of God will be known by their love. "Beloved, let us love one another; for love is of God, and he who loves is born of God and knows God" (1 Jn 4:7). The epistle, like the Gospel (Jn 13–17), teaches that the interior reality of being made a child of God will be expressed outwardly through acts of charity and lives of righteousness. Those who are children of God, Saint John makes readily clear, are really such: "See what love the Father has given us, that we should be called children of God; and so we are." This filial relationship is a present reality, but it is not static; it is ongoing and dynamic, to be fulfilled and revealed at the eschaton and the return of the Son of God: "Beloved, we are God's children now; it does not yet appear what we shall be, but we know that when he appears we shall be like him, for we shall see him as he is" (1 Jn 3:2).

The "criterion of sonship" in 1 John is found in the manifestation of righteousness, which is a gift that must be accepted, embraced,

[20] "For John, there is no middle ground. A man belongs to the Spirit or he does not. It is an 'either-or' situation; either man is of the Spirit or he is of the flesh. In this situation, Christian baptism means that man is of the Spirit. To be such is not a matter of man's personal choice. Rather, it is a matter of divine election and the gratuitous nature of this choice.... Belief in this self-revelation of the Son of Man [exalted on the Cross] is salvific. It bears with it eternal life, as God's gift of salvation to those who are born anew, in the Christian sacrament of baptism. All this is of the essence of the message of the Fourth Gospel" (Raymond F. Collins, *These Things Have Been Written: Studies on the Fourth Gospel* [Louvain: Peeters Press; Grand Rapids, Mich.: Eerdmans, 1990], 63–64, 67).

and deepened.[21] Having confessed our sins, we are cleansed "from all unrighteousness" by God, who is "faithful and just" (1 Jn 1:9) and who forgives sins because of the advocacy of "Jesus Christ the righteous", who is the "expiation of our sins" (1 Jn 2:1–2). Faith and obedience are united; they can be distinguished but not sundered. We *know* Christ "if we keep his commandments" (1 Jn 2:3, cf. v. 10), which reveal the same integral understanding of sonship, faith, and obedience found in the Gospels, along with the absolute necessity of *agape*: "Beloved, let us love one another; for love is of God, and he who loves is born of God and knows God" (1 Jn 4:7, see vv. 15–17). The filial life given by the heavenly Father shines forth in fraternal love; those who are truly born of God do not sin. On the other hand, the absence of authentic love exposes a false love, which John states is diabolical in nature (1 Jn 3:10–12). This is summarized with directness in the fourth chapter: "He who does not love does not know God; for God is love" (1 Jn 4:8). Vellanickal states,

> "To be born of God" means to receive the communication of the divine life that is essentially Trinitarian. If this Trinitarian Life of God is defined by Jn as "Love", the communication of this Life means communication of "love" that makes men "born of God" and "children of God". So, if "birth from God" and "divine sonship" consists in this participated Life of God, Who is "Love", then naturally the fact of "being born of God" should manifest itself in a "life of love" (1 John 4:7), which becomes an existential definition of "being born of God".[22]

Pauline Writings

The writings of the apostle Paul include several passages directly and indirectly addressing theosis. We will focus here on three important and closely related concepts expressed and developed by Paul that are essential to this chapter: the formula of exchange, the adoption as sons, and bearing the image of Christ.

The "formula of exchange", or *admirabile commercium*, "states that the eternal Son of God became what we are so that we could become

[21] See Vellanickal, *Divine Sonship of Christians*, 161.

[22] Ibid., 308–9. Vellanickal's study is still one of the most detailed and exhaustive when it comes to divine sonship, or theosis, in the Johannine texts.

what he is."[23] This takes on various forms in the Tradition (as subsequent chapters will detail), but is based in part on several passages from Paul's writings, including this from his second epistle to the Church in Corinth: "For you know the grace of our Lord Jesus Christ, that though he was rich, yet for your sake he became poor, so that by his poverty you might become rich" (2 Cor 8:9). The riches of the Son, as many of the Fathers pointed out, are located in his divinity, and so the riches given to us through the Son include sharing in that divinity. The young Joseph Ratzinger, in a Christmas homily given over fifty years ago, compared the commercialized and "calculated exchange" of the season with the radical, grace-filled exchange brought into history by the Incarnation, saying, "This exchange consists of God taking upon himself our human existence in order to bestow his divine existence upon us, of his choosing our nothingness in order to give us his plentitude."[24]

In Second Corinthians the emphasis is on how we are exalted and made rich because of Christ's humility, death, and Resurrection. In the famous christological hymn of Philippians 2, the emphasis is on the exaltation of Christ because of his humility.[25] "Christ Jesus," Paul wrote to the Philippians,

> who, though he was in the form of God, did not count equality with God a thing to be grasped, but emptied himself, taking the form of a servant, being born in the likeness of men. And being found in human form he humbled himself and became obedient unto death, even death on a cross. Therefore God has highly exalted him and bestowed on him the name which is above every name, that at the name of Jesus every knee should bow, in heaven and on earth and under the earth, and every tongue confess that Jesus Christ is Lord, to the glory of God the Father. (Phil 2:5–11)

This important passage can be described, writes theologian Michael J. Gorman, as "Paul's master story", which is meant to "show that Christ's kenosis (self-emptying) reveals the character of God,

[23] Daniel A. Keating, *Deification and Grace* (Naples, Fla.: Sapientia Press, 2007), 11.

[24] Joseph Ratzinger, "Three Meditations on Christmas", in *Dogma and Preaching: Applying Christian Doctrine to Daily Life* (San Francisco: Ignatius Press, 2011), 332.

[25] See Keating, *Deification and Grace*, 16–17.

summoning us to cruciformity understood as theosis".[26] This "cruciformity" involves our participation in the death and Resurrection of Christ, which is realized through the sacraments, the transforming work of the Holy Spirit, and our acts of love, sacrifice, and devotion. In that way, the exchange between the unique and uncreated Son, who is "one in being" with the Father and the Holy Spirit, is made with those servants who are made sons by grace.

Paul writes not only of the fullness of the Son's divinity but also of the fullness of time, which witnessed the Incarnation and the redemption of mankind through the Cross, Passion, and Resurrection:

> But when the time had fully come, God sent forth his Son, born of woman, born under the law, to redeem those who were under the law, so that we might receive adoption as sons. And because you are sons, God has sent the Spirit of his Son into our hearts, crying, "Abba! Father!" (Gal 4:4–6)

Paul presents here the close connection between the "formula of exchange" and adoption. "The crucial addition here," notes Daniel A. Keating, "is the link in the text between the Son (*huios*) who is sent, and the consequence of his sending, our adoption as sons (*huiothesia*)."[27] The three Persons of the Trinity are united in nature, but also in their work of imparting filial life to mankind: God the Father sends the Son, and then the "Spirit of his Son" empowers us so we can address God, not just as Creator or Maker, but as "Abba! Father!" Peace with God, as Paul explains to the Romans, is "through our Lord Jesus Christ. Through him we have obtained access to this grace in which we stand, and we rejoice in our hope of sharing the glory of God" (Rom 5:1–2). This eschatological hope, which Paul discusses in many of his writings,[28] is realized through in growing through

[26] Michael J. Gorman, *Inhabiting the Cruciform God: Kenosis, Justification, and Theosis in Paul's Narrative Soteriology* (Grand Rapids, Mich.: Eerdmans, 2009), 2.

[27] Keating, *Deification and Grace*, 17.

[28] One good example is from the opening of the Letter to the Ephesians: "Blessed be the God and Father of our Lord Jesus Christ, who has blessed us in Christ with every spiritual blessing in the heavenly places, even as he chose us in him before the foundation of the world, that we should be holy and blameless before him. He destined us in love to be his sons through Jesus Christ, according to the purpose of his will, to the praise of his glorious grace which he freely bestowed on us in the Beloved" (Eph 1:3–6). See Francois Amiot, *The Key Concepts of St. Paul* (New York: Herder and Herder, 1965), 233–85, for an excellent synthesis and summation.

sufferings, endurance, and character, and "hope does not disappoint us, because God's love has been poured into our hearts through the Holy Spirit which has been given to us" (Rom 5:5). The work of the Holy Spirit, Paul explains in detail and at length in Romans 8, includes granting sonship and giving witness to our position in Christ as children of God and heirs with Christ:

> For all who are led by the Spirit of God are sons of God. For you did not receive the spirit of slavery to fall back into fear, but you have received the spirit of sonship [*huiothesia*]. When we cry, "Abba! Father!" it is the Spirit himself bearing witness with our spirit that we are children of God, and if children, then heirs, heirs of God and fellow heirs with Christ, provided we suffer with him in order that we may also be glorified with him. I consider that the sufferings of this present time are not worth comparing with the glory that is to be revealed to us. For the creation waits with eager longing for the revealing of the sons of God; for the creation was subjected to futility, not of its own will but by the will of him who subjected it in hope; because the creation itself will be set free from its bondage to decay and obtain the glorious liberty of the children of God. We know that the whole creation has been groaning with labor pains together until now; and not only the creation, but we ourselves, who have the first fruits of the Spirit, groan inwardly as we wait for adoption as sons [*huiothesia*], the redemption of our bodies. (Rom 8:14–23)[29]

Paul's use of "adoption as his master metaphor for Christian divine sonship" draws upon both Jewish and Roman understandings of adoption.[30] This includes the Jewish apocalyptic tradition, which focused on a future hope established by God's power and judgment, and the belief that Israel was God's "child" or "son" (cf. Ex 4:22–23;

[29] Pope Francis, in a General Audience given on May 8, 2013, expressed his strong interest in this passage: "In another passage from the Letter to the Romans, that we have recalled several times, St. Paul sums it up with these words: 'For all who are led by the Spirit of God are sons of God. For you ... received the spirit of sonship. When we cry, "Abba! Father!" it is the Spirit himself bearing witness with our spirit that we are children of God, and if children, then heirs, heirs of God and fellow heirs with Christ, provided we suffer with him in order that we may also be glorified with him' (8:14–17). This is the precious gift that the Holy Spirit brings to our hearts: the very life of God, the life of true children, a relationship of confidence, freedom, and trust in the love and mercy of God. It also gives us a new perception of others, close and far, seen always as brothers and sisters in Jesus to be respected and loved."

[30] Michael Peppard, "Adopted and Begotten Sons of God: Paul and John on Divine Sonship", *Catholic Biblical Quarterly* 73 (2011): 95.

Deut 14:1; 32:5–6, 19–22; Is 1:2–4). Those who are filled with the Holy Spirit belong to "God's eschatological people, destined to inherit the ancient promises" made to Moses and the prophets.[31] The word *huiothesia*—which connotes Spirit of adoption, Spirit of sonship, divine filiation—is used in Romans 8 and three other places in the New Testament, including Galatians 4:6 as well as Romans 9:4, where it refers to the "adoption as sons" that belonged to the Israelites (also see Eph 1:5). But Paul, a Roman citizen (and writing to Christians in Rome), was also keenly aware of the privileges accorded to sons adopted in Roman families, especially that of inheritance, a theme that the apostle takes up in several places.[32] Those gifted with divine sonship are also true and full heirs, bequeathed with a divine inheritance, which is eternal glory.

These various aspects of adoption are related to Paul's teaching that those who share in the divine life are conformed to the image of the Son, "the first-born among many brethren" (Rom 8:29), and so bear "the image of the man of heaven" (1 Cor 15:49). The first man, Adam, destroyed communion with the Creator through pride and sin; the new and last Adam, Jesus Christ, restores mankind's communion with the Father through his Incarnation, suffering, death, and Resurrection—in short, through sacrificial love. The beloved Son, Paul tells the Colossians, "is the image of the invisible God, the first-born of all creation" (Col 1:15), and it is in and through him that our true image

[31] Of this connection, Vellanickal writes: "The very fact that Rom 8 speaks of an adoption that is fully realized in the final liberation from the slavery of corruption (8:21–23) seems to show that Paul had in mind a typological comparison with the liberation of Israel out of Egypt leading them to the adoption as sons of Yahweh. As Israel, the son of God, was led by God through the desert towards their heritage of the promised land, so the Christians becoming sons of God through liberation from slavery of sin, law and death are led towards their heritage—eschatological adoption at the resurrection—by the Spirit of God" (*Divine Sonship of Christians*, 80–81). For an examination within the larger scope of the epistle to the Romans, see Brendan Byrne, S.J., *Romans: Sacra Pagina* (Collegeville, Minn.: Liturgical Press, 1996), 248–51.

[32] "As research into Roman social practices has demonstrated, adoption in the Roman world was enacted for far different reasons than it is in the modern Western world; the chief impetus was the securing of an heir. Inheritance included not only land and other wealth but also the family name, the family glory, and a share of the family spirit. These are high stakes, and Paul no doubt knew that there were often disputes between biological and adopted sons, or between adopted sons and biological nephews or grandsons. His argument thus relies on a crucial feature of the social context—the *certainty* of an adopted son's right to inherit from his adoptive father. Roman laws and cultural mores clearly held that the inheritance claims of adopted sons were valid" (Peppard, "Adopted and Begotten Sons of God", 96).

(Gen 1:26–27) can be restored and elevated.[33] What emerges from 1 Corinthians 15 "is that Christ is not only a new beginning for humanity," says Bouyer, "but a new humanity. He constitutes in himself the heavenly humanity, and we must put it on, as Paul says, just as we had received from the first man a merely terrestrial humanity, which sin condemned to return to the dust from which it had been taken."[34] Through the last Adam, all of humanity—indeed, all of creation—is being reconciled to God and made radically anew (cf. 2 Cor 5:17–19; Rom 8:19–23). This has been described as "Christification".[35] Of this transformation and process, Paul states,

> And we all, with unveiled face, beholding the glory of the Lord, are being changed into his likeness from one degree of glory to another; for this comes from the Lord who is the Spirit. (2 Cor 3:18)

This verse, says Stephen Finlan, is the "most frankly theotic passage" in Paul's writings. Because they are "in Christ" and bear his image, Christians

> can fearlessly approach that which frightened Aaron and the Israelites. Moreover, believers go on to embody and to reflect the glory that they have beheld. God works within them and metamorphosizes them. While beholding Christ, believers are transformed into the same image.[36]

In sum, those united to Christ in death—that is, through baptism—will also be united with Christ in the resurrection (Rom 6:5; 1 Cor 12:13). Through his death, we are given life; the old man, sinful and doomed, has died and a new creation is born, raised up to be in Christ in "the heavenly places" (Eph 2:1–7). "For St. Paul," states Father George T. Montague, S.M., "there is no doubt that the Christian has

[33] See Keating, *Deification and Grace*, 19.

[34] Bouyer, *Christian Mystery*, 103.

[35] "The real anthropological meaning of deification is Christification.... [Paul] is not advocating an external imitation or a simple ethical improvement but a real Christification" (Panayiotis Nellas, *Deification in Christ: The Nature of the Human Person* [Crestwood, N.Y.: St. Vladimir's Seminary Press, 1987], 39).

[36] Stephen Finlan, "Can We Speak of *Theosis* in Paul?" in *Partakers of the Divine Nature: The History and Development of Deification in the Christian Traditions*, ed. Michael J. Christensen and Jeffrey A. Wittung (Grand Rapids, Mich.: Baker Academic, 2008), 76.

entered a new existence. The Christian life is defined as existing in Christ Jesus."[37]

Second Peter

The new existence given to those who are in Christ Jesus is discussed at the very start of Second Peter, in a passage that has become, in some ways, the definitive theosis text in the New Testament, so much so that one Evangelical theologian recently wrote, "This passage is the most important biblical foundation for the doctrine of *theosis*, usually translated divinization or deification."[38] The passage states:

> May grace and peace be multiplied to you in the knowledge of God and of Jesus our Lord. His divine power has granted to us all things that pertain to life and godliness, through the knowledge of him who called us to his own glory and excellence, by which he has granted to us his precious and very great promises, that through these you may escape from the corruption that is in the world because of passion, and become partakers of the divine nature. (2 Pet 1:2–4)

On one hand, this text is certainly unique, for the phrase "partakers of the divine nature" appears nowhere else in Scripture, prompting one commentator to venture that "with that remark [the author] seemingly took a step that no other writer of the New Testament dared take."[39] On the other hand, without downplaying its uniqueness, it is notable that First Peter not only contains ten references to "glory"; it contains this oft-overlooked verse: "So I exhort the elders among you, as a fellow elder and a witness of the sufferings of Christ as well as a partaker [*koinonos*] in the glory that is to be revealed" (1 Pet 5:1). This passage points to the glory to be revealed at the return of Christ, but indicates a real and current participation, "for while its full manifestation belongs to the future, he holds (cf. esp. iv. 14) that, with the End so close at hand, those who suffer for Christ already enjoy

[37] George T. Montague, S.M., "Paul's Teaching on Being and Becoming in Christ", in *Contemporary New Testament Studies* (Collegeville, Minn.: Liturgical Press, 1965), 379.

[38] Brenda B. Colijn, *Images of Salvation in the New Testament* (Downers Grove, Ill.: Inter-Varsity Academic, 2010), 264. The *Catechism of the Catholic Church* uses the phrase "partakers of the divine nature", from 2 Pet 1:4, at least six times (nos. 460, 1996, 1129, 1692, 1721, 2009). See chapter 14 of this book, "Deification in the *Catechism of the Catholic Church*".

[39] James Starr, "Does 2 Peter 1:4 Speak of Deification?", in Christensen and Wittung, *Partakers of the Divine Nature*, 81.

a foretaste of it."[40] Meanwhile, in remarking on 2 Peter 1:4, J.N.D. Kelly says that believers "will enter into true union with God, participating in His glory, immortality and blessedness".[41]

The emphasis on how partaking in the divine nature provides freedom from the corruption in the world echoes the Johannine contrast between the "children of God" and the "the children of the devil" (1 Jn 3:8–10). "Our admission to the eternal kingdom depends on the moral efforts we make," writes Norman Russell. "In other words, our sharing in the attributes of divinity is conditioned on our fully acquiring the attributes of humanity."[42] But, as Russell and Keating note, many of the early Church Fathers were wary of this verse, and it did not become widely used and referenced until the fifth century, when Cyril of Alexandria took it up "as the key text to describe the result of the Holy Spirit indwelling the faithful in baptism: We become sons by adoption through grace and attain to communion with the Triune God."[43] There is little doubt that the passage uses language taken from Hellenistic, Platonic philosophy. But, like John's use of "logos" in his famous Prologue (cf. Jn 1:1–14), the author of Second Peter employs such language for thoroughly Christian ends.[44] After all, participation in the divine nature comes through knowledge of God and "Jesus our Lord" (cf. 2 Pet 1:2, 3, 8; 2:20; 3:18), who has called us to his glory and excellence, granting his promises, which bring relief from corruption and passion. This knowledge (*epignoseos*) is "particular knowledge" and discernment that should not be confused with the secret knowledge (*gnosis*) of Gnosticism.[45]

Conclusion

Pope Benedict XVI, in his message for Lent 2013 (no. 2), reflected on a subject that was one of the abiding themes of his pontificate: the

[40] J.N.D. Kelly, *A Commentary on the Epistles of Peter and Jude* (Grand Rapids, Mich.: Baker House, 1981), 199.

[41] Ibid., 301–2.

[42] Norman Russell, *Fellow Workers with God: Orthodox Thinking on Theosis* (Crestwood, N.Y.: St. Vladimir's Seminary Press, 2009), 65–66.

[43] See ibid., 66–69, and Keating, *Deification and Grace*, 34–35. Subsequent chapters in this book will examine in detail the use of 2 Pet 1:4 by various Church Fathers.

[44] See Kelly, *Commentary on the Epistles*, 303–4.

[45] Star, "Does 2 Peter 1:4 Speak?", 84–85.

intimate and necessary relationship between charity and faith. "When we make room for the love of God," he wrote, "then we become like him, sharing in his own charity. If we open ourselves to his love, we allow him to live in us and to bring us to love with him, in him and like him; only then does our faith become truly 'active through love' (Gal 5:6); only then does he abide in us (cf. 1 Jn 4:12)." What is faith? It is, he stated,

> knowing the truth and adhering to it (cf. 1 Tim 2:4); charity is "walking" in the truth (cf. Eph 4:15).... Faith causes us to embrace the commandment of our Lord and Master [Christ]; charity gives us the happiness of putting it into practice (cf. Jn 13:13–17). In faith, we are begotten as children of God (cf. Jn 1:12ff.); charity causes us to persevere concretely in our divine sonship, bearing the fruit of the Holy Spirit (cf. Gal 5:22). Faith enables us to recognize the gifts that the good and generous God has entrusted to us; charity makes them fruitful (cf. Mt 25:14–30).

Communion with God, as Scripture explains in so many ways and places, is a gift flowing from divine love. Accepting that communion in faith and living it in love, we are made children of God, reborn as sons by grace through the work of the only begotten Son, and filled with supernatural life by the Holy Spirit. Those who are "partakers of the divine nature" live in the hope of their participation in trinitarian life being brought to fulfillment at the End. Then they will "eat of the tree of life, which is in the paradise of God" (Rev 2:7), and will dwell in the "holy city, new Jerusalem" and be in perfect communion with God, who will dwell with them (Rev 21:2–3). This truth, as the rest of this book demonstrates, has been the perennial teaching of the Catholic Church, the teaching of the truth of theosis.

Readings for Further Study

Bilaniuk, Petro B.T. "The Mystery of Theosis or Divinization". In *Studies in Eastern Christianity*, Seria Monohrafiï 25, 1:45–67. Munich/Toronto: Ukrainian Free University, 1977.

Bouyer, Louis. *The Christian Mystery: From Pagan Myth to Christian Mysticism*. London/New York: T&T Clark International, 2004.

Dauphinais, Michael, and Matthew Levering. *Holy People, Holy Land: A Theological Introduction to the Bible.* Grand Rapids, Mich.: Brazos Press, 2005.

De la Croix, Paul-Marie, O.C.D. *The Biblical Spirituality of St. John.* Staten Island, N.Y.: Alba House, 1966.

Keating, Daniel A. *Deification and Grace.* Naples, Fla.: Sapientia Press, 2007.

Vellanickal, Matthew. *The Divine Sonship of Christians in the Johannine Writings.* Analecta Biblica, vol. 72. Rome: Biblical Institute Press, 1977.

Chapter Two

DEIFICATION IN THE GREEK FATHERS

Daniel A. Keating

Deification in the Greek Fathers is a vast subject that has received serious attention by scholars in the past century.[1] The purpose of this essay, necessarily limited in scope, is to trace the main lines of development of the concept of deification in the Greek Fathers and to offer a summary understanding of the unity and variety on deification that we discover among the Greek Fathers.

As with many other Christian doctrines, the customary approach is to describe the doctrine of deification in terms of historical development from initial origins through seasons of growth to full flowering.[2] There is merit to this approach. The problem with this general model, however, arises when development is understood in terms of constant, linear progress, as if the Fathers were a set of mountain climbers in series, each one handing on the doctrine to the next in historical succession, such that the doctrine of deification is borne up a constant slope to the pinnacle of fullness.

Certainly there is historical continuity and real theological development, as each grouping of Christian teachers sought to understand and explain the faith handed on in the context of new challenges and opportunities. But progress was not constant or linear. We can

[1] Two studies on deification in the Greek Fathers stand out: Jules Gross, *The Divinization of the Christian according to the Greek Fathers*, trans. Paul A. Onica (Anaheim: A&C Press, 2002; original publication, *La divinization du chrétien d'après les pères grecs*, 1938), and Norman Russell, *The Doctrine of Deification in the Greek Patristic Tradition* (Oxford: Oxford University Press, 2004). Gross' 1938 monograph is still useful, though his investigation is colored by his preoccupation with responding to Adolf von Harnack's (1851–1930) criticisms. Russell is both up-to-date in scholarship and far more panoramic in scope. It is the single best work available.

[2] The main divisions of Gross' study display this customary pattern of development: (1) the period of formation; (2) the period of apogee; and (3) the period of consolidation.

recognize periods of great expansion in the meaning and terminology of deification, but also times when the concept was refined, chastened, and narrowed, and the terminology largely eschewed. Rather than viewing development in terms of constant linear progression, it is better to recognize a complex development, with backtracking and looping across the trails, as John McGuckin proposes: "This fertile theme [deification], then, loops its way forward rather than being linearly or progressively developed."[3] Admitting, then, the complex history of deification in the Greek Fathers, I will attempt to show the main lines of its development and identify the core features of this enigmatic doctrine.

The Roots of Deification

It is common, especially among those who reject the doctrine of deification as foreign to Christian faith, to locate the deepest roots of the Christian doctrine of deification in the social settings and philosophical currents of Greco-Roman society in the Late Antique period.[4] Certainly the social and philosophical context of the Roman world provided the *occasion* for the Christian use of deification. Christians were well aware of the notions of deification in the wider culture. But Norman Russell has argued persuasively that "in the development of the idea of deification and its distinctive vocabulary, it was Christianity that led the way."[5] From his study of the origins of deification, Carl Mosser agrees: "Careful study demonstrates that the doctrine of deification does not represent the climax of a syncretistic affair between Christianity and Hellenism", but is rather "a remarkable instance of fidelity to the early Jewish roots of Christian belief".[6]

[3] John McGuckin, "The Strategic Adaptation of Deification in the Cappadocians", in *Partakers of the Divine Nature: The History and Development of Deification in the Christian Traditions*, ed. Michael J. Christensen and Jeffrey A. Wittung (Teaneck, N.J.: Fairleigh Dickinson Press, 2007), 98.

[4] For one example, see Benjamin Drewery, "Deification", in *Christian Spirituality: Essays in Honour of Gordon Rupp*, ed. Peter Brooks (London: SCM Press, 1975), 54.

[5] Russell, *Doctrine of Deification*, 52.

[6] Carl Mosser, "The Earliest Patristic Interpretation of Psalm 82, Jewish Antecedents, and the Origins of Christian Deification", new series, *Journal of Theological Studies* 56 (2005): 73. The specifically Jewish background to Christian use of deification, often neglected, is thoroughly explored in Russell, *Doctrine of Deification*, 53–78.

The antecedents and parallels in the wider Greco-Roman culture are important to acknowledge and explore,[7] but the best explanation for the appearance of the concept and language of deification in Christian writers is to be found within the Church and from her own resources. The doctrine of deification took shape through engagement and conflict primarily within the Church, as the early Christians wrestled with and opposed the various Gnostic systems of the second and third centuries and the varieties of Arian teaching of the fourth century.

The Apostolic Fathers. In the Apostolic Fathers (late first century, early second century), we do not find the language of deification as such, but we do see "many themes associated with this concept that are destined to receive fuller treatments in the theology of Irenaeus, Clement of Alexandria, Origen, Athanasius, and others."[8] Ignatius of Antioch especially points in this direction: he identifies Christians as "Christ-bearers" (*christophoroi*) and "God-bearers" (*theophoroi*),[9] and speaks of Christians as "full of God"[10] and called to "participate in God".[11]

Psalm 82. The earliest prompt for the language of deification itself appears to have been a Christian interpretation of Psalm 82:6, which reads: "I say, 'you are gods, sons of the Most High, all of you'."[12] Justin Martyr (d. 165) is the first witness to an interpretation of this verse in terms of adoptive sonship in Christ: "It is proved that all human beings are deemed worthy of becoming gods and of having the power to become sons of the Most High."[13] Other early authors also display a similar interpretation. Irenaeus (late second century)

[7] For a wider treatment of the idea of deification in the Greco-Roman world, see Russell, *Doctrine of Deification*, 16–52, and Gross, *Divinization of the Christian*, 11–57.

[8] Vladimir Kharlamov, "Emergence of the Deification Theme in the Apostolic Fathers", in *Theōsis: Deification in Christian Theology*, ed. Stephen Finlan and Vladimir Kharlamov (Eugene, Ore.: Pickwick, 2006), 51.

[9] Ignatius of Antioch, *Letter to the Ephesians* 9.2.

[10] Ignatius of Antioch, *Letter to the Magnesians* 14.1.

[11] Ignatius of Antioch, *Letter to the Ephesians* 4.2.

[12] For a thorough exploration of Psalm 82:6 in the Fathers, see Mosser, "Earliest Patristic Interpretation of Psalm 82", 30–74.

[13] Justin Martyr, *Dialogue with Trypho* 124, trans. Russell, *Doctrine of Deification*, 99.

connects this verse to the grace of adoption (Rom 8) found in the Church:

> "God stood in the congregation of the gods, he judges among the gods." He [here] refers to the Father and the Son, and those who have received the adoption; but these are the Church.... But of what gods [does he speak]? [Of those] to whom he says, "I have said, you are gods, and all sons of the Most High." To those, no doubt, who have received the grace of the "adoption, by which we cry, Abba Father" (Rom 8:15).[14]

Clement of Alexandria (early third century) makes the connection between "becoming gods" and the event of baptism explicit:

> The same also takes place in our case, whose exemplar Christ became. Being baptized, we are illuminated; illuminated, we become sons; being made sons, we are made perfect; being made perfect, we are made immortal. "I", says He, "have said that you are gods, and all sons of the Highest." This work is variously called grace, and illumination, and perfection, and washing.[15]

Irenaeus of Lyon. If the language of Psalm 82:6 provided the first biblical warrant for speaking of Christians as "becoming gods", it is widely acknowledged that Irenaeus provided the theological framework for the doctrine of deification. Notably, Irenaeus never uses any of the technical *terms* for deification. What he provides—in response to the "Gnostic" teaching of the second century—is a vision of salvation that magnifies the glory of the Incarnation, in which Christ, the Word of God, became what we are (that is, a true and full human being) so that we could become what he is (that is, a true Son of God). He is the first to employ what is known as the "exchange formula" to sum up Christian salvation: "The Word of God was made man and he who was Son of God was made Son of Man united to the

[14] Irenaeus, *Adversus Haereses* 3.6.1, in *The Ante-Nicene Fathers* [*ANF*]*: Translations of the Writings of the Fathers Down to* A.D. *325*, vol. 1, *The Apostolic Fathers; Justin Martyr; Irenaeus*, ed. Alexander Roberts and James Donaldson (Grand Rapids, Mich.: Eerdmans, 1975), 419.

[15] Clement of Alexandria, *Paedagogus* 1.6, in *ANF*, vol. 2, *Fathers of the Second Century: Hermas, Tatian, Athenagoras, Theophilus, and Clement of Alexandria*, ed. A. Cleveland Cox (Grand Rapids, Mich.: Eerdmans, 1979), 215.

Word of God, in order that man should receive adoption and thereby become the Son of God."[16] Elsewhere he puts this more succinctly: "God made himself man, that man might become God."[17]

What Irenaeus *means* by this is concisely expressed in the following selection that embeds the exchange formula in an account of Christ as the mediator who restores the human race to friendship and communion with God:

> For it was incumbent upon the Mediator between God and men, by his relationship to both, to bring both to friendship and concord, and present man to God, while he revealed God to man. For, in what way could we be partakers of the adoption of sons, unless we had received from him through the Son that fellowship which refers to himself, unless his Word, having been made flesh, had entered into communion with us?[18]

It is this fundamental exchange at the heart of the gospel, often compressed into the "exchange formula", that will prove to be the explicit or implicit foundation for the development of the doctrine of deification in the Greek Fathers.

Appearance and Development

Clement of Alexandria. The terminology of deification first appears in Clement of Alexandria; he employs a range of words—*theopoieō*, *theioō*, *ektheoō*, and *theopoios*—to denote human deification.[19] Adopting Irenaeus' theological anthropology, Clement builds his understanding of deification on the indwelling of the Logos in the soul, but he accents the role of *imitation* in becoming like God.[20] God dwelling in us is the necessary precondition for deification, but for Clement it is becoming like God through imitation that receives the greatest emphasis.

[16] Irenaeus, *Adversus Haereses* 5 (praef.), trans. McGuckin, "Strategic Adaptation of Deification", 96.

[17] Irenaeus, *Adversus Haereses* 3.19.1, in ibid., 96–97.

[18] Irenaeus, *Adversus Haereses* 3.18.7, in *ANF*, 1:448.

[19] See Russell, *Doctrine of Deification*, 122–23; see also 333–44, where Russell provides an excellent summary of the Greek vocabulary of deification found in the Fathers.

[20] See ibid., 124, 128, 134.

Origen. The next critical figure for our tracing of the doctrine of deification is the great scholar and teacher Origen of Alexandria (d. 254). What are the marks of Origen's account of deification? On the one hand, he narrows the range of vocabulary in comparison with Clement, preferring the term *theopoieō* to describe Christian deification; on the other hand, he broadens the conceptual understanding of deification by using the language of participation. For Origen, "deification takes place through a spiritual participation in the logos."[21] Moreover, Origen is the first Christian writer to apply 2 Peter 1:4, "partakers of the divine nature", to our participation in God.[22] The following selection from his *Commentary on Romans* shows how Origen conceives of our participation in the divine nature through the gift of the indwelling Spirit:

> From the fullness of the Spirit, the fullness of love is infused into the hearts of the saints [Rom 5:5] in order to receive participation in the divine nature, as the apostle Peter has taught [2 Pet 1:4], so that through this gift of the Holy Spirit, the word which the Lord said might be fulfilled, "As you, Father, are in me and I in you, may they also be one in us" [Jn 17:21]. This is, of course, to be sharers of the divine nature by the fullness of love furnished through the Holy Spirit.[23]

Both the concept of participation and the use of 2 Peter 1:4 will prove important for the expansion of the doctrine of deification in later writers.

[21] Ibid., 143.

[22] For Origen as the first Christian writer to cite 2 Pet 1:4, see Russell, *Doctrine of Deification*, 151, and A.L. Kolp, "Partakers of the Divine Nature: The Use of II Pet. 1:4 by Athanasius", *Studia Patristica* 17 (1982): 1018. Russell says that "there seems to be an allusion to 2 Peter 1:4" in Tertullian (*Adv. Marc.* 2.25) that would predate Origen's use by a decade (*Doctrine of Deification*, 326). But it is questionable whether Tertullian's phrase "taking humanity into divinity" is an allusion to 2 Pet 1:4. When patristic authors allude to 2 Pet 1:4, they almost always make use of the term "partaker" or the phrase "divine nature". Neither appears in Tertullian's phrase, and in fact there is no verbal link between the two passages. Tertullian is clearly teaching a form of deification in this text, but there really is no echo of 2 Pet 1:4 here.

[23] Origen, *Commentary on Romans* 4.9.12, trans. Thomas P. Scheck, *Commentary on the Epistle to the Romans: Books 1–5*, Fathers of the Church 103 (Washington, D.C.: Catholic University of America Press, 2001), 292–93.

At the same time, though for Origen baptism is the beginning of Christian deification, he does not emphasize or develop the sacramental locus of deification.[24] Origen is, in fact, sometimes critiqued for his ambivalent attitude toward the body in general, drawing back from the rich theological anthropology found in Irenaeus.[25] As is true with so many other areas of his thought, Origen's account of deification displays genuine insights that will be crucial for later writers, but also contains ambiguities that will need to be clarified.

Athanasius. With the towering figure of Athanasius we arrive at a new stage in the use of the concept of deification. He follows Origen in both the use of participation language and in applying 2 Peter 1:4 to our adoptive sonship in Christ, and he uses terms for deification more frequently than any writer before him.[26]

Athanasius' earliest and best known statement on deification occurs in his work *On the Incarnation*, where he offers an unadorned version of the exchange formula: "For he was made man that we might be made God."[27] An expansion of this formula appears in a later work against the Arians: "He himself has made us sons of the Father, and deified men by becoming himself man. Therefore he was not man and then became God, but he was God, and then became man, and that to deify us."[28] Notably, Athanasius employs the terminology of deification in a new context—namely, to defend the full divinity of the Son and Spirit. He *assumes* that human destiny is to share in the divine nature, and uses this to argue that the Son and Spirit *must be* divine if they genuinely give us a share in the divine nature (as the Scripture testifies for Athanasius): "Further it is through the Spirit that we are all said to be partakers of God.... But if, by participation

[24] See Russell, *Doctrine of Deification*, 153.

[25] See ibid., 153. Andrew Louth claims that in Origen the Incarnation is only a stage to a higher union of the soul with God and that "Origen's mysticism centred on Christ is ultimately transcended by a mysticism centred on the eternal Word" (*The Origins of the Christian Mystical Tradition: From Plato to Denys* [Oxford: Clarendon Press, 1981], 65).

[26] Athanasius' use of the term *theopoiēsis* is the first instance of this word used in Greek Christian writing (see Russell, *Doctrine of Deification*, 168).

[27] Athanasius, *De Incarnatione* 54, in *Nicene and Post-Nicene Fathers* [*NPNF*]*: A Select Library of the Christian Church*, 2nd series, ed. Philip Schaff and Henry Wace (Peabody, Mass.: Hendrickson Pubs., 1995), 4:65. Russell translates this as follows: "He became human that we might become divine" (*Doctrine of Deification*, 169).

[28] Athanasius, *Contra Arianos* 1.38–39, in *NPNF*, 2nd series, 4:329. See also *Contra Arianos* 1.9 and 3.53.

in the Spirit, we are made 'sharers in the divine nature' (2 Pet 1:4), we should be mad to say that the Spirit has a created nature and not the nature of God."[29]

Faced with sophisticated attacks on the full divine status of the Son and Spirit, Athanasius drew selectively on the inheritance from Origen to produce an account of deification that was more scripturally and theologically integrated than any before him. Deification functions as a kind of lynchpin that brings together the doctrine of the Trinity, the Incarnation of the Son, and our share in the Son through the Spirit given through baptism. It implicates the whole of the Christian mystery and is centered on our divine filiation. Vladimir Kharlamov concludes: "More clearly than any Christian writer before him, Athanasius makes a direct identification between deification and divine sonship."[30]

The Cappadocian Fathers. The theme of deification appears in all three Cappadocian Fathers—Basil the Great, Gregory Nazianzen, and Gregory of Nyssa—but in varied ways. Basil is the most tentative in his use of this notion and its terminology. Norman Russell judges that Basil's understanding of deification is closer to Clement's view—pointing more to imitation of Christ and growth in virtue—than to Athanasius' account, which is grounded in a more ontological participation in Christ.[31] Still, Basil conceives of life in Christ through the Spirit as one of ongoing and increasing deification:

> So also Spirit-bearing souls, illuminated by the Spirit, are themselves becoming spiritual, and send forth their grace to others. Hence comes foreknowledge of the future, understanding of mysteries, apprehension of what is hidden, distribution of charismata, heavenly citizenship, a place in the chorus of angels, joy without end, abiding in God, likeness to God, and what is most desirable, being made God.[32]

[29] Athanasius, *Epistle to Serapion* 1.24, trans. C.R.B. Shapland, *The Letters of Saint Athanasius concerning the Holy Spirit* (New York: Philosophical Library, 1951), 125–26.

[30] Vladimir Kharlamov, "Rhetorical Application of Theosis in Greek Patristic Theology", in Christensen and Wittung, *Partakers of the Divine Nature*, 121.

[31] See Russell, *Doctrine of Deification*, 212. For Basil's approach to deification, see also Paul M. Collins, *Partaking in Divine Nature: Deification and Communion* (London and New York: T&T Clark, 2010), 66.

[32] Basil the Great, *De Spiritu Sancto* 9.23, cited in John Behr, *The Nicene Faith*, pt. 2 (Crestwood, N.Y.: St. Vladimir's Seminary Press, 2004), 316.

Gregory of Nazianzus uses the language of deification freely and dramatically and is the originator of the term "theosis".[33] Sometimes he appears to use the terms of deification simply as titles of honor, yet he plainly follows Athanasius in grounding our deification in the deifying activity of the Son and Spirit and anchors deification in the event of baptism: "Were the Spirit not to be worshipped, how could he deify me through baptism?"[34] Moreover, the exchange formula guides his understanding of our participation in the divine nature through Christ, as the following eloquent statement displays:

> O the paradoxical blending! He who is comes into being, and the uncreated is created, and the uncontained is contained.... The one who enriches becomes poor; he is made poor in my flesh, that I might be enriched through his divinity. The full one empties himself; for he empties himself of his own glory for a short time, that I may participate in his fullness.[35]

Norman Russell judiciously sums up Nazianzen's approach to deification as grounded in the Incarnation (what Russell calls the "realistic" sense of deification) but emphasizing the "ethical" aspect of deification as growth through ascetical practice.[36] We will see these two aspects of deification emerge even more clearly in the writings of Cyril of Alexandria and Maximus the Confessor.

With Gregory of Nyssa we confront a writer who is hesitant in his use of the terminology of deification, yet who appears to deepen the *concept* of deification considerably. John McGuckin observes that, though Nazianzen more readily uses the language of deification, it is Gregory of Nyssa who develops more deeply the implications of being assimilated to God and participating in God.[37] Nyssen offers his own version of the exchange formula, grounded in the Incarnation: "[The Word became incarnate] so that by becoming as we are, he

[33] See Russell, *Doctrine of Deification*, 214. The term "theosis" has become the most commonly used word for deification in the Byzantine tradition.

[34] Gregory of Nazianzus, *Oration* 31.28, trans. Frederick Williams and Lionel Wickham, *On God and Christ: The Five Theological Orations and Two Letters to Cledonius* (Crestwood, N.Y.: St. Vladimir's Press, 2002), 139.

[35] Gregory of Nazianzus, *Oration* 38.13, trans. Nonna Verna Harrison, *Festal Orations: St. Gregory of Nazianzus* (Crestwood, N.Y.: St. Vladimir's Seminary Press, 2008), 71.

[36] Russell, *Doctrine of Deification*, 222.

[37] See McGuckin, "Strategic Adaptation of Deification", 107.

might make us as he is."[38] But notably he ties our deification also to participation in the Eucharist:

> Since, then, that God-containing flesh partook for its substance and support of this particular nourishment also, and since the God who was manifested infused himself into perishable humanity for this purpose, viz. that by this communion with Deity mankind might at the same time be deified, for this end it is that, by dispensation of his grace, he disseminates himself in every believer through that flesh, whose substance comes from bread and wine, blending himself with the bodies of believers, to secure that, by this union with the immortal, man, too, may be a sharer in incorruption.[39]

A final word in this section should be offered on the Antiochene Fathers of the late fourth and early fifth centuries (for example, Diodore, Theodore of Mopsuestia, John Chrysostom). The striking thing about their theology overall is the absence of the language and conceptuality of deification. We do find a carefully stated version of the exchange formula in Chrysostom ("He became Son of man, who was God's own Son, in order that he might make the sons of men to be children of God"),[40] but especially in the works of Theodore we find no reference to or notion of deification. Nonna Verna Harrison suggests that Theodore redefines the goal of salvation not as participation in the divine nature in the traditional sense, but as "sinlessness and immortality in the age to come".[41]

Controversy, Broadening, and Maturing

In the fifth century we find a more hesitant use of the *terminology* of deification than we discovered in the fourth. The exact causes of

[38] Gregory of Nyssa, *Antirrheticus* 11, cited in Russell, *Doctrine of Deification*, 229.

[39] Gregory of Nyssa, *Catechetical Oration* 37, in *NPNF*, 2nd series, 5:506. In his *Mystagogical Catecheses* (4.3), Cyril of Jerusalem, a contemporary of Nyssen, also links the Eucharist to our participation in the divine nature (see 2 Pet 1:4).

[40] John Chrysostom, *Homilies on John* 11.1, in *NPNF*, 1st series, ed. Philip Schaff (Peabody, Mass.: Hendrickson Pubs., 1978), 14:38.

[41] Nonna Verna Harrison, "Women, Human Identity, and the Image of God: Antiochene Interpretations", *Journal of Early Christian Studies* 9 (2001): 222. For the absence of a theology of divinization in Theodore, see also Richard A. Norris, *Manhood in Christ: A Study of the Christology of Theodore of Mopsuestia* (Oxford: Clarendon, 1963), 190.

this more circumspect use of deification language are not certain, but they are commonly traced first to the Origenist and Anthropomorphite controversies of the late 390s and early 400s, and then to the outbreak of the Nestorian controversy in 429. As debate arose over the proper way to speak about the image of God in the human race on the one hand, and about the Incarnation on the other, theological language concerning human participation in the divinity became more chastened. At the same time, one could argue that through these controversies the *concept* of deification was deepened and found its most mature exponent to date in Cyril of Alexandria (d. 444).

Cyril of Alexandria. Cyril of Alexandria was in the thick of each of these controversies, either as a young protégé of his uncle Theophilus, the archbishop of Alexandria, or as one of the main protagonists in the later conflict with Nestorius. We find in Cyril's early works a use of the terminology of deification similar to his primary theological mentor, Athanasius, but with less frequency. With the onset of the Nestorian controversy, however, the technical terminology of deification disappears and is replaced by the frequent citation of 2 Peter 1:4 ("partakers of the divine nature"). Indeed, Cyril cites this text more frequently by far than any other Christian writer in the patristic period.

Like Irenaeus and Athanasius before him, Cyril anchors his understanding of deification in the Incarnation of the Word and the exchange at the heart of the gospel, as this sweeping statement from his *Commentary on John* displays:

> Therefore his only-begotten Word has become a partaker of flesh and blood, that is, he has become man, though being life by nature, and begotten of the life that is by nature, that is, of God the Father, so that, having united himself with the flesh which perishes according to the law of its own nature ... he might restore it to his own life and render it through himself a partaker of God the Father.... And he wears our nature, refashioning it to his own life. And he himself is also in us, for we have all become partakers of him, and have him in ourselves through the Spirit. For this reason we have become "partakers of the divine nature" (2 Pet 1: 4), and are reckoned

> as sons, and so too have in ourselves the Father himself through the Son.[42]

For Cyril it is by means of the divine life implanted within us—primarily through the gift of the Spirit in baptism and the Eucharist—that we grow progressively into the fullness of the divine image.

> For just as the root of the vine ministers and distributes to the branches the enjoyment of its own and inherent natural quality, so the only-begotten Word of God, by putting his Spirit within them, imparts to the saints, as it were, a kinship to his own nature and the nature of God the Father, inasmuch as they have been united with him through faith and complete holiness of life; and he nourishes them to godliness, and works in them the knowledge of all virtue and well doing.[43]

We find in Cyril an integration of what Norman Russell calls the "realistic" and "ethical" aspects of deification—that is, what God has done for us in Christ through the Spirit on the one hand, and our task of appropriating the grace of deification through a progressive advance toward the divine image and likeness on the other.[44] Jules Gross sums up this accomplishment: "With Cyril of Alexandria the doctrine of divinization indeed appears as the sum total of all that the previous fathers have written on this theme."[45]

The Monastic Tradition and Maximus the Confessor. After Cyril of Alexandria the doctrine of deification in the Greek world fell temporarily on hard times: "With Cyril's death in 444 deification disappears from view."[46] When it does reappear, it finds a new home in the monastic spirituality of Dionysius the Areopagite (early sixth century). Dionysius is especially well known for his simple formulation of the meaning of deification (or theosis). Theosis is according to

[42] Cyril of Alexandria, *Commentary on John 14:20*, trans. Daniel Keating, *Deification and Grace* (Naples, Fla.: Sapientia Press, 2007), 21.

[43] Cyril of Alexandria, *Commentary on John 15:1*, in ibid., 65.

[44] Russell, *Doctrine of Deification*, 9. For a detailed study of deification in Cyril, see Daniel Keating, *The Appropriation of Divine Life in Cyril of Alexandria* (Oxford: Oxford University Press, 2004).

[45] Gross, *Divinization of the Christian*, 233.

[46] Russell, *Doctrine of Deification*, 237.

Dionysius "the attainment of likeness to God and union with him so far as possible".[47]

But it is especially in the theology of Maximus the Confessor (d. 662) that we discover a remarkable melding of the earlier patristic tradition on deification with spiritual teaching drawn from the monastic life. Norman Russell claims that "the key to understanding Maximus in his monastic perspective.... The whole thrust of his writings is directed towards assisting his monastic or ascetically minded lay correspondents to advance in the spiritual life."[48]

What are the chief marks of Maximus' teaching on deification? First, our deification is entirely grounded in the coming of the Word into our flesh in the Incarnation:

> For just as having loosed the laws of nature supernaturally he was made low for us without change—a human being as we are, sin alone excepted—so also shall we consequently come to be above because of him—gods as he is by the mystery of grace—altering nothing at all of our nature.[49]

That deification occurs by grace means that our nature is not changed into another nature but elevated beyond its own natural limits.

Second, deification originates and is strengthened through the sacramental mediation of baptism and the Eucharist—this is fully in accord with the approach of Athanasius and especially Cyril.[50] But perhaps the hallmark of Maximus' teaching is his emphasis on the full exercise of personal freedom in the development of deification in the believer.

> For it was not possible in any other way for a created human being to be proved a son of God and a god through deification by grace unless

[47] Dionysius, *Ecclesiastical Hierarchy* 1.3, trans. Norman Russell, *Fellow Workers with God: Orthodox Thinking on Theosis* (Crestwood, N.Y.: St. Vladimir's Press, 2009), 21–22.

[48] Russell, *Doctrine of Deification*, 262. McGuckin identifies a similar spiritual-ascetical element in Maximus' doctrine of deification: "This powerful theologian amplified the ascetical context of the doctrine [of deification]" ("Strategic Adaptation of Deification", 98).

[49] Maximus the Confessor, *Ambigua* 7, trans. Adam G. Cooper, *The Body in St. Maximus the Confessor: Holy Flesh, Wholly Deified* (Oxford: Oxford University Press, 2005), 112.

[50] For the sacramental grounding of deification in Maximus, see Elena Vishnevskaya, "Divinization and Spiritual Progress in Maximus the Confessor", in *Theōsis: Deification in Christian Theology*, ed. Stephen Finlan and Vladimir Kharlamov (Eugene, Ore.: Pickwick, 2006), 141, and Russell, *Doctrine of Deification*, 294–95.

> first he had been born in the Spirit by choice, through the independent power of self-determination that naturally dwells within him.[51]

"For the Confessor, the essential conditions for fulfilling the divinizing process are the magnanimous divine initiative and willing human cooperation."[52]

Another noteworthy feature of Maximus' theology of deification is the role he accords to love: the love of God for us and our responsive love for God: "For nothing is more truly godlike than divine love, nothing more mysterious, nothing more apt to raise up human being to deification."[53] The accent on love in Maximus echoes the prominence of this theme in the theology of Augustine.

Finally, what we see in the Confessor's theology of deification is a thoroughgoing penetration of the divine and human resulting in the most exalted statements of our participation in God: "The whole of the human being is interpenetrated by the whole of God and becomes all that God is, excluding identity of essence. The human being receives to itself the whole of God and, as a prize for ascending to God, inherits God himself."[54] The clarity with which Maximus unites and distinguishes the human and divine natures in Christ enables him to speak of deification in the fullest possible sense without falling prey to pantheistic notions. Norman Russell concludes that Maximus' teaching on deification "represents the true climax of the patristic tradition" and that "the Irenaean and Alexandrian principle that God became man in order that man might become god receives in his hands its greatest elaboration and most profound articulation."[55]

[51] Maximus the Confessor, *Ambigua* 42, trans. Russell, *Doctrine of Deification*, 282.

[52] Vishnevskaya, "Divinization and Spiritual Progress", 134.

[53] Maximus the Confessor, *Epistle* 2, trans. Andrew Louth, *Maximus the Confessor* (London and New York: Routledge, 1996), 85.

[54] Maximus the Confessor, *Ambigua* 41, trans. Vishnevskaya, "Divinization and Spiritual Progress", 141.

[55] Russell, *Doctrine of Deification*, 8, 262. While this conclusion is fully warranted, I find Russell at points overstating the differences between Maximus and the earlier tradition of Athanasius and Cyril. He proposes that Maximus "abandoned the Christological use of the term and developed it in a completely new way", but many of Maximus' most profound statements on deification are centered on the Incarnation, the exchange formula, and the full reality of Christ's divine and human natures, which Russell himself acknowledges (294). Maximus certainly develops the spiritual implications of deification in a new monastic setting, but to claim as Russell does that with Maximus "we are almost in a different world here than Athanasius and Cyril" (*Fellow Workers*, 46) would seem to undervalue the profound continuities between the two approaches.

John of Damascus. The period of the Fathers in the East is normally understood to run at least as far as John of Damascus (d. 750). As is typical with John, we find an eloquent synthesis of the patristic teaching on deification—synthesizing the Alexandrians, the Cappadocians, and Maximus—but little elaboration. As Andrew Louth observes: "John himself does not use the language of deification very much, although he does regard the deification of human kind as the 'ultimate mystery.'"[56] The following selection displays John's approach to deification and brings to a close this brief survey of the development of deification in the Greek Fathers:

> Thus, because we did not keep what he had imparted to us, his own image and his own Spirit, he now participates in our poor weak nature so that he may render us pure and incorrupt and make us once more participators in his divinity.... Let us receive the divine burning coal, so that the fire of the coal may be added to the desire within us to consume our sins and enlighten our hearts, and so that by this communion of the divine fire we may be set afire and deified.[57]

Understanding Deification in the Greek Fathers

Attempts at synthesis often flatten the rich and varied elaboration on deification that we find in the actual writings of the Fathers, but notwithstanding this risk it is nonetheless important to identify the primary elements that comprise the doctrine of deification in the Greek Fathers.

1. Deification is grounded in the entire economy of salvation, and especially in the Incarnation of the Son of God and the exchange that occurred through his assumption and transformation of our nature. "For you know the grace of our Lord Jesus Christ, that for your sake he became poor, though being rich, so that by his poverty you may become rich" (2 Cor 8:9).[58] Deification for the Greek Fathers is not a separate and exotic path off on its own, but the culmination of all

[56] Andrew Louth, *St. John Damascene: Tradition and Originality in Byzantine Theology* (Oxford: Oxford University Press, 2002), 179.

[57] John of Damascus, *De Fide Orthodoxa* 4.13, trans. Frederic H. Chase, Jr., *St. John of Damascus: Writings*, Fathers of the Church 37 (Washington, D.C.: Catholic University of America Press, 1958), 355, 359.

[58] Translation by the author.

that the Father has done for the human race through the Son and in the Spirit.

2. The primary resources for the origination of the doctrine of deification came from the Scriptures, read in the light of the experience of faith in Christ within the Church. It was a reading of Psalm 82:6 (and later 2 Peter 1:4), interpreted within the wider biblical testimony of participation in Christ and the Spirit, especially in Paul and John, that provided the context for the concept and terminology of deification to emerge.[59]

3. God effectively dwelling in us is the source and cause of our deification. What Christ accomplished through his Passion, death, and Resurrection must be appropriated through the Church, and especially through the gift of the Spirit in baptism and the Eucharist. Indeed, deification in its primary sense is a way of speaking about adoptive sonship in Christ through the Spirit. Some Fathers are more explicit about the sacramental grounding of deification than others, but it is present in many of them and the best accounts display this clearly.

4. One of the hallmarks of the Eastern account of deification is the requirement of personal freedom for the reception of, and growth in, deification. Though personal freedom is not absent from Western accounts, it is much more fully emphasized and prized in the East. Perhaps this is one reason why the "ethical" aspect of deification seems to receive more attention in the East. Our full and free cooperation in our deification is not just a necessary instrument, but is itself *part* of being transformed into the image and likeness of Christ.

5. For the Greek Fathers, our deification is "by grace and not by nature". They are concerned to avoid any sense of pantheism, any confusion of human nature with the being and nature of the triune God. Paradoxically, though deification raises us to a participation in God that is above our nature, it does not bring about a *change* in our nature. Rather, through deification our nature is exalted, glorified, and brought to the goal for which we were made. Andrew Louth sums this up: "Deification, then, is not a transcending of what it means to be human, but the fulfillment of what it is to be human."[60]

[59] For a concise summary of the key biblical texts that served as the context for the doctrine of deification, see Keating, *Deification and Grace*, 16–20.

[60] Andrew Louth, "The Place of *Theosis* in Orthodox Theology", in Christensen and Wittung, *Partakers of the Divine Nature*, 39.

How should we evaluate the distinction between "image" and "likeness" that came to be an accepted theological principle in later Byzantine theology? According to this distinction, the "image" refers to humanity's created structure and is not lost through Adam's sin; the "likeness" is forfeited through Adam's sin, regained in Christ, and is something that we must personally attain as a result of ascetic effort.[61] Is this distinction found already in the Greek Fathers, and is it somehow intrinsic to the Eastern account of deification? This distinction appears in a first sketch in Irenaeus (though he also equates the two terms), and then is found in several of the Eastern Fathers (Clement of Alexandria, Basil the Great, Maximus, and John of Damascus). But notably the terms are not distinguished, but rather equated, in other prominent Greek Fathers (Athanasius, Gregory of Nyssa, Cyril of Alexandria), among whom we find a full and impressive elaboration of the doctrine of deification.[62] Given this range, we can conclude that a theological distinction between these terms *may* be useful for explicating deification, but is certainly not essential or integral to the doctrine itself.

In his impressive study *The Doctrine of Deification in the Greek Patristic Tradition*, Normal Russell proposes a system of classification—a threefold typology—for the different senses of deification, in an attempt to come to terms with the variety that we find in the Greek Fathers. He divides the senses of deification into *nominal*, *analogical*, and *metaphorical*. The nominal sense is simply honorific and occurs when the title "god" is given to humans as a way to honor their status. The analogical is defined as the stretching of the nominal, as when humans are spoken of as "gods by grace". The metaphorical sense is further divided into the "realistic" (the idea that human beings are somehow transformed and participate in God) and the "ethical" (the ascetic effort to attain likeness to God by imitation of him).[63] In a later volume, *Fellow Workers with God: Orthodox Thinking on Theosis*, Russell primarily employs the latter distinction between the realistic and the ethical sense.[64]

[61] Russell, *Fellow Workers*, 80.

[62] See ibid., 77–86, for an overview of the image-likeness distinction in the Greek Fathers.

[63] Russell, *Doctrine of Deification*, 1, 9, 14.

[64] Russell, *Fellow Workers*, 25–26. He also calls the realistic sense a "theological theme" and the ethical sense a "spiritual teaching" (23).

Identifying a nominal or honorific sense is useful, even if it is somewhat rare in the Greek Fathers. But the analogical sense as defined by Russell (the stretching of the nominal) misidentifies what the Fathers are saying when they claim that we are "gods by grace". This is not nominal language, but a formulaic way of expressing our *realistic* participation in Christ through the Spirit. Further, the category of "metaphorical" is ambiguous and (I believe) unhelpful. In one sense, all language of deification is metaphorical, because we do not become "God" by nature and essentially, but "by grace", and therefore (in a sense) metaphorically.

Consequently, I would recommend retaining three of the terms he uses (nominal, realistic, and ethical), with the first indicating *merely* an honorific use, and the second two necessarily paired together to convey the true content of deification. The realistic and ethical senses of deification parallel in a striking way the christological (or allegorical) and moral senses of interpreting the Bible. Just as the Fathers interpret the whole of the Bible in terms of its *telos* in Christ himself (his saving work), so they also employ the moral sense to show how the Scripture now applies to us.

In the same way, the ethical sense of deification—our progress in deification through ascetical effort and the full use of our graced capacities—must be founded on the realistic sense of deification and draw energy from what Christ has already done, and from the real indwelling of the Spirit (and so of the triune God) in the soul. Russell himself arrives at a similar position—that the ethical and realist senses must go together: "Neither approach is independent of the other. The realist needs the ethical, and the ethical the realistic. Participation and imitation go hand in hand."[65] And, I would add, the ethical needs to *follow in principle* upon the realistic, for if Christ has not redeemed our nature in himself and granted to us a share in that redeemed nature through the Spirit in baptism, we have no ability to exert ourselves and so grow into the fullness of the divine likeness.

We find in some Greek Fathers an accent on the realistic sense of deification, and in others an accent on the ethical sense. But even among the latter the *foundation* in the realistic sense is there, either explicitly or implicitly. And the fullest accounts of deification, found

[65] Ibid., 26.

in Cyril and Alexandria and Maximus the Confessor, impressively combine both senses and show their interrelation, and so display in a marvelous way "what God has prepared for those who love him" (1 Cor 2:9).

Readings for Further Study

Christensen, Michael J., and Jeffrey A. Wittung, eds. *Partakers of the Divine Nature: The History and Development of Deification in the Christian Traditions*. Teaneck, N.J.: Fairleigh Dickinson Press, 2007.

Gross, Jules. *The Divinization of the Christian according to the Greek Fathers.* Translated by Paul A. Onica. Anaheim: A&C Press, 2002.

Keating, Daniel A. *The Appropriation of Divine Life in Cyril of Alexandria.* Oxford: Oxford University Press, 2004.

Russell, Norman. *The Doctrine of Deification in the Greek Patristic Tradition.* Oxford: Oxford University Press, 2004.

Chapter Three

DEIFICATION IN THE LATIN FATHERS

Jared Ortiz

The Latin patristic understanding of deification is a vast topic that has not received the scholarly attention it deserves. Indeed, it has become something of a commonplace to say that the Latin Fathers did not really hold a doctrine of deification, that the few exceptions to this learned it from the Greeks, and that the Latins are generally guilty of losing sight of the big picture of salvation (becoming God) by reducing it to a narrow conception of redemption (overcoming sin).[1] While there are many good studies of deification in the Greek Fathers, it would not be possible, the argument runs, to write a parallel study on the Fathers of the Latin Church.[2]

[1] In one of the only surveys of Latin patristic thought on deification, Gustave Bardy (in the very first sentence) asserts that "Latin theology has always insisted much less than Greek theology on the divinization of man" ("Divinisation: Chez les Pères Latins", in *Dictionnaire de Spiritualité, ascétique et mystique doctrine et histoire*, ed. Charles Baumgartner and Marcel [Paris: Beauchesne, 1957], 1390). Bardy also argues that it was Greek patristic thought that influenced the Latin Fathers on deification (1393). In their collection of essays on the development of the doctrine of deification, Michael J. Christensen and Jeffrey A. Wittung do not include any discussion of the Latin Fathers (*Partakers of the Divine Nature: The Historical Development of Deification in the Christian Tradition* [Grand Rapids, Mich.: Baker Academic, 2007]). Andrew Louth's essay in the Christensen-Wittung volume, "The Place of *Theosis* in Orthodox Theology", offers the criticism that the West has reduced salvation to redemption and cites the Easter *Exsultet* as evidence (34–35). In *The Doctrine of Deification in the Greek Patristic Tradition* (repr., Oxford: Oxford University Press, 2009), Norman Russell says, "Deification is also found in the Latin tradition, but, with the exception of St. Augustine, very sparsely" (325). He discusses deification in three Latin Fathers briefly and fairly in an appendix (325–32). Daniel Keating, in his *The Appropriation of Divine Life in Cyril of Alexandria* (Oxford: Oxford University Press, 2004), includes a chapter comparing the Latin Fathers Augustine and Leo to Cyril as well as a thoughtful assessment of the "perceived East-West differences" on deification. There are a few scattered studies of individual Latin Fathers (mostly of Hilary and Augustine), but I am aware of no other major treatment of deification in the Latin Fathers.

[2] Bardy, "Divinisation: Chez les Pères Latins", 1390.

This essay cannot go into the history of how these opinions have arisen. Rather, through an attentive survey of the Latin tradition, it aims to demonstrate that deification is an essential part of the grammar of Latin patristic thought.[3] Like the Greek Fathers, the Latin Fathers do not all equally develop or employ deification, nor do they always understand it the same way.[4] Like the Greeks, many Latin Fathers are reticent to use the word "deification", though by drawing on a range of complementary terms—ascent, adoption, grace, contemplation, vision, knowledge, likeness to God, imitation, perfection, sanctification, participation, union, angelic life, immortality—they all, to greater or lesser degrees, point to the same *reality* of deification. Like the Greeks, there is variety to the place and role of deification in the thought of different Latin Fathers. Because the Latin patristic tradition of deification has hitherto not been explored, this essay will be broad, seeking to show the richness, diversity, and near ubiquity of deification in early Latin Christian thought. It is hoped that the discussion here can help overcome some of the commonplaces that have thus far inhibited serious study of deification in the Latin Fathers.

Lex Orandi, Lex Credendi

"The law of praying is the law of believing", or, more simply put, how the Church prays reflects and determines what she believes. This ancient principle has often been invoked in doctrinal controversies in order to establish what the Church really teaches: if the Church worships in such a way, then she must actually believe such things are the case. The question, then, is, are Latin Christians praying deification in the patristic period?

[3] Augustine is not included this survey because his contribution is treated in the following chapter.

[4] As a working definition of deification, I follow John McGuckin: "The concept of deification is the process of the sanctification of Christians whereby they become progressively conformed to God; a conformation that is ultimately demonstrated in the glorious transfiguration of the 'just' in the heavenly Kingdom, when immortality and a more perfect vision (and knowledge and experience) of God are clearly manifested in the glorification (Δόξα) of the faithful" ("The Strategic Adaptation of Deification in the Cappadocians", in Christensen and Wittung, *Partakers of the Divine Nature*, 95). Like the Greeks, the Latin Fathers will emphasize, modify, add, or refine one or another aspect of this definition.

A study of the liturgical language of the Latin West turns up a wealth of references to deification. For example, during the Christmas Mass, it was not uncommon for a Latin bishop to pray a collect like this:

> O God, You who have wondrously created the dignity of human nature and more wondrously reformed it, grant us, we pray, to be sharers of the divinity of your Son, Jesus Christ, who deigned to become a participator of our humanity.[5]

In the fifth century, the Basilica of Saint Mary Major in Rome—which then as now houses the relics of Christ's manger and therefore has always had a particular devotion to the mystery of the Incarnation—prayed this antiphon at vespers on the Feast of the Circumcision:

> O wondrous exchange!
> The Creator of the human race,
> Assuming an ensouled body,
> Deigned to be born of a Virgin,
> And coming forth as a man, without a seed,
> He bestowed on us his deity [*deitatem*].[6]

Even the *Exsultet* sung at Easter Vigil, which is often pointed to as evidence that the West has reduced salvation to redemption, begins by locating the redeemed congregation in heaven with the angels and culminates with this mystical invocation: "O truly blessed night ... in which heaven is united to earth, and God to man."[7] This theme is developed the next day in the Solemn Preface to the Canon of the Easter Day Mass, which powerfully brings together the Latin understanding of redemption and deification:

[5] Translation by the author. Original Latin can be found in *Sacramentarium Veronense*, ed. Leo Eizenhöfer, Cunibert Mohlberg, and Petrus Siffrin (Rome: Herder, 1956), 1239. See also antiphons 1258 and 1260. This sacramentary was compiled in the sixth century, though the prayers could have originated any time before this.

[6] Translation by the author. For original Latin text and lovely commentary, see Éamonn Ó Carragáin, *Ritual and the Rood: Liturgical Images and the Old English Poems of the Dream of the Rood Tradition* (Toronto: University of Toronto Press, 2005), 288.

[7] Translation by the author. Original Latin can be found in the *Missale Romanum ex Decreto Sacrosancti Oecumenici Concilii Vaticani II instauratum auctoritate Pauli VI promulgatum, Ordo lectionum Missae* (Vatican City: Vatican Polyglot Press, 1970), 273. This sequence was likely composed in the fourth or fifth century.

> It is truly right and just in every time, but especially on this day, that we should praise, bless, and proclaim you, because Christ, our Paschal Sacrifice, was offered, through whom the sons of light rise into eternal life, the halls of the kingdom of heaven are opened to the faithful, and by the law of blessed exchange human things are changed into divine. For the death of all of us has been redeemed by the cross of Christ and the life of all has been resurrected in his Resurrection.[8]

In the liturgical prayers of the Latin West, the Incarnation and the Resurrection are understood as uniting God and man, and as changing the latter into the former. The liturgies celebrating those events make this deifying reality present or, more accurately, advance the process of deification, a fact profoundly underscored by the Latin understanding of the sacraments. These examples show that deification informs Latin Christian prayer and so must also inform Latin Christian belief.

Third Century

The Latin language does not become widely used in the Roman Empire until the third century, where it appears first in North Africa and only later in Rome and beyond. Before this time, there were many Greek-speaking Christians who lived in the West and taught deification—Irenaeus, Justin Martyr, and Hippolytus, among the most notable. Their influence on the Latin Church is debated, though the fact that they all took deification for granted and lived in the West suggests that the idea is, at least, not geographically foreign. Their contributions have been well treated in other places,[9] so we will turn to the first Latin-speaking Christians who touched on the theme of deification.

North African Martyrs. The prison writings of the North African martyrs, collected and edited (likely by Tertullian) in *The Passion of*

[8] Translation by the author. Original Latin can be found in *The Gelasian Sacramentary: Liber Sacramentorum Romanae Ecclesiae*, ed. Henry Austin Wilson (Oxford: Clarendon Press, 1894), 90.

[9] See, for example, Russell, *Doctrine of Deification*, 96–112, and references therein.

the Holy Martyrs Perpetua and Felicity, are some of the earliest (ca. 203) and most remarkable Latin Christian documents we have. They are an eloquent testimony to the Latin understanding of martyrdom and attest to the prevalence of deification themes available to African Christians at an early date.[10] For Perpetua and her companions, dying for Christ meant transformation into Christ; it meant ascent to paradise, divine adoption, and immersion into loving communion with God. In a vision granted to the newly baptized Perpetua, she sees a golden ladder, hemmed on both sides by instruments of torture, which reaches from earth to heaven, but guarded by a dragon at the bottom.[11] As she begins to ascend the narrow path, she, like another Christ, tramples the head of the dragon. At the top of the ladder, Perpetua sees a white-haired shepherd, surrounded by thousands of martyrs, tending his sheep in a garden, who welcomes her as "daughter" and gives her "as it were a little cake".[12] Upon waking, she still can taste the indescribable sweetness of this heavenly Eucharist—something of heaven, communion with Christ, is already being experienced here, even in the darkness of prison.

Because their martyrdom is imminent, there is no real sense of advancing in deification or of progressive participation in the life of God. Transformation is identification, an idea echoed by Perpetua's slave Felicity, who, when mocked by the guards because of her pains while giving birth in prison, retorts, "Now it is I that suffer what I suffer; but then [when thrown to the beasts] there will be another in me, who will suffer for me, because I also am about to suffer for Him."[13] There is though a real sense of continuity between the joy of suffering here and the joy to be experienced in heaven: "Thanks be to God," Perpetua says to Saturus in his vision, "that joyous as I was in the flesh, I am now more joyous here."[14]

[10] Some of these themes are reminiscent of Jewish apocalyptic thought. See ibid., 53–79.

[11] See *The Passion of the Holy Martyrs Perpetua and Felicity* 1.3, trans. R. E. Wallis, in *Ante-Nicene Fathers* [*ANF*], eds. Alexander Roberts and James Donaldson, vol. 3 (Peabody, Mass.: Hendrickson Pubs., 1995), revised and edited for New Advent by Kevin Knight, 2009, http://newadvent.org/fathers/0324.htm.

[12] Ibid.

[13] *Passion of the Holy Martyrs Perpetua and Felicity* 5.2. These same themes are present in the vision of Perpetua's companion Saturus (4.1–3), though he emphasizes the idea of martyrdom as a sharing in the life of the angels.

[14] *Passion of the Holy Martyrs Perpetua and Felicity* 4.2.

Tertullian. Fluent in Latin and Greek, the North African Tertullian was likely familiar with deification ideas from both traditions. Tertullian, though, was not simply borrowing from others, but was creatively working through a variety of biblical texts to articulate his understanding of deification. For example, in interpreting God's comment, "Adam has become as one of us" (Gen 3:22), Tertullian says that this is "in consequence of the future taking of the man into the divine nature".[15] In the Incarnation, Christ has united both human and divine nature in himself; "He has fitted them together as bride and bridegroom in the reciprocal bond of wedded life."[16] By dying, Christ has redeemed us and given us the Holy Spirit, who, Tertullian says, is responsible for disciplining our moral mediocrity and bringing us to perfection (that is, advancing godlikeness).[17] But because Christ has risen and ascended, he has already "carried our flesh with him into heaven as a pledge of that complete entirety which is one day to be restored to it"[18]—that is, when our bodies will be glorified in the resurrection. The Transfiguration, Tertullian says, proves that this glorification will not destroy our nature, for Christ himself retained both his human and divine nature intact when transfigured, while Moses and Elias were shown still to be fully human in their glorified state.[19] Highlighting the related moral and ontological dimensions of deification, Tertullian eloquently sums up the hope Christ has given us: "God held converse with man, that man might learn to act as God. God dealt on equal terms with man, that man

[15] Tertullian, *Against Marcion* 2.25, trans. Peter Holmes, in *ANF*, eds. Alexander Roberts, James Donaldson, and A. Cleveland Coxe, vol. 3 (Buffalo, N.Y.: Christian Literature Publishing, 1885), revised and edited for New Advent by Kevin Knight, 2009, http://newadvent.org/fathers/03122.htm.

[16] Tertullian, *On the Resurrection of the Flesh* 63, trans. Peter Holmes, in *ANF*, eds. Alexander Roberts, James Donaldson, and A. Cleveland Coxe, vol. 3 (Buffalo, N.Y.: Christian Literature Publishing, 1885), revised and edited for New Advent by Kevin Knight, http://newadvent.org/fathers/0316.htm. See also *On the Resurrection* 8.

[17] See the following, where he describes the "stages of growth" through which the Spirit leads us: Tertullian, *On the Veiling of Virgins* 1, trans. S. Thelwall, in *ANF*, eds. Alexander Roberts, James Donaldson, and A. Cleveland Coxe, vol. 4 (Buffalo, N.Y.: Christian Literature Publishing, 1885), revised and edited for New Advent by Kevin Knight, 2009, http://newadvent.org/fathers/0403.htm. See also *On the Resurrection* 9.

[18] Tertullian, *On the Resurrection* 51.

[19] See ibid., 55. See also *Ad Martyras* 2, trans. S. Thelwall, in *ANF*, eds. Alexander Roberts, James Donaldson, and A. Cleveland Coxe, vol. 3 (Buffalo, N.Y.: Christian Literature Publishing, 1885), revised and edited for New Advent by Kevin Knight, 2009, http://www.newadvent.org/fathers/0323.htm.

might be able to deal on equal terms with God. God was found little, that man might become very great."[20]

Cyprian. Cyprian was an avid reader of Tertullian, yet his thought on deification developed in its own distinctive way.[21] Cyprian emphasizes the interrelated sacramental and ethical dimensions of deification, more so than Tertullian, though he also seems to have lost something of Tertullian's dynamic understanding of the deification process. For Cyprian, baptism makes us sons and daughters of God, and this awesome change must be manifest in a Christlike way of life. Of baptism and the moral life, Cyprian says,

> For this is to change what you had been, and to begin to be what you were not, that is, sons of God by grace, that the divine birth might shine forth in you, that the godly discipline might respond to God, the Father, that in the honour and praise of living, God may be glorified in man.[22]

Cyprian often comments on how our union with Christ is made possible by the Incarnation and is realized in the celebration of the Eucharist:

> For because Christ bore us all, in that He also bore our sins, we see that in the water is understood the people, but in the wine is showed the blood of Christ. But when the water is mingled in the cup with wine, the people is made one with Christ, and the assembly of believers is associated and conjoined with Him on whom it believes; which association and conjunction of water and wine is so mingled in the Lord's cup, that that mixture cannot any more be separated.[23]

[20] Tertullian, *Against Marcion* 2.27; see also 3.24.

[21] Bardy says that Cyprian can be passed over completely (see "Divinisation: Chez les Pères Latins", 1394).

[22] Cyprian, *On Jealousy and Envy* 15, trans. Robert Ernest Wallis, in *ANF*, eds. Alexander Roberts, James Donaldson, and A. Cleveland Coxe, vol. 5 (Buffalo, N.Y.: Christian Literature Publishing, 1885), revised and edited for New Advent by Kevin Knight, 2009, http://newadvent.org/fathers/050710.htm. See also ibid., 14; *Epistle* 1.3 and 80.2; *On the Lord's Prayer* 9–11.

[23] Cyprian, *Epistle* 62.13, trans. Robert Ernest Wallis, in *ANF*, eds. Alexander Roberts, James Donaldson, and A. Cleveland Coxe, vol. 5 (Buffalo, N.Y.: Christian Literature Publishing, 1885), revised and edited for New Advent by Kevin Knight, 2009, http://newadvent.org/fathers/050662.htm.

The Incarnation and the sacraments unite us to Christ and so make us holy. "And therefore we ask that our bread—that is, Christ—may be given to us daily, that we who abide and live in Christ may not depart from His sanctification and body."[24] For Cyprian, there does not seem to be much sense that one progresses in likeness to Christ or that one advances in "godly discipline". Rather, in baptism, one is sanctified and the task of the Christian is to *maintain* that sanctification by a holy way of life.[25]

Novatian. Turning from Africa to Rome, we come upon Novatian, the first Roman author to write in Latin. His *De Trinitate* displays a highly developed understanding of deification. According to Novatian, God gave man freedom as a fitting complement to the dignity of being made in his image. He was invited to use this freedom to obey God and thus win for himself immortality. Instead, man plunged himself into mortality, "by hurrying to be God under the influence of perverse counsel".[26] Novatian is alluding to Satan's promise of (self- and therefore false) deification in Genesis 3:5, an interpretation of this passage which is surprisingly uncommon in both Latin and Greek literature.[27] Christ came to restore us to immortality which, Novatian says, "is the fruit of divinity".[28] Christ offers us a share in his own divine life and this proves that Christ is divine as well: "by giving divinity by immortality, He proves Himself to be God by offering divinity, which if He were not God He could not give."[29] Christ's offer of deification—which is here assumed—is proof that Christ is God. This offer would be meaningless, though, if God had not also truly become man. In the Incarnation, God became "a

[24] Cyprian, *On the Lord's Prayer* 18, trans. Robert Ernest Wallis, in *ANF*, eds. Alexander Roberts, James Donaldson, and A. Cleveland Coxe, vol. 5 (Buffalo, N.Y.: Christian Literature Publishing, 1885), revised and edited for New Advent by Kevin Knight, 2009, http://newadvent.org/fathers/050704.htm.

[25] See ibid., 12. See also *Epistle* 14 and *On the Dress of Virgins* 3.

[26] Novatian, *On the Trinity* 1, trans. Robert Ernest Wallis, in *ANF*, eds. Alexander Roberts, James Donaldson, and A. Cleveland Coxe, vol. 5 (Buffalo, N.Y.: Christian Literature Publishing, 1886), revised and edited for New Advent by Kevin Knight, 2009, http://newadvent.org/fathers/0511.htm.

[27] See, though, Augustine, *City of God* 22.30.

[28] Novatian, *On the Trinity* 15.

[29] Ibid.

sharer in our body" so that "our body should be in Him", for otherwise salvation would not be possible for us.[30]

Novatian locates his understanding of the deification process in his trinitarian theology. Through Christ, the Holy Spirit brings about the saving effects of baptism and "effects with water the second birth as a certain seed of divine generation, and a consecration of a heavenly nativity, the pledge of a promised inheritance, and as it were a kind of handwriting of eternal salvation".[31] The Spirit thus becomes "an inhabitant given for our bodies and an effector of their holiness" who works "in us for eternity".[32] Perhaps drawing on a theme from Irenaeus, Novatian says that the Holy Spirit acclimates human beings to God over time,[33] "for our bodies are both trained in Him and by Him to advance to immortality, by learning to govern themselves with moderation according to His decrees."[34] This process will be completed only when the Holy Spirit produces "our bodies at the resurrection of immortality".[35]

Fourth Century

Lactantius. The early fourth-century convert and Christian apologist Lactantius quotes approvingly an insight from Seneca: "Virtue is the only thing which can confer upon us immortality, and make us equal to the gods."[36] Lactantius thinks that Seneca does not really understand the deep truth of what he has said, so he develops the idea in its properly Christian context. Lactantius roots the transformation of man into god-equality in the mediation of Christ, who is both God and man. Although Lactantius has something of a muddled Christology (claiming that Christ, though truly divine and human, is a "middle

[30] Ibid., 10.

[31] Ibid., 29.

[32] Ibid., 15.

[33] Ibid. Cf. Irenaeus, *Against Heresies* 3.17.1, 3.20.2, 4.38.1, and 5.7.1.

[34] Novatian, *On the Trinity*, 29.

[35] Ibid.

[36] Lactantius, *Divine Institutes* 3.12, trans. William Fletcher, in *ANF*, eds. Alexander Roberts, James Donaldson, and A. Cleveland Coxe, vol. 7 (Buffalo, N.Y.: Christian Literature Publishing, 1886), revised and edited for New Advent by Kevin Knight, 2009, http://newadvent.org/fathers/07013.htm.

substance"), he still understands that the purpose of the Incarnation is that Christ "might be able, as it were, to take by the hand this frail and weak nature of ours, and raise it to immortality".[37]

Hilary. From his exile among the Greeks, Hilary of Poitiers likely learned to use deification as an argument for the divinity of Christ against the Arians. In his *De Trinitate*, he shows how it cannot be the case, as the Arians claimed, that the Father and Son share only a unity of will and not of nature. For "God the Word became flesh, that through His Incarnation our flesh might attain to union with God the Word."[38] So, "while, we abiding in Him, He abode in the Father, and as abiding in the Father abode also in us; and so we might arrive at unity with the Father, since in Him Who dwells naturally in the Father by birth, we also dwell naturally, while He Himself abides naturally in us also."[39] The fact that we are destined for union with God—that we will be deified—proves that Christ is also God.

While Hilary probably acquired these anti-Arian arguments from the Greeks, they found such a ready audience because Hilary was already versed in the deification tradition before his exile. In his pre-exilic commentary on the Gospel of Matthew, he says,

> He calls the flesh that he had assumed a city because, as a city consists of a variety and multitude of inhabitants, so there is contained in him, through the nature of the assumed body, a certain assembly of the whole human race. And thus he becomes a city from our assembly in him and we become the dwelling of this city through consort with his flesh.[40]

The Incarnation, the young Hilary holds, brings about a real change in our humanity. A recent student of Hilary's deification thought

[37] Ibid., 4.13; see also 4.25.

[38] Hilary, *On the Trinity* 1.11, trans. E. W. Watson and L. Pullan, in *Nicene and Post-Nicene Fathers* [*NPNF*]*: A Select Library of the Christian Church*, 2nd series, vol. 9, eds. Philip Schaff and Henry Wace (Buffalo, N.Y.: Christian Literature Publishing, 1899), revised and edited for New Advent by Kevin Knight, 2009, http://newadvent.org/fathers/330201.htm.

[39] Ibid., vol. 8, http://newadvent.org/fathers/330208.htm, and *Tractatus super Psalmos* 67.37.

[40] Hilary, *In Matthaeum* 4.12, trans. Ellen Scully, in "The Assumption of All Humanity in Saint Hilary of Poitiers' *Tractatus super Psalmos*" (Ph.D. diss., Marquette University, Milwaukee, Wisc., 2011), 89.

comments boldly on what this means: "Every human being now born, because of his very human nature—the nature that Christ assumed—is conformed to the body of Christ and, through this mediation, is assumed into a unity with the paternal glory, that is, into participation in divine life. Unity with God is now an ontological fact that precedes any individual's act of the will."[41] This change needs to be "ratified" by the sacraments, but the Incarnation itself changes us and gives us a profound hope. Hilary returns to this idea again and again and even incorporates it into one of his hymns:

> With what strong hopes have I faithfully believed in Christ,
> Who by His Birth taketh me to Himself through His Flesh....
> This lasting gift of God (Christ) offereth to His saints,
> To live hereafter with Him in a body like his own.[42]

In Hilary of Poitiers, the West finds its most eloquent spokesman for the transformative effects of the Incarnation itself.

Marius Victorinus. Drawing heavily on his training in Neoplatonic philosophy, the famous philosopher and convert Marius Victorinus comes to understand the effects of the Incarnation in a similar way to Hilary. For Victorinus, Christ is primarily understood as the Logos, the Word, through whom all things were made. He is present to and the principle of all things that exist. "It is not astonishing then that the *Logos* has taken flesh mysteriously to come to the aid of the flesh and of man."[43] When the Logos becomes flesh, he assumes a whole man, body and soul. But he does not just take a particular body and soul, but the universal body and soul, the logos of body and the logos of soul; in other words, the Logos takes to himself "the totality of all souls and all bodies".[44] "These universals [of flesh

[41] Scully, "Assumption of All Humanity", 117. Cf. *Tractatus super Psalmos* 125.6 and 66.7.

[42] Hilary, Hymn II, trans. Walter Neidig Myers, "The Hymns of Saint Hilary of Poitiers in the *Codex Aretinus*: An Edition, with Introduction, Translation and Notes" (master's thesis, University of Pennsylvania, Philadelphia, 1928). See also *On the Trinity* 9.4–5 and 11.49.

[43] Marius Victorinus, *Against Arius III* II.2.3, trans. Mary T. Clark, *Theological Treatises on the Trinity*, Fathers of the Church 69 (Washington, D.C.: Catholic University of America Press, 1981), 225.

[44] Aloys Grillmeier, *Christ in Christian Tradition*, vol. 1 (Atlanta: John Knox Press, 1975), 406.

and soul] have been raised upon the cross and purified by the Savior God, the *Logos*, the universal of all universals."[45] In the Incarnation (including the Cross and Resurrection), the Logos raises up "souls and bodies through the operation of the Holy Spirit to life again, to divine and life-giving understanding, uplifted by knowledge, faith, and love".[46] The taking up of the whole man transforms all men. Now, through the Holy Spirit, the Logos is not only present in men, but their actions become actions of the Logos, who "projects, so to speak, its power towards inferiors and towards actions, while it fills the world and worldly things".[47]

Ambrose. Like Hilary, Ambrose assumes the doctrine of deification as a principle from which he can argue. Against those who would deny the divinity of the Holy Spirit, Ambrose says, "Who, then, can dare to say that the Holy Spirit is separated from the Father and the Son, since through Him we attain to the image and likeness of God, and through Him, as the Apostle Peter says, are partakers of the divine nature?"[48] Polemics, though, are not the primary place Ambrose develops his understanding of deification; rather, he explores it in his mystical reading of the Song of Songs and in his reflections on the life of virginity.

> Virginity has brought from heaven that which it may imitate on earth. And not unfittingly has she sought her manner of life from heaven, who has found for herself a Spouse in heaven. She, passing beyond the clouds, air, angels, and stars, has found the Word of God in the very bosom of the Father, and has drawn Him into herself with her whole heart.[49]

[45] Victorinus, *Against Arius III* II.2.3.

[46] Victorinus, *Against Arius IB* 58. For more on how these Victorine themes are experienced in the Christian life, see his Hymns to the Trinity II and III.

[47] Victorinus, *Against Arius III* III.2.12. Grillmeier uses this quotation to point out an aspect of "cosmic redemption" in the thought of Victorinus (*Christ in Christian Tradition*, 406).

[48] Ambrose, *On the Holy Spirit* 1.6.80, trans. H. de Romestin, E. de Romestin, and H. T. F. Duckworth, in *NPNF*, 2nd series, ed. Philip Schaff and Henry Wace, vol. 10 (Buffalo, N.Y.: Christian Literature Publishing, 1896), revised and edited for New Advent by Kevin Knight, 2009, http://newadvent.org/fathers/34021.htm. See also *On Christian Faith* 5.14.180–81.

[49] Ambrose, *On Virginity* 1.3.11, trans H. de Romestin, E. de Romestin, and H. T. F. Duckworth, in *NPNF*, 2nd series, ed. Philip Schaff and Henry Wace, vol. 10 (Buffalo, N.Y.: Christian Literature Publishing, 1896), revised and edited for New Advent by Kevin Knight, 2009, http://newadvent.org/fathers/34071.htm. See also *On the Mysteries* 7.37–42 and *On Death as a Good* 5.20.

Virginity is an angelic way of life, for Christ brought it down from heaven when he joined himself to an earthly body. "Then a Virgin conceived," Ambrose says, "and the Word became flesh that flesh might become God."[50] In a number of treatises, Ambrose develops a spiritual itinerary of the soul espoused to God,[51] which he develops in surprising ways. Not only does the espoused soul ascend so as to delight in God himself, but because the soul is transformed by deifying virtue, Christ himself delights and even feeds on the soul. "Christ dines on such food in us, He drinks such drink in us."[52] And yet, even Christ's feeding on us is a spur to further advancement into godlikeness, for "with the intoxication of this drink, He challenges us to make a departure from worse things to those that are better and best"—that is, to God himself.[53]

Jerome. Like Ambrose, Jerome links deification with the life of virginity. "Great and precious are the promises attaching to virginity which He has given us, that through it we may become partakers of the divine nature."[54] Later in the same treatise, Jerome explains what this means: "You see, then, that we are privileged to partake of His essence, not in the realm of nature, but of grace, and the reason why we are beloved of the Father is that He has loved the Son; and the members are loved, those namely of the body."[55] We are adopted sons, Jerome says, but this can only be understood properly in light of a true understanding of the Incarnation: "The Word was made flesh that we might pass from the flesh into the Word. The

[50] Ambrose, *On Virginity* 1.3.11. See also *On Christian Faith* 5.14.178 and *On the Holy Spirit* 1.9.107.

[51] See Ambrose, *On Isaac, or the Soul* 4.11, in *Seven Exegetical Works*, trans. Michael P. McHugh, Fathers of the Church 65 (Washington, D.C.: Catholic University of America Press, 1972), 18–19. See also *Epistle* 71.

[52] Ambrose, *On Isaac* 5.49; see also 6.53, and *On Death as a Good* 5.19.

[53] Ambrose, *On Isaac* 5.49; see also 6.52–54; *On the Death of Satyrus* 2.54; *On Death as a Good* 5.16–17.

[54] Jerome, *Against Jovinianus* 1.39, quoting 2 Pet 1:4, trans. E.W. Watson and L. Pullan, in *NPNF*, eds. Philip Schaff and Henry Wace, 2nd series, vol. 6 (Buffalo, N.Y.: Christian Publishing, 1899), revised and edited for New Advent by Kevin Knight, http://newadvent.org/fathers/30091.htm.

[55] Jerome, *Against Jovinianus* 2.29, trans. W.H. Fremantle, G. Lewis, and W.G. Martley, in *NPNF*, eds. Philip Scaff and Henry Wace, 2nd series, vol. 6 (Buffalo, N.Y.: Christian Publishing, 1893), revised and edited for New Advent by Kevin Knight, http://newadvent.org/fathers/30092.htm.

Word did not cease to be what He had been; nor did the human nature lose that which it was by birth. The glory was increased, the nature was not changed."[56] For Jerome, deification is a theological commonplace from which he argues other things. He does, though, give us a spiritual gem from his own ascetic experience about how he understands deification as "angelification". Discussing his sojourn in the desert, Jerome tells a friend, "There, also—the Lord Himself is my witness—when I had shed copious tears and had strained my eyes towards heaven, I sometimes felt myself among angelic hosts, and for joy and gladness sang: 'because of the savour of your good ointments we will run after you'."[57]

Fifth Century

Prudentius. The most famous work of the Spanish poet Prudentius is his *Psychomachia*, variously translated as "Spiritual Warfare" or "Battle for the Soul". It is conceived as an extended allegory on the life of the soul in which virtues and vices wage war. In one section, after Chastity has killed Lust with a sword-thrust through the throat, Prudentius comments on how such a victory has become possible:

> In that virgin mother
> Human nature lost its primal stain and
> Power from above made flesh new.
> A maid unwed gave birth to God, Christ,
> Man from his Mother,
> God from his Father.
> From that day all flesh is divine,
> For flesh gave him birth and by this union
> Shares in God's nature.
> The word made flesh ceased not to be
> What he was before, though joined to flesh.

[56] Ibid.

[57] Jerome, *Letter* 22, quoting Song 1:3–4, trans. W.H. Fremantle, G. Lewis and W.G. Martley, in *NPNF*, eds. Philip Schaff and Henry Wace, 2nd series, vol. 6 (Buffalo, N.Y.: Christian Publishing, 1893), revised and edited for New Advent by Kevin Knight, http://newadvent.org/fathers/3001022.htm.

Not made less by commerce with flesh
His majesty lifts up unhappy men.
What he always was he remains, and
What he was not he begins to be.
Now we are not what we were,
But born to better things.
He gives to me yet remains himself.
By becoming what is ours God is not less,
In giving us what is his he lifts us to heavenly gifts.[58]

Prudentius roots his account of the triumph of virtue in deification: because of the Incarnation, we partake of God's nature and so acquire God's strength and attributes.

Cassian. Though from Gaul, Cassian spent much of his time learning from the monks of Egypt, and it is largely through him that the Latin West was introduced to the wisdom of Eastern monasticism. According to Cassian, the ultimate goal of the monastic life is the Kingdom of God; the means or immediate goal is purity of heart, which Cassian, following Saint Paul, understands as a process of sanctification.[59] Accordingly, the main efforts of the monk should be directed toward what Cassian calls "divine contemplation", by which "the soul may ever cleave to God and to heavenly things."[60] Aided by frequent reception of the Eucharist,[61] this happens through meditating on the Sacred Scriptures, which "fills your heart, and fashions you so to speak after its own likeness, making of it, in a way, an ark of the testimony".[62] In moving terms, Cassian says that the monk who attains

[58] Quoted in Robert Louis Wilken, *The Spirit of Early Christian Thought* (New Haven, Conn.: Yale University Press, 2003), 234. Wilken says that this poem was so popular and influential in the Middle Ages that it rivals Augustine's major works for the number of manuscript copies. The editions are richly illustrated and were much read both in Latin and in vernacular languages (228).

[59] See Cassian, *Conferences* 1.4–5, referring to Rom 6:22, trans. C.S. Gibson, in *NPNF*, eds. Philip Schaff and Henry Wace, 2nd series, vol. 11 (Buffalo, N.Y.: Christian Publishing, 1894), revised and edited for New Advent by Kevin Knight, http://newadvent.org/fathers/350801.htm. See also ibid., 1.13–14, and *On the Incarnation of the Lord* 5.4.

[60] Cassian, *Conferences* 1.8; see also 10.6.

[61] See ibid., 23.21.

[62] Ibid., 14.10.

purity of heart can, to some extent, adapt this earthly life to the life of bliss promised to the saints when God will be "all in all" (1 Cor 15:28, DR):

> And this will come to pass [in this life] when God shall be all our love, and every desire and wish and effort, every thought of ours, and all our life and words and breath, and that unity which already exists between the Father and the Son, and the Son and the Father, has been shed abroad in our hearts and minds, so that as He loves us with a pure and unfeigned and indissoluble love, so we also may be joined to Him by a lasting and inseparable affection, since we are so united to Him that whatever we breathe or think, or speak is God.[63]

Even now, Cassian says, the monk can begin to have a foretaste "of that celestial life and glory".[64]

Maximus of Turin. Another neglected witness to deification in the Latin West is the North Italian Maximus, the bishop of Turin at the turn of the fifth century. In one of his homilies, Maximus beautifully describes the transformative effects of the Incarnation:

> And when He began to spread Himself about through the whole earth by the power of His divinity, He immediately drew the entire human race into His substance by His own strength. Thus, in pouring out the energy of His Spirit on all the saints, He made every Christian to be what Christ is. For when the Lord Jesus was a man in the world, alone and by Himself like leaven hidden in a lump of dough, He made it possible for everyone to be what He Himself was. Whoever, therefore, sticks to the leaven of Christ becomes in turn leaven as useful to himself as he is helpful to everyone else and, certain of his own salvation, he is made sure of the redemption of others.[65]

Maximus' teaching on deification clearly influenced his Latin hearers as can be seen in a sermon attributed to him, but likely delivered by a now unknown disciple of his:

[63] Ibid., 10.7.

[64] Ibid.; see also 9.25.

[65] Maximus of Turin, *Sermon* 33.3, in *The Sermons of St. Maximus of Turin*, trans. Boniface Ramsey, Ancient Christian Writers 50 (New York: Newman Press, 1989), 80. Cf. *Sermon* 25.2, p. 61.

> Beloved brethren, we should always remember and have before our eyes the fact that the Lord Jesus Christ came from heaven to earth for this reason—to bestow eternal life on us. Therefore, although He was the Son of God, He preferred to become a son of man so that He might make us, who were men, sons of God.[66]

Peter Chrysologus. Peter Chrysologus, archbishop of Ravenna in the time leading up to the great christological Council of Chalcedon, rarely missed an opportunity to emphasize that deification is the goal of the Christian life. In his explanation of the Our Father to catechumens preparing for baptism, he explains how wondrous it is that God has made us his sons and daughters:

> Yet, why is it strange if He has made men devoted sons of God, since He gave Himself and made Himself into the Son of Man? At that time He raised the nature of flesh into one divine, when He brought His divinity down to human nature. At that time He made man co-heir with Himself among the dwellers of heaven, when He made Himself the sharer of the things of earth.[67]

Chrysologus tells the catechumens that their lives should mirror who they in fact are: "Understand that you, whose Father is in heaven, have a lineage derived from heaven. So act, too, that you become your Father's image by your holy way of life."[68] The fact of divine sonship means we should act like God's children; this, in turn, advances our likeness to the Father. It is the redemption, Chrysologus says, that makes this godly life possible:

> He supports man, that he may be unable to fall now. He made into a heavenly being him whom He had made an earthly one. He vivifies with a divine life man once animated with human life. Thus He raises the whole man toward God, to leave in him nothing of sin, or of death, or of labor, or of suffering, or of earth.[69]

[66] Maximus of Turin, *Sermon* 90. See also *Sermon* 111.

[67] Peter Chrysologus, *Sermon* 70, trans. George E. Ganss, *Saint Peter Chrysologus: Selected Sermons and Saint Valerian: Homilies*, Fathers of the Church 17 (New York: Fathers of the Church, 1953), 119–20.

[68] Chrysologus, *Sermon* 67.

[69] Chrysologus, *Sermon* 148; cf. *Sermon* 3 and 115.

Chrysologus does not neglect the sacramental dimension of deification either. In one sermon, he uses the story of the Centurion's Servant as a parable of deification with appropriately Eucharistic overtones: "But since God, when he wills, makes what is human become divine, and, when he sees fit, changes what is of our flesh into his own Spirit, he does not disdain either dwelling in the flesh or coming under the roof of our body."[70]

Leo the Great. One of the great synthesizers of the Latin tradition—and therefore an important witness to the Latin patristic understanding of deification—Pope Leo the Great preached the content of deification in a variety of contexts. Leo roots his understanding of deification in a clear Christology, affirming the Catholic faith that in Christ there is both an integral divine and human nature in one Divine Person.[71] Neither nature cancels out the other, and this means that Christ unites "humanity to Himself as to remain immutably God" and imparts "Godhead to man as not to destroy but enhance him by glorification".[72] The noncompetition of the two natures inseparably united in Christ brings about our divinization without violating our human nature.

For Leo, we appropriate this salvation through baptism, the efficacy of which is also rooted in the Incarnation. In baptism, "a man is made the body of Christ, because Christ also is the body of a man."[73] Similarly, the Eucharist is the "celestial food" that causes us to "pass into the flesh of Him, who became our flesh".[74] As we become conformed to our Head, we are not only called to imitate him, but are enabled to do so because God has given us of his own life.

> Thus it is that God, by loving us, restores us to His image, and, in order that He may find in us the form of His goodness, He gives us

[70] Chrysologus, *Sermon* 102.6, trans. William B. Palardy, *Selected Sermons*, vol. 3, Fathers of the Church 110 (Washington, D.C.: Catholic University of America Press, 2005), 120.

[71] Leo the Great, *Sermon* 91.2, trans. Charles Lett Feltoe, in *NPNF*, eds. Phillip Schaff and Henry Wace, 2nd series, vol. 12 (Buffalo, N.Y.: Christian Publishing, 1894), revised and edited for New Advent by Kevin Knight, http://newadvent.org/fathers/360391.htm. All Leo the Great quotations come from this volume.

[72] Ibid. See also *Sermon* 20.1; 22.4–5; 26.2; and 72.2.

[73] Leo the Great, *Letter* 59.4, http://newadvent.org/fathers/3604059.htm. See also *Sermon* 63.6–7.

[74] Leo the Great, *Letter* 59.2. See also *Sermon* 63.7.

> that whereby we ourselves too may do the work that He does, kindling that is the lamps of our minds, and inflaming us with the fire of His love, that we may love not only Himself, but also whatever He loves.[75]

From this arises a unity of will that makes us friends with God—that is, a kind of "equal" because we have attained "the dignity of the Divine Majesty"[76], not, of course, by nature, but by the grace of the Incarnation and the sacraments, which makes us like God.

Sixth Century

Boethius. In his *Consolation of Philosophy*, written in prison shortly before his death, Boethius discusses his troubles with Lady Philosophy. At one point in the discussion, she has shown him that "both happiness and God are supreme goodness, so that it follows that supreme happiness is identical with supreme divinity."[77] Lady Philosophy then draws the corollary of this:

> Since it is through the possession of happiness that people become happy, and since happiness is in fact divinity, it is clear that it is through the possession of divinity that they become happy. But by the same logic as men become just through the possession of justice, or wise through the possession of wisdom, so those who possess divinity necessarily become divine. Each happy individual is therefore divine. While only God is so by nature, as many as you like may become so by participation.

In reverent awe, Boethius responds, "What you say is beautiful and valuable." Boethius stands in the Tradition, also seen in Augustine,[78] that thinks the truth of deification (though not the attaining of it) is available to reason; it necessarily follows from a true understanding of the nature of God.

[75] Leo the Great, *Sermon* 12.1, trans. Charles Lett Feltoe, in *NPNF*, eds. Phillip Schaff and Henry Wace, 2nd series, vol. 12 (Buffalo, N.Y.: Christian Publishing, 1894), revised and edited for New Advent by Kevin Knight, http://newadvent.org/fathers/360312.htm.

[76] Ibid.

[77] Boethius, *Consolation of Philosophy*, trans. Victor Watts (London: Penguin, 1999), bk. 3, proem 10, p. 71. All quotations come from this section.

[78] See Augustine, *Confessions* 7.10.16.

Benedict. The monastic tradition of the West, especially that flowing from Benedict of Nursia, is another important, though neglected, source for thinking about deification. Benedict's understanding of the monastic life is grounded in sonship, the divine sonship by which we have become adopted sons of God and the monastic sonship under the abbot, which is an imitation of it.[79] The monastery is a "school of the Lord's service"[80] in which monks are trained in holiness; it is a place where transformed senses open the path for interior transformation into God: "Let us open our eyes to the deifying light [*deificum lumen*], and our ears to the voice from heaven."[81] By doing good deeds, with God's help, the monk will be able to "dwell in your tent, Lord" and "rest on God's holy mountain" (Ps 14:1).[82] Compelled by love "to pursue everlasting life",[83] the monk not only follows the narrow way, but "runs on the path of God's commandments, with a heart expanded (*dilitato corde*) with the inexpressible sweetness of love".[84] Benedict says here that the monastic life "stretches" the monk's soul so he can joyfully live the ineffable delight of eternal life he has tasted. Benedict hopes that the monastic community "might participate (*participemur*) in the sufferings of Christ, so that we may merit to be sharers (*consortes*) in his kingdom."[85] The monastery, then, could be understood as a kind of "heaven on earth", which prepares the monk for eternal life.[86]

Gregory the Great. The great monk and pope Gregory shows how the ethical dimension of deification is ordered toward the "higher" or more advanced deification of contemplation. "For man was made to contemplate his Creator, that he might ever be seeking after His

[79] See *The Rule of St. Benedict*, ed. Timothy Fry (Collegeville, Minn.: Liturgical Press, 1982), prologue, 1 and 5; cf. 2.2–3.

[80] Ibid., prologue, 45.

[81] Ibid., prologue, 9; translation modified by author.

[82] Ibid., prologue; 23ff.

[83] Ibid., 5.10.

[84] Ibid., prologue, 49; translation modified by author.

[85] Ibid., prologue, 50. The language of participation and sharing may be an allusion to 2 Pet 1:4, and the goal of the Kingdom is likely drawn from Cassian, explicitly recommended at 73.5 (see above for Cassian).

[86] See ibid., 73.1–9.

likeness, and dwell in the festival [*solemnitate*] of His love."[87] By living a holy life and meditating on the Scriptures, the purified mind "feeds upon the contemplation of eternity and comprehends the joys of the Heavenly Kingdom" so that he ascends beyond temporal things and enters into the mysteries of eternity.[88] For Gregory, the goal of life is the vision of God, a vision that makes us like God.

In Gregory's *Life of Benedict*, we see both the ethical and contemplative dimensions of deification in a rather striking way. Most of the *Life* concerns Benedict's miracles, which, Gregory explains, are brought about not only through prayer, but also through *Benedict's own volition.*[89] According to Gregory, Benedict can do this because he "possessed the spirit of Christ"[90]—that is, because Benedict had become godlike. Benedict is one with God, already, in a sense, transformed into God, whose will is God's will, whose powers are God's powers, and whose acts are God's acts. Benedict is the holy one or, we could say, the deified man.[91]

Still, Gregory shows that even the tremendous holiness displayed in Benedict's way of life is ordered toward something higher, toward further transformation into godlikeness. One night—sometime after the remarkable meeting with his twin sister, Scholastica, when Benedict famously did *not* get to do his will and which marks the end of his miracles—Benedict stays awake to pray in anticipation of the night office, when, suddenly "the whole world was brought before his eyes, apparently drawn together beneath a single ray of sunlight."[92]

[87] Gregory the Great, *Morals on the Book of Job* 8.18.34 (London: J. G. F. and J. Rivington, 1844), 440–41. For Gregory, as for Benedict, there is a strong emphasis on divine sonship, rooted in a clear Christology. See ibid., 2.23.42, and *Homilies on the Gospels* 2.2 and 30.9.

[88] Gregory the Great, *Homilies on the Book of the Prophet Ezekiel* 2.8.4, trans. Theodosia Gray (Etna, Calif.: Center for Traditionalist Orthodox Studies, 1990), 247. Compare this description with Gregory's own experience in the monastery as described in the *Dialogues* 1, preface. See also *Homilies on Ezekiel* 1.7.8, and Gregory's *Commentary on the Song of Songs* 2.

[89] Gregory the Great, *Life of Benedict* 30.2, trans. Carolinne White, *Early Christian Lives* (London: Penguin Books, 1998), 161–204. The *Life of Benedict* forms book 2 of Gregory's *Dialogues*.

[90] Ibid., 8.9.

[91] Compare with Gregory's description of the "two lives" of the Church in his *Homilies on Ezekiel* 2.10.4.

[92] Gregory the Great, *Life of Benedict* 35.3. The description is reminiscent of both the first day of creation (cf. Gen 1:3–4) and of the description of Christ, the light who shines in the darkness (cf. Jn 1:3–5). See also *Morals on the Book of Job* 1.35.48.

Picking up a phrase from the *Rule*, Gregory tells us that Benedict sees God and all the world with "a mind expanded" (*animus dilatatus*):[93]

> the whole of creation is small to the soul that sees the Creator. Although it has seen only a tiny part of the Creator's light, all that has been created becomes small to him because in the light of the vision the folds of the innermost mind are relaxed and it expands in God to such an extent that it becomes larger than the world.[94]

Gregory's depiction of Benedict shows how he understands what it means to progress in deification, to advance in godlikeness throughout a holy life. In another work, Gregory makes a relevant distinction that helps illumine the complementary ethical and contemplative dimensions of deification shown in the *Life of Benedict*: "the likeness of Christ's life is now drawn in the conduct of the elect"[95]—this is what was shown in a radical way in Benedict's life and miracles—"and in the Resurrection the likeness of eternity will follow in the mind, since we shall see Him as He is";[96] remarkably, this is what happens in Benedict's "vision" described at the end of the *Life*. Benedict has been graced to experience the "likeness of eternity" while still in this life. With a mind and heart expanded, Benedict was allowed to see God, thereby becoming more like God and seeing all things as God sees them.

Conclusion

The doctrine of deification is the common patrimony of the Christian East and West, amply and ably received and handed on by both the Greek and Latin Fathers of the Universal Church. Although the vocabulary and emphases vary between and within each tradition, the *res* is the same. The breadth of the Latin patristic understanding of

[93] Gregory the Great, *Life of Benedict* 35.7. See *Rule of St. Benedict*, prologue, 49, quoted above: the monk "runs on the path of God's commandments, with a heart expanded (*dilitato corde*) with the inexpressible sweetness of love".

[94] Gregory the Great, *Life of Benedict* 35.6.

[95] Gregory the Great, *Homilies on the Book of the Prophet Ezekiel* 1.2.21.

[96] Ibid.

deification displayed here will hopefully provide a warrant that further research into this topic is not only needed, but would be richly rewarded. In doing so, we might make it a little easier to recognize that this central teaching about the meaning of salvation is the rightful inheritance of all Christians everywhere.

Readings for Further Study

The secondary literature on deification in the Latin Fathers is limited, and what is available is of mixed value. In particular, the piece by Michael Azkoul should be read with a critical eye. While providing helpful references, his work is marred by unfortunate prejudices. The other studies below offer the first and some of the only tentative forays into the theme of deification in the Latin Fathers.

Azkoul, Michael. *Ye Are Gods: Salvation according to the Latin Fathers*. Dewdney, B.C.: Synaxis Press, 2002.

Bardy, Gustave. "Divinisation: Chez les Pères Latins". In *Dictionnaire de Spiritualité, ascétique et mystique doctrine et histoire*, edited by Charles Baumgartner and Marcel Viller, 3:1389–98. Paris: Beauchesne, 1957.

Keating, Daniel. "Cyril in Comparison: Augustine of Hippo" and "Leo the Great". In *The Appropriation of Divine Life in Cyril of Alexandria*, 227–93. Oxford: Oxford University Press, 2004.

Ladner, Gerhart. *The Idea of Reform: Its Impact on Christian Thought and Action in the Age of the Fathers*. Cambridge, Mass.: Harvard University Press, 1959.

Mersch, Émile. *The Theology of the Mystical Body*. Translated by Cyril Vollert. Saint Louis: Herder, 1951.

_____. *The Whole Christ: The Historical Development of the Doctrine of the Mystical Body in Scripture and Tradition*. Eugene, Ore.: Wipf and Stock, 2011.

Russell, Norman. "Appendix I: The Latin Tradition". In *The Doctrine of Deification in the Greek Patristic Tradition*, 325–32. Reprint, Oxford: Oxford University Press, 2009.

Scully, Ellen. "The Assumption of All Humanity in Saint Hilary of Poitiers' *Tractatus super Psalmos*". Ph.D. diss., Marquette University, Milwaukee, Wisc., 2011.

Wild, Philip. "The Divinization of Man according to St. Hilary". Ph.D. diss., Mundelein, 1950.

Chapter Four

NO LONGER A CHRISTIAN BUT CHRIST: SAINT AUGUSTINE ON BECOMING DIVINE

David Vincent Meconi, S.J.

Saint Augustine of Hippo (354–430) is best known for his expression that the human heart is restless until it rests in God: "You have made us and drawn us to yourself, and our heart is unquiet until it rests in you."[1] As perennial as this image has been for centuries of Christian seekers, it is scarcely a glimpse into the heart's ultimate end for this great Christian teacher. For Augustine, each person is made not simply to rest in God but *to become God*. This is the entire purpose of God's creating and God's becoming human in the Son's Incarnation: that individual persons come to share in and thus appropriate for themselves God's very life. While this volume endeavors to show how this is a teaching central throughout Catholicism, Augustine's unique emphasis lies in his unmatched awareness that love transforms the lover into the beloved. Simply, we become what we love. For Augustine, a person's love determines his identity: "Do you love the earth? You will be earth. Do you love God? What shall I say? That you will be God? I don't dare to say this on my own. Let us listen to the scriptures. ... *You are gods and sons of the Most High* (Ps 82:6)."[2] Presenting Christianity as our "becoming gods" in Christ will guide the following study into human deification as Augustine came to use it in his preaching and throughout his writing.

[1] Saint Augustine, *Confessions* 1.1.1, in *The Confessions: With an Introduction and Contemporary Criticism*, trans. Maria Boulding, ed. David Vincent Meconi, S.J., Ignatius Critical Editions (San Francisco: Ignatius Press, 2012), 3; hereafter, I shall simply use the standardized citation "*Conf.*" with book, section, and paragraph number, followed by the corresponding page in Boulding.

[2] Saint Augustine, *Homilies on the First Epistle of John* 2.14, trans. Boniface Ramsey, *Homilies*, vol. I/14 (Hyde Park, N.Y.: New City Press, 2009), 51 (emphasis in original).

Among academic theologians, Augustine is normally not associated with those Church Fathers who expounded the glorious transformation of the human person in Christ. Yet, more and more studies are showing how he did in fact understand Christianity in terms of deification. In granting Augustine his own chapter, this essay aims to bring to light just how important he has been in the history of Christian deification. Confessedly, eighteen appearances of the term *deificare* in a literary corpus of almost 5.5 million words seem economic at best; the reality of becoming "gods", "other Christs", and extensions of Christ's own body proves to be the primary way that Augustine presents one's new life as a lover of Jesus. To show how this is done, I have chosen to elucidate four main points: (1) Augustine's theology of humanity's beginnings in Eden, (2) the purpose of the Son's Incarnation, (3) the Holy Spirit's uniting created persons in and to love, and (4) the role of the Church not only as the Body of Christ but as the "whole Christ", the *totus Christus*, Augustine's favored ecclesial image.

The life of Augustine is perhaps the best chronicled of all the Church Fathers. He was born in the middle of the fourth century in modern-day Algeria to his Christian mother, Monica, and to his rather stern, pagan father, Patricius; Augustine had one brother and one sister. At an early age he excelled at studies, and after teaching Roman rhetoric in various schools in Carthage and Rome, he was invited to Milan to become the imperial rhetor, placing his tongue in "the marketplace of speechifying ... to lying follies and legal battles".[3] As the young Augustine sought true knowledge, he was drawn into the Manichean sect and their facile answer to the problem of evil in the world: the terrestrial order is actually the result of two equally sovereign and eternal enemies, the Wholly Good (*summum bonum*) and the Wholly Evil (*summum malum*). Evil in this world is thus an inevitable by-product of this cosmic war with the (convenient) result that no true seeker can be blamed for his malicious deeds but must simply acknowledge the ineluctability of wrongdoing. For nine years Augustine tells us he adhered to such folly, but while in Milan he read "the books of the Platonists" and began to see how there was only one ultimate source of reality and that all of creation is good.

[3] *Conf.* 9.2.2; 227.

This allowed him to see that all things in this world are participants in the divine and that evil was not a positive, efficient force but in fact the exact opposite—a parasitic, deficient lack of what should be there. Evil was not something to which one could point but was the result of a fallen perversity when free creatures made for greatness chose lesser and lesser goods when infinite joy was offered to them.

Milan also providentially introduced him to the city's great bishop, Ambrose (ca. 330–397). Through Ambrose he came to understand that not all Scripture is to be read literally but that a deeper, allegorical sense could be applied to those passages that were inspired to convey the more mysterious images and meanings of God's providence. When Augustine sailed from Ostia (where Saint Monica died and was buried)[4] back to North Africa in 387, he sought to fulfill his dream of beginning a quasi-monastic community where studious Catholic men could live together and tranquilly seek the life of prayer and study that had won Augustine over. As his biographer Possidius relates, however, God had different plans.[5] The aging bishop of Hippo, Valerius, recruited Augustine first as a priest (391) and then as a coadjutor bishop (395). For the next thirty-five years Augustine would labor as both a tireless bishop within Christ's Church, as well as an influential leader in North African society, defending his flock, adjudicating legal disputes, and even acting as important counsel to imperial statesmen.

During this time, his three most formidable opponents were (1) the non-Christian, staunchly pagan aristocrats, who were unwilling to let go of the long-standing gods and goddesses of ancient Rome; (2) the Donatist Christians, who broke off after some Catholic clerics colluded with the Roman army during the persecutions of the emperor Diocletian (ca. 303–311/313); and (3) the Pelagians, who argued that the individual person had all he needed for salvation and simply needed to keep his eyes and heart on Christ's example of innocence.[6] The occasions Augustine faced to defend or explicate

[4] See *Conf.* 9.11.27–13.37; 253–62.

[5] Possidius was Augustine's final secretary and composed the definitive hagiographical life, *The Life of St. Augustine* (or *Vita Sancti Augustini*); for this instance of Augustine's recruitment into presbyteral office, see no. 4, as found in *The Western Fathers*, ed. and trans. F.R. Hoare (New York: Harper Torchbooks, 1954), 197–98.

[6] For more on Augustine's life, see two standard biographies: Peter Brown, *Augustine of Hippo* (1967; Berkeley: University of California Press, 2000), and Serge Lancel, *St. Augustine* (London: SCM Press, 2002).

some aspect of Church teaching were thus as numerous as his literary output. As we sift through the writings of the most copious patristic author (totaling over one hundred separate theological treatises, nearly five hundred homilies, and around three hundred letters), we should therefore never make the methodological mistake of limiting a study of Augustine to any one time period or any one adversary.

In analyzing Augustinian deification, therefore, we extend our study from the few places where the term *deificare* appears, and instead examine the reality of the deified life as presented in his preaching and writings. In so doing, we shall encounter his use of myriad biblical, creedal, and theological metaphors that seek to strengthen his Christian faithful's hope that their lives in Jesus are no longer merely human, that the baptized must no longer live simply in their fallen state but have now been granted access to perfect love and mercy, wisdom, and immortality. Reading Augustine in this way is to refuse to limit our understanding of him to any one particular period of his life, especially late in his episcopate when he is constructing his far-reaching and influential anti-Pelagian works, stressing the depravity of sinful humanity and the utter, unshakeable need for God's grace in all things but sin. This teaching that the individual person is unable to save himself is part of Augustine, to be sure, but it neither explains nor exhausts who he is and what his vision of Christianity entails. Given the forty-plus years he was theologically and pastorally active, given all the various schismatics, heretics, and pagans with whom he contended, it was inevitable that he would highlight some partial truths of the faith more at one time than at another. However, throughout all these decades of priestly and intellectual service, one common thread runs through Augustine's thought—that out of perfect love, God has become human so as to enable humans to become one with God.

Divine Images Restless for Divinity

Accordingly, Augustine came to affirm both the goodness of the creation as well as the freedom of the human person, made for divine likeness but also given free will and thereby able to turn sinfully away from God if so desired. This entire drama is captured in the opening pages of Scripture. In fact, Augustine was the first Christian author to notice that the sixth day never receives its own final approval from God—that is, on the eve of the sixth day, we read how "God saw *everything* that he had made, and behold, it was very good. And there was evening and there was morning, a sixth day" (Gen 1:31; emphasis added). Whereas other days received their own stamp of approval ("God saw it was good"), Augustine here comments that God did not finalize the sixth day, because the human person was purposefully made incompletely—that is why God "did not say individually about the human creature, as in the other cases, *And God saw that it was good*, but after the man was made and given rights, whether to rule or to eat, he concluded about them all: *And God saw all the things that he had made, and behold they were very good*." So why does Genesis avoid calling Adam and Eve good in and of themselves? The former Manichee is sure to note that it is not because they were not good; it is because they were "not yet completed" in that they "would foreshadow something yet to come.... And so it was arranged that something should be said which would be both true in the present [that, in fact, the human person is good] and would signify foreknowledge of the future."[7] Made in the divine image and likeness, Adam and Eve thirst to be completed in and by God. The first Adam thus foreshadows the Second Adam, in whom humanity and divinity are perfectly reconciled. The first Adam is "incomplete" because, in Augustine's estimation, we were never made simply to be "merely" human but in time to be invited to become even more than human (*ultra homines*) as the divine image and likeness in humans was fulfilled.[8]

In other words, Augustine's famous "restless heart" points us to a human creature who remains incomplete and unsteady, stressed and stretched, until he realizes union with God. This inescapable desire to be one with God was examined very early on in the *Soliloquies* (a term Augustine here invents) where Augustine [A] depicts himself talking with Reason [R] personified:

[7] Augustine, *On Genesis* 3.24.36–37; trans. Edmund Hill, *Genesis* (Hyde Park, N.Y.: New City Press, 2002), 239 (emphasis in original).

[8] Augustine, *The Trinity* 1.6.11; the Latin is found in the *De Trinitate*, *Corpus Christianorum Latinorum* (*CCL*) series, vol. 50 (Turnhout: Brepols, 1968), 40.

R: Does it not seem to you that your image in a mirror wants, in a way, to be you and is false because it is not?

A: That certainly seems so.

R: Do not all pictures and replicas of that kind and all artists' works of that type strive to be that in whose likeness they are made?

A: I am completely convinced that they do.[9]

Or a few years later as he is composing his *Confessions*, Augustine admits that "I shudder inasmuch as I am unlike him, yet I am afire with longing for him because some likeness there is."[10] In creating us in his own image and likeness, God made us for himself, and although we can try to slake that sacred desire with creatures, that only brings "shuddering", while the closer we draw to God, we experience greater ardor and sweeter desires to become fully who we are meant to be.

Sin is accordingly explained as trying to be God without God. Augustine sees all sin as a false imitation of the divine majesty. Sin is not the choosing of evil but the choosing of a lower good (oneself) when a higher good is available (God). The human person is allured by the goodness of the world, and often instead of praising the Creator through and on account of those goods, fallen men and women seek to usurp such beauty of themselves. Augustine the astute pastor thus knows how the human mind should see all things,

> in that more excellent nature which is God; but instead of staying still and enjoying them as it ought to, it wants to claim them for itself, and rather than be like him by his gift it wants to be what he is by its own right. So it turns away from him and slithers and slides down into less and less which is imagined to be more and more; it can find satisfaction neither in itself nor in anything else as it gets further away from him who alone can satisfy it.[11]

Instead of using all things to enjoy God, however, the soul is allured by what it finds in creation and desires to usurp reality and beauty

[9] Augustine, *Soliloquies* 2.9.17, trans. Kim Paffenroth (Hyde Park, N.Y.: New City Press, 2000), 72–73.

[10] *Conf.* 11.9.11; 338.

[11] Augustine, *The Trinity* 10.5.7; trans. Edmund Hill, *The Trinity* (Hyde Park, N.Y.: New City Press, 1991), 292.

for itself. Such aversion from God results only in the soul's distorting creatures for their Creator.[12]

In the drama of Genesis Augustine finds the reason why this is so. On the natural level Adam and Eve had everything they could have possibly desired while in Eden. They lacked one thing only, and this could not be found in creation but solely in that divine relationship for which they were brought into existence. What other than God could those made for God desire? That is why, Augustine argues, the fallen intellect of the Enemy knew precisely how he could tempt our first parents. To tempt them with better creatures was impossible, so he instead exploited the innate desire for divinity implanted within each of our souls: "Our first parents could not have been persuaded to sin unless they had been told, *You will be like gods*."[13] The deifying union for which we have been made was the only promise able to entice our otherwise perfect protoparents. In one way, Augustine admits, the Enemy did not lie here at Genesis 3:5—for we shall be like gods—but the deception came through his feigning that such divinity was his to give. Our godliness could come only through the one God-Man, and it is to this divine descension we now turn.

God Becomes Human So Humans Can Become God

For Augustine, the entire work of the Son's Incarnation is aimed at our deification. To make us like himself is God's sole purpose in the Son's assuming human flesh to his divine self: "In order to make gods of those who were merely human, one who was God made himself human."[14] Like his Greek predecessors, lines like this abound in Augustine's theology, always uniting language of deification with the Son's enfleshment, as every instance of mankind's "becoming gods" is inextricably linked to Jesus Christ's work on earth. This is the reason for the Incarnation and the entire essence of love: to unite and thus transform the beloved into the lover.

[12] This is consistent with Augustine's long-standing definition of sin: "Sinfulness in the human person is a disorder and a perversion: an aversion to the creator who should be chosen, and a conversion to the creature who should be inferior" (*To Simplicianus* 1.2.18; my translation).

[13] Augustine, *The Trinity* 11.5.8; Hill, *Trinity*, 310 (emphasis in original).

[14] Augustine, *Sermon* 192.1; Hill, *Sermons*, vol. III/6 (Hyde Park, N.Y.: New City Press, 1993), 46.

To show this, let us examine a homily Augustine delivered while traveling in Carthage sometime during the dreary winter months of (most likely) early 404. That particular Sunday, Augustine probably chose to preach on the Psalm for that Mass because he knew in Carthage that the hostilities between faithful Catholics and polytheist pagans were especially very real. Since the Christian Scriptures talk at times about "gods", Augustine used the occasion of Psalm 82:1—"God has taken his place in the divine council; in the midst of the angels he holds judgment"—to exhort his faithful to understanding how the one true God wants to make them all like him, participants in his own divinity. He thus begins:

> To what hope the Lord has called us, what we now carry about with us, what we endure, what we look forward to, is well known.... We carry mortality about with us, we endure infirmity, we look forward to divinity. For God wishes not only to vivify, but also to deify us. When would human infirmity ever have dared to hope for this, unless divine truth had promised it?[15]

The opening of his sermon brings the people immediately into their own "restless heart" and the innate desire for perfection, eternal life, unalloyed joy—in short, divinity. This is what every individual soul yearns for, and this is precisely what God promises us. For he created us not only to give us natural life (vivification) but supernatural life (deification) as well.

And how does he accomplish such a feat? Through the Incarnation of the Son, God unites himself to all mankind, and in Christ all those who used to be human only, have been given a new life and are thereby rendered into created "gods". We therefore hear next:

> Still, it was not enough for our God to promise us divinity in himself, unless he also took on our infirmity, as though to say, "Do you want to know how much I love you, how certain you ought to be

[15] Augustine, *Sermon* 23B.1 (lines 1–6); Hill, *Sermons*, vol. III/11 (Hyde Park, N.Y.: New City Press, 1997), 37. This sermon belongs to one of the twenty-six "Dolbeau" sermons. In 1990, the French scholar François Dolbeau chanced upon a volume of unknown homilies of Augustine while in the main library of Mainz, Germany. Fortunately at the end of his life, Augustine's secretary, Possidius, drew up an *indiculum*, recording the first few words of each homily Augustine gave, thereby allowing us to match these newly discovered sermons with Augustine's own list.

> that I am going to give you my divine reality? I took to myself your mortal reality." We mustn't find it incredible, brothers and sisters, that human beings become gods, that is, that those who were human beings become gods.[16]

This is particularly Augustinian: love not only unites; it transforms the beloved into the lover insofar as it is able. The ultimate charity is the movement of God into humanity, the hypostatic union of natures in Christ Jesus; and gazing upon this new and unmatchable image of God-made-flesh, we are all invited to see true love, our truest selves. This is what perfect divinity longs to do: to unite itself with those it loves—that is why God has become human. In return, Augustine exhorts, we too must imitate such love and become gods!

In such a move, Augustine of course is not envisioning any sort of polytheism, nor is he suggesting that we creatures ever cease being wholly dependent upon and eternally subordinated to God himself. In his language of "becoming gods", Augustine is showing us that those in Christ no longer need to act simply as fallen humans but are given the ability to be like God and to move from being vengeful to being loving, from being ignorant to being wise, from being mortal to becoming incorruptible! This is the great exchange of natures: the Son's humanity for our "divinity", and the consequent ability to participate in God's attributes in a way that perfects those made in God's image and made unto his likeness.

So although the Father has one Son by nature, he wills to have myriad sons and daughters by grace. For this Christ has united all of mankind in himself, thereby not only redeeming fallen mankind (justification), but also working so as to transform us into his own filial belovedness before the Father. In this we are made into brothers and sisters, and thus coheirs, with Christ:

> He who justifies is the same who deifies because by justifying he made [human persons] into children of God: *he gave them power to become children of God* (John 1:12). If we are made God's children, we are made gods: but this is through the grace of the one who adopts and not through the nature of the one who begets. For there is only one Son of God: our Lord and Savior Jesus Christ.... The rest who have

[16] Augustine, *Sermon* 23B.1 (lines 10–14); Hill, *Sermons*, III/11, p. 37.

been made into gods are thus made by his grace and not born from his own substance, so as to be what he is, but they come to him through his generosity and are thus Christ's coheirs.[17]

Again and again Augustine stresses the transformative essence of love and grace. Here he easily relies on the scriptural language of divine adoption to provide yet one more image of how God longs to make us his own. He is never afraid to call this adoption our "becoming gods" as long as he (1) stresses how this is the result of union with Christ and no other supposed "deity" who claims to make its adherents into gods, and (2) highlights how this process of deification is achieved not through the abolishing of our human nature but by its perfection in and through grace.

This participation in God is no mere metaphor for Augustine but proves to be the heart of the Christian life. In many beautiful ways Augustine presents Christianity as mankind's mirrored response to the Incarnation: as Jesus is a Divine Person now personally united to a human nature, human persons are called to participate in the divine nature. Just as God is now able to live a human life in Christ, Christians are called to live a divine life in Christ. Whereas Jesus sends the Holy Spirit to sanctify the world, those in the world are to receive the same Holy Spirit and thus become one not only with God but with all of God's people: "We are bidden to imitate this mutuality by grace, both with reference to God and to each other ... because it is by his gift that we are one with each other; with him we are one spirit (1 Cor 6:17), *because our soul is glued on behind him* (Ps 63:8). And *for us it is good to cling to God* (Ps 73:27)."[18]

The Love Poured into Our Resting Hearts

This "glue" and this "clinging" between persons is nothing other than the Gift of God, the Holy Spirit. His role eternally is to unite Father and Son; in the economy he continues this operation of bringing persons into union. Moreover, this indwelling in the created soul

[17] Augustine, *Expositions of the Psalms* 49.2, trans. Maria Boulding, *Expositions*, vol. III/16 (Hyde Park, N.Y.: New City Press, 2000), 381(emphasis in original).

[18] Augustine, *The Trinity* 6.5.7; Hill, *The Trinity*, 209 (emphasis in original).

re-creates otherwise "merely" humans into divinely adopted sons and daughters of God. While the incarnate reality of Jesus Christ is both the cause and the pattern of this new life in God, the Holy Spirit is the one who unites us both to Christ as well as to his Christian people. The love that God pours into our hearts (cf. Rom 5:5, Augustine's most cited scriptural verse—well over two hundred times) is the Holy Spirit himself. Whereas we are originally introduced to the Spirit that hovers over all of creation, thereby establishing true order and beauty throughout, the same Holy Spirit moves from simply being present (*praesans*) to actually taking up residence (*habitatio*) in the souls of those conforming to Christ.[19] When this happens, two new aspects of the Christian life occur: (1) the Christian soul is made into a divine temple now fitted for God's own indwelling, and (2) the creature begins to dwell at a supernatural level, thus exhibiting superhuman qualities and abilities.

First, when true love is personally present in the heart of men and women, they can truly be said to have God dwelling within them. This is how Augustine interprets the Pauline taxonomy of the baptized becoming the new temples of God on earth (cf. 1 Cor 6:19). In fact, against the Pneumatomachi and those later Arians who denied the divinity of the Holy Spirit, Augustine relies on the Spirit's divinizing presence within us to prove the Spirit's consubstantiality with the Father and the Son—that is, if the Spirit has the power to render creatures into temples, into "gods" who are made such, the Spirit is obviously divine per se. Commenting on the Nicene Creed, then, Augustine explains why the section on the Church follows immediately from our profession of the Spirit's divinity:

> So neither the whole Church nor any part of it desires to be worshipped instead of God, nor does anybody want to be a god to those who belong to the temple of God which is built of those made into gods by the uncreated God (*ad templum dei quod aedificatur ex diis quos facit non factus deus*). So the Holy Spirit, if he were a creature and not creator, would certainly be a rational creature—for rational creatures are the highest of creatures—and so would not be placed before the Church in the rule of faith, since he also would be a member of

[19] For example, see Augustine, *Epistle* 187.5.16.

> the Church in that part of it which is in heaven, and would have no temple himself but be himself a temple. But he has a temple, of which the apostle says *do you not know that your body is a temple of the Holy Spirit within you, which you have from God?* (1 Cor 6:19).[20]

Clearly, any true member of Christ's Church does not wish to be worshipped—nor could those Christians made into "gods" wish to be honored as such. Such "gods" become so only through grace and participation in the one who alone is worthy of praise. For it is the indwelling of the Holy Spirit that renders Christians divine. Through proper profession (God the Holy Spirit before and infinitely superior to the Church) and reception of God's own divine life within one's soul, creatures are elevated to the divine and allowed to experience new agency, new life.

Very cleverly, then, Augustine sees there are in fact three ways of coming from God the Father. Using the three closely connected Latin terms *natus* (born), *datus* (given), and *factus* (made), Augustine argues that proceeding from the Father (1) there is the *natus*-God, the eternal, only begotten Son; (2) the *datus*-God, the Holy Spirit, who is the Gift between the Father and the Son; and (3) the *factus*-god, the creature made divine through the lordship of the Son's Incarnation and the inhabitation of the Holy Spirit.[21] When this happens, created persons made godly are no longer bound by the limitations of this world, no longer allured by the fallenness of sin and decay. This is what it means to be transformed in Christ, to become a new creature, a temple of God, a child of the Father—to be so united with God, one is led and wholly informed by him: "The Lord makes those whom he wishes devout so that they have recourse to the Lord and desire to be ruled by him and make their will dependent upon his will and, by constantly clinging to him, become one spirit with him."[22] Taken out of "the world", the deified are no longer conformed to creation but to God and to his ways.

[20] Augustine, *The Enchiridion* 15.56, trans. Bruce Harbert, *Enchiridion* in the collection of many of Augustine's doctrinal works, *On Christian Belief*, vol. I/8 (Hyde Park, N.Y.: New City Press, 2005), 307 (emphasis in original).

[21] Cf. Augustine, *The Trinity* 15.14.15.

[22] Augustine, *The Grace of Christ and Original Sin* 1.46–51, trans. Roland Teske, *Answer to the Pelagians*, vol. I/23 (Hyde Park, N.Y.: New City Press, 1997), 428.

Such conformity is most properly the work of the Holy Spirit because, as we mentioned as quintessentially Augustinian, it is the result of love's nature to transform: "Through love we become conformed to God and out of this conformity and figuration and separation from the world we are no longer confounded by those things which should be subject to us. Such conformity is through the Holy Spirit."[23] For Augustine, then, it is through loving rightly that one begins to realize God's own divine presence within: "Begin to love, to be made perfect. Have you begun to love? God has begun to dwell in you. Love him who has begun to dwell in you, so that by dwelling in you more perfectly he may make you perfect.... Ask your heart. If it is filled with charity, you have God's Spirit."[24] As the sign of God's presence within a creature, the Spirit as perfect charity achieves a formal union between creature and Creator, thus enabling the individual person to operate on a level that transcends any created and fallen nature. In the Holy Spirit, Christian souls are equipped to live holy lives, to be wise, to love, and to live forever. This is what Augustine calls the "spiritual person", the one who is able to discern the highest of truths. This spiritualization of the individual person is not the result of study or even moral rectitude for Augustine. It is an ecclesial process wherein an individual adheres to God with and through God's people. Deification is not an isolating but a communal event; for the bishop of Hippo, becoming God means being made a member of the *ecclesia perfecta*.

The Whole Christ

The locus of Christian deification is the Catholic Church. Only here can a spiritual identity and a mystical union between Christ and Christian be achieved. This is where Augustine the preacher can proclaim to his flock, in no uncertain terms, "Let us congratulate ourselves then and give thanks for having been made not only Christians but Christ. Do you understand, brothers and sisters, the grace of God upon us; do

[23] Augustine, *The Catholic Way of Life and the Manichean Way of Life* 1.13.23, trans. Roland Teske, *The Manichean Debate*, vol. I/19 (Hyde Park, N.Y.: New City Press, 2006), 42.

[24] Augustine, *Homilies on the First Epistle of John* 8.12, trans. Ramsey, *Homilies*, 127–28.

you grasp that? Be filled with wonder, rejoice and be glad: we have been made Christ. For, if he is the head, and we the members, then he and we are the whole man."[25] In the Church believers are grafted onto Christ as branches onto the vine, watered through the graces of baptism and sustained by the nourishment of the Eucharist.

To describe this union, Augustine uses the term for the "whole Christ", teaching how Christ is truly complete only with his disciples in eternal communion with him. Out of his infinite love, Jesus longs to identify himself with those must vulnerably entrusted to him: the poor and the persecuted. For we are his Body, and in us Christ continues to be encountered, continues to be emptied:

> Now, however, I wonder if we shouldn't have a look at ourselves, if we shouldn't think about his body, because he is also us (*quia et nos ipse est*). After all, if we weren't him, this wouldn't be true: *When you did it for one of the least of mine, you did it for me* (Matt 25:40). If we weren't him, this wouldn't be true: *Saul, Saul, why are you persecuting me?* (Acts 9:4). So we too are him, because we are his organs, because we are his body, because he is our head, because the whole Christ is both head and body.[26]

The "whole Christ" is a concept unique to Augustine, and with it he is able to show how the Mystical Body of Christ continues through the generations and across the globe. This whole Christ refuses to be limited simply to a biological being but is an entire assembly of those whose love unites and transforms them into one. For the Church is nothing other than the baptized being incorporated into "the structure of Christ's body, and there shall be one Christ loving himself (*erit unus Christus amans se ipsum*)."[27] This "one Christ" is the Head and the body, the Savior with all the saved, Christ with all the Christians.

In this way, Augustine proves to have a more extensive definition of *ecclesia* than most of the Church Fathers. For him, the Church began not with Peter's profession of faith, but at creation with the genesis of the good angels, thereby consisting of the holy men and

[25] Augustine, *Homilies on the Gospel of John* 21.8, trans. Edmund Hill, vol. III/12 (Hyde Park: New City Press, 2009), 379.

[26] Augustine, *Sermon* 133.8; Hill, *Sermons*, III/4, p. 338 (emphasis in original).

[27] Augustine, *Homilies on the First Epistle of John* 10.3, trans. Ramsey, *Homilies*, 148.

women of the Old Testament (cf. *Sermon* 4.11), and all who have sought to do the will of Jesus Christ. Today the Church is the visible Catholic Church, the maternal corollary to God's paternity, from whom schismatics and heretics have divided themselves:

> If any, though, have cut themselves off from the Church by the division of schism, even though they may seem to themselves to be holding on to the Father, they are most perniciously forsaking their mother, while those who relinquish both Christian faith and mother church (*fidem christianam et matrem eccleisam*) are deserting both parents. Hold on to your Father, hold on to your mother. You are a little child; stick to your mother. You are a little child, suck your mother's milk, and she will bring you, nourished on milk, to the table of the Father.[28]

The table of the Father is the Body of Jesus Christ, the living altar of our faith. When we are brought here, Augustine teaches, we begin to see the deepest truth of our life, that we are extensions of Christ's own self.

Christ continues his life in those humble enough to approach and to feed on him in Holy Communion. This is the way the enfleshed God comes to those in the flesh, and while Augustine uses terms like "mystical" and "spiritual" presence, he does so at a time when these terms stressed the pervading presence of Christ but were never meant to speak against the Real Presence. For example, we hear Augustine often preach how it is in the consuming of the Lord's sacred Body and Blood that he comes to dwell in us, effecting that unity which is a sign of true charity:

> The eating of his flesh and the drinking of his blood is that its whole purpose is for us to abide in him and him in us. Now we abide in him when we are his members, while he abides in us when we are his temple. But for us to be his members, we have to be bonded together by unity. What makes unity bond us together? What else but charity? And where does the charity of God come from? Question the apostle. *The charity of God*, he says, *has been poured out in our hearts through the Holy Spirit.*[29]

[28] Augustine, *Sermon* 198.42; Hill, *Sermons*, III/11, p. 212.

[29] Augustine, *Homilies on the Gospel of John* 27.6, trans. Hill, *Homilies*, 470 (emphasis in original).

The Body and Blood of Christ, however, do not belong simply to Christ. As members and extensions of his body, we too are involved in the sacramental economy of the "whole Christ".

In an oft-quoted sermon, dated to the Feast of Pentecost around the year 408, Bishop Augustine asks his congregation to gaze upon the sacred Host and to realize that while they may see one thing, they must also understand something else—that is, they see bread, but they are to understand that this is actually the Body of Christ. Yet, they have come to Mass not simply to see Jesus but to become him! Therefore, Augustine teaches, if we really want to understand what is on the altar of God, we should also see ourselves:

> So if it's you that are the Body of Christ and its members, it's the mystery meaning you that has been placed on the Lord's table. What you receive is the mystery that means you. It is to what you are that you reply "Amen," and by so replying you express your assent. What you hear, you see, is "The Body of Christ," and you answer, "Amen." So, be a member of the Body of Christ, in order to make that "Amen" true.[30]

Augustine taught a sacramental realism, never wavering that what the priest celebrated on the altar at every Mass is in fact the sacred Body and Blood of Jesus Christ. Yet, establishing this Real Presence is rarely his aim when preaching about the Eucharist. He instead stresses the recipients' role in receiving and thus becoming this Christ.

We can see ourselves in him only because he first identifies himself with us. This is the purpose of Christ's incessant advent: not only to unite each to himself in the Spirit but to gather a people unto himself, his Body, the Church. Here the Lord continues to empty himself so as to live the life of each of his members. This is the ongoing emptying of the Son into mankind. His kenosis hence becomes our theosis. In his Mystical Body on earth, then, Jesus Christ continues to

> identify his members with himself, just as he did when he said, *I was hungry and you fed me* (Matt 25:35), and as he identified us with himself when he called from heaven to the rampaging Saul who was persecuting God's holy people, *Saul, Saul, why are you persecuting me?* (Acts

[30] Augustine, *Sermon* 272, trans. Hill, *Sermons*, III/7, p. 300; slightly adjusted; quoted in *CCC* 1396.

> 9:4), though no one was laying a finger on Christ himself. ... "See yourself reflected in me," Christ says.[31]

When we begin to see ourselves and others this way—in Christ, even *as* Christ—we begin to become what Augustine calls (again, drawing from Saint Paul) spiritual people. The "spiritual person" for Augustine can be found only around the altar. For becoming "spirit" is never to denigrate the flesh but the exact inverse: to see the Lord's ongoing Incarnation in all we meet.

Such identification between God and his people is expressed beautifully in the final book of Augustine's *Confessions*. Whereas we began this essay with that work's "restless heart", we conclude by examining how the final rest for which all seek is found solely in Christ's Church, wherein creatures are filled with Christ's Spirit and thus enabled to live and act divinely—that is, we are made "spirit-filled ... in your Church, O God, persons gifted with the Spirit judge of spiritual things in virtue of the grace you have given".[32] And while Augustine charitably warns against ever using this spiritual power to judge both the things of God (who is above our judgment) as well as the souls of others (whose judgment belongs to God alone), he hears God saying to his saints, "What you see through my Spirit, I see, just as what you say through my Spirit, I say. You see these things in terms of time, but I do not see in time, nor when you say these things in temporal fashion do I speak in a way conditioned by time."[33] Human divinization thus allows the creature to see and to speak like God but in a way commensurate with still and always being a creature.

Life is therefore changed for those living in Christ. No longer does the human agent have to act alone. For Christ now dwells in and through and even as each of his own. In the state of grace, they are Christ's eyes that see within ours, his mind that knows by means of ours. Augustine accordingly continues:

> It is different for people who see creation through your Spirit, for you are seeing it through their eyes.... No one knows the reality of

[31] Augustine, *Expositions of the Psalms* 32, exp. 2.2; Boulding, *Expositions*, III/15, p. 393 (emphasis in original).

[32] *Conf.* 13.23.33; 441.

[33] Ibid., 13.29.44; 452–53.

> God except the Spirit of God. How, then, can we too know the gifts that God has given to us? This is the answer that comes to me: if we know something through his Spirit, it is still true to say that *no one knows it except God's own Spirit*; for just as it could rightly be said to people who spoke in the Spirit of God, *It is not you who are speaking* (Matt 10:20), so too is it rightly said to those who know anything in the Spirit of God.[34]

The story of each soul begins with the "restless heart" searching for its final and true home. The narrative of Augustine's *Confessions* concludes with those who have allowed their life's story to be written by God's providential grace, coming to experience their creaturely life now in union with the Spirit of God. They are bound forever by the Spirit of unity, the Spirit of charity. Originally created in that same God's image and likeness, they now find the only true fulfillment possible, the godliness for which they were first brought into being. The saints thus enjoy forever God's divine life, having been rendered everlasting participants in his own perfection.

Conclusion

The legacy of Augustinian studies has not always acknowledged his teaching on the possibility of mankind being deified in Christ. In fact, many scholars have maintained that deification, the central soteriology of Catholicism, is in fact impossible in Augustine's way of envisioning God, the individual person, and the world in general. Major figures in both the academy and the *ecclesia* argue that while the Greek Fathers and the Orthodox Church boast the splendor of human deification, the Western Church has suffered for centuries under Augustine's inability to see how human nature is not simply justified but glorified in its eternal appropriation of God's own attributes.[35] Surely, however, more and more students of Augustine are awakening to how he employed various images and metaphors of deification.

[34] Ibid., 13.31.46; 453–54 (emphasis in original).

[35] For the history of this, see David Meconi, S.J., *The One Christ: St. Augustine's Theology of Deification* (Washington, D.C.: Catholic University of America Press, 2013), xiii–xv.

This essay set out to show not only that deification is a fundamental teaching throughout Augustine's thought, but also to show exactly what that teaching entails. Perhaps the most lapidary formula for his doctrine of deification is that individuals "are not gods by nature", but have instead been "formed by the Father, through the Son, by the gift of the Holy Spirit".[36] Made for perfect union with the Father, we are claimed by the Incarnation of the Son and are so joined together by the Gift of Love, the Holy Spirit. In Jesus Christ, God becomes like us so, with and through Christ, we in return could become like God—loving, wise, merciful, and eternal.

This process is achieved most clearly in the Church of Christ. Here is the "whole Christ", where the divine head and creaturely members become one, sharing and identifying in each other's lives and qualities. Here the Son of God continues to pour himself out in exchange for the fullness of life in those he has made his coheirs before the Father. The indwelling of the Holy Spirit unites us to the Blessed Trinity, achieving both a divine adoption and an eternal participation in God's own nature, thus achieving the Lord's own declaration, "You are gods" (Ps 82:6; Jn 10:34). This doctrine of deification thus allows Augustine to interpret such seemingly polytheistic scriptural statements in an orthodox manner. Yet, even more important, it enables him to present the Christian life not as a mere keeping of the law but as a transformation in Christ, where humanity and divinity are perfectly joined.

Readings for Further Study

Augustine of Hippo, Saint. *The Confessions: With an Introduction and Contemporary Criticism*. Translated by Maria Boulding, O.S.B. Edited by David Vincent Meconi, S.J. Ignatius Critical Editions. San Francisco: Ignatius Press, 2012.

Lancel, Serge. *St. Augustine*. Translated by Antonia Nevill. London: SCM Press, 2002.

Meconi, David Vincent, S.J. *The One Christ: St. Augustine's Theology of Deification*. Washington, D.C.: Catholic University of America Press, 2013.

[36] Augustine, *On Faith and the Creed* 9.16, trans. Michael Campbell, in *On Christian Belief*, 166.

Chapter Five

DEIFICATION IN THE DOMINICAN TRADITION: ALBERT, THOMAS, AND CATHERINE

Andrew Hofer, O.P.

According to Dominican tradition, the Mother of God interceded for the salvation of souls, and her Son answered her prayer by saying that he would send to the people "preachers and men of truth, through whom the world shall be enlightened and reclaimed".[1] From this heavenly mission, Saint Dominic de Guzman founded the Order of Preachers for preaching the gospel and the salvation of souls. Confirmed by Pope Honorius III on December 22, 1216, Dominic's fledgling community was destined to bring forth many "champions of the Faith and the true lights of the world."[2] As such, the sons and daughters of Dominic—friars, contemplative nuns, sisters, those in clerical and lay fraternities, and others who participate in his charism—have long preached how God the Father saves us through Jesus Christ his Son in the grace of the Holy Spirit. Generation after generation, for eight hundred years now, Dominicans have looked, under the patronage of Our Lady, to their holy father Dominic as the "Preacher of Grace" and "Doctor of Truth" for his help in bringing people to this new life of God, "who called you out of darkness into his marvelous light" (1 Pet 2:9).[3]

[1] Gerard de Frachet, *Lives of the Brethren of the Order of Preachers 1206–1259*, trans. Placid Conway, O.P. (London: Blackfriars Publications, 1955), 4.

[2] Pope Honorius III, quoted in Pope Benedict XV, *Fausto Appetente Die*, Encyclical on Saint Dominic, June 29, 1921, no. 2.

[3] Due to the complexity of the sources, the scriptural quotations in this essay come from a variety of translations.

Of the many thousands of Dominicans who have instructed people in the way of holiness, three have been named Doctors of the Universal Church: the Universal Doctor, Saint Albert the Great (d. 1280); the Common Doctor, Saint Thomas Aquinas (d. 1274); and the Doctor of Unity, Saint Catherine of Siena (d. 1380). In order for us to see the Dominican contribution to the history of theological reflection on deification, we can do no better than to consider deification in the doctrine of these exemplary teachers.

Saint Albert the Great

Albert is in the unfortunate situation of being widely known but little studied, in comparison with his student Thomas Aquinas, who surpassed him. Yet, it is Albert who received the rare title "the Great". Moved by grace, Albert proved himself in a myriad of ways as preacher, teacher, priest, bishop, philosopher, theologian, natural scientist, mystic, and so forth. To others, he seemed more than simply human. Ulrich of Strasbourg, another of Albert's students, referred to his master as "so godlike (*divinus*) in every branch of knowledge that he can aptly be called the wonder and the miracle of our time."[4]

Because the topic of deification in Albert the Great's teaching is vast, this very brief treatment focuses on a select consideration of his commentaries on the Pseudo-Dionysian corpus. Albert held a fascination for Pseudo-Dionysius that was unsurpassed in the thirteenth century. He commented on all of Pseudo-Dionysius' extant writings: *On the Celestial Hierarchy*, *On the Ecclesiastical Hierarchy*, *On the Divine Names*, *On Mystical Theology*, and the Pseudo-Dionysian letters (the ten letters traditionally established, plus an eleventh attached to the collection). Albert, like others throughout the Middle Ages, thought that the author was the eponymous disciple converted by Paul in Athens (cf. Acts 17). As such, Pseudo-Dionysius held a nearly apostolic authority. Now he is believed to have been a monk,

[4] Ulrich of Strasbourg, *Summa de Bono* IV tr. 3, chap. 9, in *Albert and Thomas: Selected Writings*, trans. Simon Tugwell, O.P., Classics of Western Spirituality (New York: Paulist Press, 1988), 3; Tugwell's introduction (3–129) to Albert is an excellent resource for learning about this Dominican Doctor.

[5] For introductions, see Paul Rorem, *Pseudo-Dionysius: A Commentary on the Texts and an Introduction to Their Influence* (New York: Oxford University Press, 1993), and Andrew Louth, *Denys the Areopagite*, Outstanding Christian Thinkers (New York: Continuum, 1989).

probably from Syria, writing around A.D. 500.[5] Pseudo-Dionysius wrote about deification in various ways throughout his works, and so the translations of his texts into Latin, at different times in the Middle Ages, provided a valuable source for Western speculation about how God transforms man to share in his divine nature. Scholars classify two distinct interpretations of Pseudo-Dionysian mysticism among Western scholastics—the affective and the intellective.[6] Albert is a leader among the intellective interpreters.

In commenting upon Pseudo-Dionysius' *Ecclesiastical Hierarchy*, Albert came across this definition of deification: "both the likeness to God and unity, inasmuch that is possible".[7] This has been called the first formal definition of deification in Christian history.[8] Albert interprets this to mean that deification should be thought of in two respects, both created and Uncreated. He writes, "'Likeness' refers to the created habitus of glory, which one acquires by being conjoined to God, and 'unity' refers to the object of beatitude, which is the Uncreated Beatitude."[9] In other words, Albert believes that participation in God by a creature results in the creature receiving a new created disposition by which it is made to be like God. This occurs first in grace during this life on earth, and then, even more significantly, in the glory of heaven. Yet, this created effect of deification comes about precisely because of unification with, inasmuch as possible, God, the source of all happiness who alone is happiness itself. Holding both of these ideas about the created and the Uncreated together is of the greatest significance for understanding the reality of deification. There needs to be a real change in the rational creature that makes it resemble God more by grace than by what it had by nature, without itself being obliterated in the presence of God.

[6] See Bernard McGinn, *The Harvest of Mysticism in Medieval Germany*, vol. 4 of *The Presence of God: A History of Western Christian Mysticism* (New York: Crossroad Publishing Company, 2005), 13.

[7] Pseudo-Dionysius, *Ecclesiastical Hierarchy* 1.3. For Albert's commentaries on Pseudo-Dionysius, see volumes 36.1–2 and 37.1–2 in the critical edition sponsored by the Institute of Albert the Great, Cologne, published by Aschendorff (1972–1999). Here I am translating the Pseudo-Dionysian Latin text read by Albert. For a complete English translation of the Greek treatise, see *Pseudo-Dionysius: The Complete Works*, trans. Colm Luibheid, with collaboration by Paul Rorem, Classics of Western Spirituality (New York: Paulist Press, 1987), 193–259.

[8] See Norman Russell, *The Doctrine of Deification in the Greek Patristic Tradition*, Oxford Early Christian Studies (Oxford: Oxford University Press, 2004), 1.

[9] Albert the Great, *Super Dionysium De Ecclesiastica Hierarchia* 1, 36.2:14.

Albert expounds more upon a double sense of deification when he comments on Pseudo-Dionysius' *Epistle* 2, to Gaius. Rather than considering deification from the perspective of a focus on the deified, Pseudo-Dionysius focuses on what deifies. In this letter, Pseudo-Dionysius asks how the One who transcends everything is above all divinity and the source of goodness. Is not God divinity and the source of goodness itself? How can God be above divinity and the source of goodness? Pseudo-Dionysius is emphasizing that God is far above all things that share in God's nature through deification, as those things could be seen in an inferior way as divinity and the source of goodness. Elucidating Pseudo-Dionysius' point, Albert writes again with a distinction about how God transcends all things that participate in God so that in deification there are always both the created and the Uncreated:

> It must be said that something is the source of deification in two ways, namely effectively (and thus God alone is the deifying source) and also something deifies formally, just as the participation of deity is assimilating to God either through grace or through glory, and this is something other than God. If therefore divinity is called the deifying source effectively, then God is not above divinity, but God is above that divinity which is the deifying source formally.[10]

Albert is using the Aristotelian distinction between efficient and formal causality in order to analyze Pseudo-Dionysius' Neoplatonism.[11] Only God is the efficient cause, or the agent, of divinization, making others like himself both during this life on earth and in their entrance into heaven. However, others could be called "divinity" or a "source of goodness" in that God uses them to be formal causes, allowing them to shape the divinization of others.

After these emphases on the created and Uncreated, we now focus simply on Albert's understanding of how the intellect is transformed and raised to be conformed to God through the Pseudo-Dionysian mystical theology. This theology is not a mere university discipline that uses books and has a grade at the end. Rather, Albert uses a scriptural verse as a *thema* to open up the vast meaning of the *Mystical Theology*, Pseudo-Dionysius' shortest treatise. He chooses "Truly God

[10] Albert the Great, *Super Dionysii Epistulas* 2, 37.2:483.

[11] I am grateful for Daria Spezzano's keen insight here and elsewhere in improving this essay.

of Israel, the Savior, you are a hidden God" (Is 45:15). Albert shows how this verse gives insight to the four characteristics of mystical theology's nature, content, audience, and objective. Mystical theology's nature is scriptural, as Albert shows not only by quoting the prophet Isaiah, but also in explicating how "Truly" from Isaiah 45:15 should be understood. Sacred Scripture does not rest on human arguments, so fraught with uncertainty and error, but on the authority of divine inspiration, on undoubted truth itself. In Scripture, we are in contact with God himself. Yet, as for the content of this mystical theology, we find that God is "a hidden God".[12] Albert quotes 1 Timothy 6:16 and John 1:18 to show that God dwells in inaccessible light and no one has ever seen God. As for the audience, those meant to have this mystical theology, Albert focuses on the word "Israel". Albert takes up ancient definitions of Israel meaning "very straight" or "a man seeing God".[13] One cannot practice this theology without first having a purified life that enables one to have right behavior and sharpness of understanding. Finally, what is the objective or goal of mystical theology? That is suggested by the use of the term "Savior" in Isaiah 45:15. Albert writes with a typical Dominican abhorrence, both to useless ivory tower speculation and to moralism preoccupied with laws governing acts. The goal is something more than mere thinking or acting. This teaching's goal "is not just that we should acquire knowledge or, as in ethics, that we should 'become good' by doing good works, but that we should go further and attain to everlasting salvation, where we shall encounter openly and without veil what is at present left hidden from us about God by way of negations."[14] Albert then gives the following two Old Testament quotations: "To know you is the consummation of righteousness, and the knowledge of your righteousness and truth is the root of immortality" (Wis 15:3), and "I have seen the Lord face to face and my soul is saved" (Gen 32:30). This experience is the salvation of being deified through mystical theology.

An example of one deified in true theology, for both Pseudo-Dionysius and Albert, is the Evangelist John, the supposed recipient

[12] Translated in *Albert and Thomas: Selected Writings*, trans. Simon Tugwell, O.P., Classics of Western Spirituality (New York: Paulist Press, 1988), 134.

[13] Jerome rejects the explanation of the name of Israel as a "man seeing God" and favors "straight". See Tugwell's explanation in ibid., 135, n. 3.

[14] Albert the Great, *Super Mysticam Theologiam* 1, 37.2:454, trans. Tugwell, in *Albert and Thomas*, 136.

of Pseudo-Dionysius' *Epistle* 10.[15] At the end of this letter to John in exile, the author writes, "You will be sent away and return to the land of Asia and there you will perform imitations of the good God and you will hand on to those who will come after you."[16] Albert gives two possible interpretations to this letter's conclusion, both of which communicate something of Albert's spirituality of deification. Albert first comments, "*You will perform imitations of the good God*, by preaching and working for the salvation of others, just as Christ did, *and*, that is also, *you will hand on* your doctrine *to those who will come after you* by writing books."[17] Second, the Dominican Doctor gives this alternative explanation: "*You will perform*, that is you will write, *the imitations of the good God*, that is the actions and doctrines of Christ, which are propounded so that we may imitate them, because he wrote the Gospel after his return from exile, just as Jerome says in his preface to the Gospel."[18] Interestingly, Albert's commentary concerning the Evangelist John reflects Albert's own Dominican vocation in an imitation of Jesus Christ himself. For Albert, as for his Order, deification occurs through the communication of the gospel and the salvation of souls.

Saint Thomas Aquinas

It is a wonderful thing to be a student of a Doctor of the Church. But the more significant honor in this case is for the student to surpass his great teacher and rise to be unparalleled among teachers in the Catholic faith. Only Saint Thomas Aquinas is named by the Second Vatican Council[19] and the 1983 Code of Canon Law (can. 252 §3) as

[15] For a study of Albert's Johannine mysticism, see Andrew Hofer, O.P., "He Taught Us How to Fly: Albert the Great on John the Evangelist", *Angelicum* 87 (2010): 569–89. The following paragraph is based upon the research in pages 586–88. Scholars say that the Pseudo-Dionysian collection of ten letters is hierarchically arranged, with the exception of *Epistle* 8, to a monk who disrupted hierarchy. The very order signifies that John the Evangelist, receiving the tenth letter, has a preeminent role in deification.

[16] Albert the Great, *Super Dionysii Epistulas* 10, 37.2:548.

[17] Ibid., p. 550 (emphasis in original).

[18] Ibid. (emphasis in original).

[19] See Vatican Council II, Decree on Priestly Training, *Optatam totius*, October 28, 1965, no. 16; cf. Vatican Council II, Declaration on Christian Education, *Gravissimum educationis*, October 28, 1965, no. 10. More recently, consider Pope Benedict's repetition of what Paul VI said: "All of us who are faithful sons and daughters of the Church can and must be his

the special teacher of men studying theology for the priesthood. His writings prove to be an extraordinary resource for scholars in search of the truth about God and the world over seven centuries after his life.[20]

Unlike Albert, Thomas may suffer from an "overfamiliarity" in which people presume they know what the Common Doctor teaches. Yet, when we read Thomas' writings through the lens of deification, we can see some wonders of his profound teaching that would otherwise be missed. Daria Spezzano argues that "throughout the *Summa* a theology of deification [is present] which, though sometimes hidden, is always at work."[21] God, who is present to us, transforms us in the *habitus* of created grace so as to be united to him, the Uncreated One, through the theological virtues, especially charity, and the gifts of the Holy Spirit, especially wisdom. By raising intellect and will to acts beyond their nature, deification in this life prepares us for the loving union of God in heaven's beatific vision. The following merely sketches Thomas' profound theology of deification, present in many of his writings.

Near the beginning of the *Summa*, Thomas asks thc following question: "Can creatures be said to be like God?"[22] This has great

disciples, at least to some extent!" Pope Benedict XVI, "General Audience" (Paul VI Hall), June 23, 2010, quoting Pope Paul VI's Address to People in the Square at Aquino, September 14, 1974.

[20] There are many fine introductions to Thomas' thought. One of special value in understanding his writings is Jean-Pierre Torrell, O.P., *Saint Thomas Aquinas*, vol. 1, *The Person and His Work*, rev. ed., trans. Robert Royal (Washington, D.C.: Catholic University of America Press, 2005). For my application of Thomas' understanding of deification to the liturgy, see Andrew Hofer, O.P., "Aquinas, Divinization, and the People in the Pews", in *Divinization: Becoming Icons of Christ through the Liturgy*, ed. Andrew Hofer, O.P. (Chicago: Hillenbrand Books, 2015), 54–72.

[21] Daria Spezzano, "The Grace of the Holy Spirit, the Virtue of Charity, and the Gift of Wisdom: Deification in Thomas Aquinas' *Summa Theologiae*" (Ph.D. diss., University of Notre Dame, 2011), 468. Spezzano deepens the important study of A.N. Williams, *The Ground of Union: Deification in Aquinas and Palamas* (New York: Oxford University Press, 1999). For example, Spezzano corrects Williams by defending the importance of "created grace" in the *Summa Theologiae*. For a brief treatment of divinization focusing on Aquinas' scriptural commentaries, see Daniel Keating, "Justification, Sanctification and Divinization in Thomas Aquinas", in *Aquinas on Doctrine: A Critical Introduction*, ed. Thomas Weinandy, O.F.M. Cap., Daniel Keating, and John Yocum (London: T&T Clark, 2004), 139–58. Spezzano's dissertation has now been revised and published as *The Glory of God's Grace: Deification according to St. Thomas Aquinas* (Washington, D.C.: Sapientia Press, 2015).

[22] Thomas Aquinas, *The Summa Theologica of St. Thomas Aquinas*, trans. Fathers of the English Dominican Province (New York: Benziger, 1947), I, q. 4, a. 3 (hereafter *STh*). At times, I slightly alter the translation to be more faithful to the Latin text.

importance in understanding the language of deification, as theologians have reflected on our talk about God, how we know God, and who God really is, in vastly different ways. Thomas takes as his first objection an argument proceeding from Psalm 86:8: "There is none like you among the gods, O Lord." The objection says that the more excellent creatures are called "gods" by participation. If even they are not like God, then how much more unlike God are all other creatures. Aquinas responds with an explanation from Pseudo-Dionysius that when Sacred Scripture denies that anything is like God, "it is not the contrary of likeness to him, for the same things are both like God and unlike. They are like inasmuch they imitate him, who is not perfectly imitable, and they are unlike inasmuch as they fall short of their cause."[23] With careful metaphysical precision, Aquinas refutes various ways of likeness between God and creatures, such as likeness within a common genus, but affirms the likeness revealed by Scripture. Thomas underscores the analogy of a cause, outside the genus of its effect, which makes an effect like it. These effects are like God, through this analogy of participation.[24] For Thomas, ultimately, we must speak of creatures being like God, because that is what the Bible says: "Let us make man in our image, after our likeness" (Gen 1:26); "[W]hen he appears we shall be like him" (1 Jn 3:2).[25] Creatures participate in the being of God, and can even be said to be "partakers of the divine nature" (2 Pet 1:4).[26]

In various writings, it is clear that Aquinas speaks of deification because he reads it in Sacred Scripture. Aquinas writes that several scriptural passages call those who are justified by divine grace "children of God" or "begotten of God", such as in John 1:12; Romans 8:16; 1 John 3:1, 9; and James 1:18. Even more startling, the name of divinity is ascribed to mere human beings. Aquinas cites Exodus 7:1: "I make you as God to Pharaoh"; Psalm 82:6: "I say, 'You are gods, sons of the Most High, all of you'"; John 10:35: "[H]e called them gods, to whom the word of God came"; and 2 Peter 1:4: "That through these you may escape from the corruption that is

[23] *STh* I, q. 4, a. 3 ad 1; cf. *On the Divine Names* 9.7.

[24] See *STh* I, q. 4, a. 3 ad 3.

[25] See *STh* I, q. 4, a. 3, sed contra.

[26] For Thomas' use of this verse in his theology of grace, see especially *STh* I–II, q. 110, a. 3, and *STh* III, q. 62, a. 1.

in the world because of passion, and become partakers of the divine nature."[27] Because of this scriptural warrant, Aquinas can also use patristic texts that speak of deification as well as develop his own way of speaking about this mystery of sanctification.

Thomas uses the verb *deifico* quite frequently, many times to speak of what happens to Christ's own humanity in the Incarnation.[28] To avoid heresies that do not affirm Christ's true divinity or separate Christ's humanity as a person coexistent with the person of his divinity, Thomas will need to distinguish. Is Christ simply deified as an outstanding saint? No, he is the eternal Son of God, who became incarnate for our salvation. As Thomas says, "Christ, therefore, who both sanctifies and forgives sins, is not called God as they are called gods who are sanctified, and whose sins are forgiven, but as one who has the power and the nature of divinity."[29] At the Incarnation, Christ's own humanity is radically deified through the hypostatic union, a union different from the sanctification of others.[30]

Thomas can also speak of what happens to us in grace by deification through the Incarnation. Examining the fittingness of the Incarnation for the restoration of the human race, he considers deification both in terms of bringing us close to God and delivering us from evil. He says that the Incarnation is for our "full participation in divinity" and quotes Saint Leo's Christmas preaching: "O Christian, acknowledge your dignity; and having becoming a sharer in the divine nature, do not return to the old filth by a degenerate way of life."[31] It is precisely through Christ's grace as head of the Church that we receive grace, saving us from evil and transforming us to be more and more like God. In one place, he quotes Athanasius in saying that the Son

[27] *Summa contra Gentiles* 4.4.2–3 (hereafter *ScG*); cf. *ScG* 1.42.22. For an English translation of its four books, see *Summa contra Gentiles*, trans. Anton C. Pegis et al. (Notre Dame, Ind.: University of Notre Dame Press, 1975). At times, I slightly alter the translation to be more faithful to the Latin text.

[28] According to Torrell's research through the *Index Thomisticus*, Thomas uses the verb *deifico* thirty-four times, seventeen of which are in a christological context. See Jean-Pierre Torrell, O.P., *Saint Thomas Aquinas*, vol. 2, *Spiritual Master*, trans. Robert Royal (Washington, D.C.: Catholic University of America Press, 2003), 126–27, n. 3. Similarly, Thomas uses *deiformitas* fifty-one times, many of which have an intellectual connotation not present in *deifico*. See Torrell, *Spiritual Master*, 127, n. 4.

[29] *ScG* 4.4.15; cf. *ScG* 4.34.25.

[30] See *STh* III, q. 2.

[31] *STh* III, q. 1, a. 2, quoting Leo the Great, Sermon 51 (*Patrologia Latina* 54.192).

of God "became man, and was circumcised in the flesh, not for his own sake, but that he might make us gods through grace, and that we might be circumcised in the spirit".[32] Thomas does not simply "think the world" of grace; grace is more than the world. As should be widely known, Thomas posits that "the good of grace in one is more than the good of nature in the whole universe."[33] This grace transforms our souls and provides the basis for Thomas' examination of the many virtues, gifts, and fruits of the Holy Spirit and beatitudes in the *Summa*'s *Secunda Secundae*.

Earlier we saw Albert commenting on Pseudo-Dionysius on what is the cause of deifying, and what is not in different respects. Similarly, Thomas asks, "Whether God alone is the cause of grace?" He replies:

> It must be said that nothing can act beyond its species, since the cause must always be more powerful than its effect. Now the gift of grace surpasses every capability of created nature, since it is nothing short of a partaking of the divine nature, which exceeds every other nature. And thus it is impossible that any creature should cause grace. For it is as necessary that God alone should deify (*solus Deus deificet*), bestowing a partaking of the divine nature by a participated likeness, as it is impossible that anything except fire should enkindle.[34]

This emphasis on God alone as the proper cause of deification helps us understand Thomas' emphasis on the sacraments, and especially the sacrament of the Holy Eucharist. The Holy Eucharist has a particular prominence in Thomas' teaching, for that is the sacrament of sacraments as the presence of Christ himself, and all other sacraments are ordered to it and lead to its reception.[35] In celebrating the Solemnity of the Body and Blood of Christ, the Church takes for the second lesson in the Office of Readings a passage from Thomas' work on the Feast of Corpus Christi featuring deification: "Since it was the will of God's only-begotten Son that men should share in

[32] *STh* III, q. 37, a. 3 ad 2, quoting Athanasius, *Fragments on Luke* (*Patrologia Graeca* 27.1396). The English Dominican Province translation has "God's", and the Blackfriars, Gilby translation has "sons of God", but the Latin text of *deos* should be translated as "gods". Certain twentieth-century English Thomists were even more squeamish about deification terminology than was Thomas!

[33] *STh* I–II, q. 113, a. 9 ad 2.

[34] *STh* I–II, q. 112, a. 1.

[35] Cf. *STh* III, q. 65, a. 3.

his divinity, he assumed our nature in order that by becoming man he might make men gods."[36] In his question from the *Summa* on the effects of the Holy Eucharist, Aquinas quotes John Damascene as his authority in the sed contra of one article: "The fire of that desire which is within us, being kindled by the burning coal [that is, this sacrament], will consume our sins, and enlighten our hearts, so that we shall be inflamed and be deified (*deificemur*)."[37] This burning fire thus transforms devout recipients to be more and more members of Christ, sharing in the *res*, or reality, of the Eucharist, which is unity with God and one another in his Church.

To round off this brief sketch, we can see that Thomas teaches also on the deification that occurs in the entry of the saints to the beatific vision. The saints in heaven, raised up in the light of glory, see God face-to-face in a vision without intermediary. Their intellects thus receive what Thomas calls "deiformity", fulfilling the passage from 1 John 2:2: "When he shall appear we shall be like him, for we shall see him as he is."[38] Deification during this life on earth can only be complete in the loving sight of God in everlasting happiness. Thomas, like the Order he entered, lifts people up through preaching to hope in the complete salvation found only in heaven.

Saint Catherine of Siena

It is said that at the age of six, little Catherine saw a vision of Jesus Christ above the church of the friars preachers at Siena. During this vision of the Lord, Catherine was "transformed into him upon whom her loving gaze was fixed".[39] This transformation prepared Catherine for further experiences of transformation. In declaring her a Doctor of the Church, Pope Paul VI recounts the story of Catherine

[36] Thomas Aquinas, *Opusculum* 57.1, in *The Liturgy of the Hours according to the Roman Rite*, vol. 3, trans. International Commission on English in the Liturgy (New York: Catholic Book Publishing, 1975), 610. Cf. *CCC* 460.

[37] *STh* III, q. 79, a. 8, sed contra.

[38] *STh* I, q. 12, a. 5.

[39] See Raymond of Capua, *The Life of Catherine of Siena*, trans. Conleth Kearns, O.P. (Wilmington, Del.: Michael Glazier, 1980), no. 30, p. 29. Blessed Raymond of Capua, Catherine's confessor and disciple, wrote her life after her death. Among valuable studies of Catherine's life, see Suzanne Noffke, O.P., *Catherine of Siena: Vision through a Distant Eye* (Collegeville, Minn.: Liturgical Press, 1996).

speaking in a divine way to a consistory of cardinals: "Never has man spoken thus," her hearers said, "and it is beyond doubt that it is not this woman who is speaking, but indeed the Holy Spirit."[40] She even received the stigmata of the Lord, which she wished would be hidden from view. The wounds visibly appeared after her death on April 29, 1380, at the age of thirty-three, when her prayer that she would give up her life for the sake of the Church was accepted.

Through her *Dialogue*, over 380 letters, and more than two dozen prayers, Catherine of Siena is a profound teacher of God's transformative love. She writes, "Love transforms one into what one loves."[41] Thomas McDermott comments, "This statement, more than any other, expresses the whole of Catherine of Siena's spiritual thought."[42] It expresses her understanding of deification. Yes, Catherine can give variations on that classic deification formula, uttered as a divine communication from God to her as in, "I, God, became a man and humanity became God through the union of my divine nature with your human nature. This greatness is given to every person in general."[43] It can also be found within her following prayers: "You, God, became human and humanity became God"; "We are your image, and now by making yourself one with us you have become our image, veiling your eternal divinity in the wretched cloud and dung heap of Adam. And why? For love! You, God, became human and we have been made divine!"[44] What is more, Catherine offers a fascinating range of ways to express deification within the Dominican tradition.

The theme of deification immediately strikes the reader when opening Catherine's book, *The Dialogue*. She says that by continual

[40] Pope Paul VI, Apostolic Letter *Mirabilis in Ecclesia Deus*, October 4, 1970, trans. W.B. Mahoney, O.P.,www.drawnbylove.com, accessed January 5, 2013.

[41] God says to Catherine: "I will show myself to them, just as my Truth said: 'Those who love me will be one with me and I with them, and I will show myself to them and we will make our dwelling place together.' This is how it is with very dear friends. Their loving affection makes them two bodies, because love transforms one into what one loves. And if these souls are made one soul [with me], nothing can be kept hidden from them. This is why my Truth said, 'I will come and we will make a dwelling place together.' That is the truth." See Catherine of Siena, *The Dialogue*, trans. Suzanne Noffke, O.P., Classics of Western Spirituality (New York: Paulist Press, 1980), chap. 60, pp. 115–16.

[42] Thomas McDermott, O.P., *Catherine of Siena: Spiritual Development in Her Life and Teaching* (New York: Paulist Press, 2008), 320, n. 2.

[43] Catherine of Siena, *Dialogue*, chap. 110, p. 205.

[44] Prayer 11 in *The Prayers of Catherine of Siena*, trans. Suzanne Noffke, O.P., 2nd ed. (San Jose, Calif.: Authors Choice Press, 2001), 102; and *Dialogue*, chap. 13, p. 50.

humble prayer, "the soul is united with God, following in the footsteps of Christ crucified, and through desire and affection and the union of love he makes of her another himself." She goes on to explain Christ's words: "If you will love me and keep my word, I will show myself to you, and you will be one thing with me and I with you"[45] (cf. Jn 14:21–23). And we find similar words in other places from which we can see it is the truth that by love's affection the soul becomes another Christ.

Catherine is perhaps more famous for her endearing title of "Christ on earth" for the pope than for her spirituality of deification. But such a title should be seen in relation to her profound insight that each Christian, moved by God's transforming love, can become one that the Lord finds to be "another himself". Still in *The Dialogue*'s Prologue, Catherine reports the Lord's message of love: "Open your mind's eye and look within me," says the Lord, "and you will see the dignity and beauty of my reasoning creature." This teaching, as is Dominican preaching in general, is firmly founded in the goodness of nature. *The Dialogue* continues, "But beyond the beauty I have given the soul by creating her in my image and likeness, look at those who are clothed in the wedding garment of charity, adorned with many true virtues. They are united with me through love." Catherine thus sees that the life of grace, offering the theological virtues, raises the soul to be in union with the Lord in his own divine charity. "So I say, if you should ask me who they are, I would answer," said the gentle, loving Word, "that they are another me; for they have lost and drowned their own will and have clothed themselves and united themselves and conformed themselves with mine."[46]

Arguably more than any Western male Doctor of the Church, Catherine constantly employs images to communicate the doctrine of the faith. For some common examples from dietary symbols, she can teach on the Trinity through speaking of table (Father), food (Son), and waiter (Holy Spirit), on the Incarnation through writing about dough baked in the Virgin Mary, and on working for salvation through urging people to eat souls. Given this exaltation of the

[45] Catherine of Siena, *Dialogue*, chap. 1, p. 25.

[46] Ibid., pp. 25–26. For an account of this in Catherine's spirituality of transformation, see Denis Vincent Wiseman, O.P., *Jesus Christ Crucified and Gentle Mary: Salvation and Mary in the Life and Writings of Catherine of Siena*, Marian Library Studies, new series 27 (Dayton, Ohio: University of Dayton, 2005–2006), 168–70; cf. p. 83.

common to understand heaven's work, we turn now to her images of marriage, fire, and water that describe the mystery of divinization.

Bridal imagery in Western mysticism, so rooted in the revelation of both Old and New Testaments, conveys considerable possibilities for understanding deification. In Catherine's approach, the bride is frequently the holy Church, also known as the Mystical Body of Christ.[47] By God's love, the Church is chosen and transformed to be like her divine Spouse, who shed his blood for her. In a beloved phrase, Catherine expresses this transformation in various letters by talking about the color of the Church, like a woman with bright cheeks.[48] Bridal imagery can also be used for the individual soul's deification. For example, Catherine writes to the wife of Milan's twice-excommunicated tyrant, "A servant maid would become a great lady should the emperor make her his wife. By her union with him she would become an empress—not by her own merit (for she was only a servant), but because of his dignity as emperor." With this image implanted in Regina's mind, Catherine then has her turn to God: "Just think, dearest mother in Christ gentle Jesus! The soul who has fallen in love with God, she who is a servant and slave ransomed by the blood of God's Son, attains such great dignity that she cannot be called a servant now, but an empress, spouse of the eternal emperor!"[49] Just as a maid becomes an empress through marital union with the emperor, so a creature becomes deified through a union with God made possible by the Passion of Christ.

Catherine loves to speak of fire. In a striking phrase, she prays to God about how her nature is that of the Creator: "In your nature, eternal Godhead, I shall come to know my nature. And what is my nature, boundless Love? It is fire, because you are nothing but a fire of love. And you have given humankind a share in this nature, for by the fire of love you created us."[50] This fire blazes up through charity,

[47] For Catherine's sacramental understanding of *il corpo mistico*, see Catherine of Siena, *Dialogue*, 36, n. 15, and *Prayers*, 131–32, n. 1.

[48] For the complete translation of the letters, see *The Letters of Catherine of Siena*, vols. 1–4, trans. Suzanne Noffke, O.P., Medieval and Renaissance Texts and Studies, vols. 202–3, 329, and 355 (Tempe, Ariz.: Arizona Center for Medieval and Renaissance Studies, 2000–2008). For examples of the Church as a woman with bright cheeks, see Letter T177/G29/DT61 in *Letters of Catherine of Siena* 3:100; Letter T16/G38 in *Letters of Catherine of Siena* 3:117; and Letter T331/G7/DT77 in *Letters of Catherine of Siena* 3:217.

[49] Letter T29/G319/DT18, in *Letters of Catherine of Siena* 1:207–8.

[50] Prayer 12, in Catherine of Siena, *Prayers*, 117–18; cf. prayer 13 in *Prayers*, 130.

sharing in the intensity of the divine life. For Catherine, God's children in the advanced stages of the spiritual journey, who experience increased suffering and are "fattened" in charity, are "like the burning coal that no one can put out once it is completely consumed in the furnace, because it has itself been turned into fire. So it is with these souls cast into the furnace of my charity, who keep nothing at all, not a bit of their own will, outside of me, but are completely set afire in me." The will, now completely transformed by God's love, has no selfishness in it, but is completely divinized. God continues to assure Catherine about his power for those who have completely accepted his love: "There is no one who can seize them or drag them out of my grace. They have been made one with me and I with them."[51]

This divine perfection is offered to all in the Church—clerical, religious, lay, both married and celibate. For example, in a letter to two married couples in Florence, Catherine writes:

> I long to see you set ablaze and consumed in the fire of divine charity. This is the fire that in burning does not consume us but makes our soul fat, and unites us with and transforms us into itself, a fire of divine love. Once we see that we have our being from God alone, we will also see that God has in love given us all the graces and gifts that have been given us besides.... Oh boundless love! Oh immense charity! Oh fire of divine charity! What heart could see that it is loved with such blazing love and not melt with love and be totally transformed in it?[52]

In another letter, to a young Sienese nobleman and poet, Catherine similarly writes about how "it is the nature of fire to burn and transform into itself whatever comes near it." Catherine continues, "So we, when we contemplate our Creator's love, are drawn at once to love him and turn our affection completely to him. In him all the dampness of selfishness is dried up, and we take on the likeness of the Holy Spirit's fire."[53] No wetness of sin can withstand this divine fire.

Yet, Catherine also loves to talk about God with an image quite different from fire: water. In this case, too, she speaks of how a totality

[51] Catherine of Siena, *Dialogue*, chap. 78, p. 147.

[52] Letter T48/G29, in *Letters of Catherine of Siena* 3:311–12.

[53] Letter T228/G278, in ibid., 2:15.

occurs in coming completely into God's life. Catherine uses the metaphor of a fish in the sea for describing the immersion in God that occurs when receiving the Holy Eucharist. *The Dialogue* relates, "In communion the soul seems more sweetly bound to God and better knows his truth. For then the soul is in God and God in the soul, just as the fish is in the sea and the sea is in the fish."[54] Later in the book, God tells her, "Dearest daughter, contemplate the marvelous state of the soul who receives this bread of life, this food of angels, as she ought. When she receives this sacrament she lives in me and I in her. Just as the fish is in the sea and the sea is in the fish, so am I in the soul and the soul in me, the sea of peace."[55] This Eucharistic immersion in God, as in a sea, means a complete conformity of the soul's will to God's will. Saint Catherine prays, "I proclaim and do not deny it: you are a peaceful sea in whom every soul is immersed who conforms her will with your eternal will."[56]

Finally, following upon this Catherinian emphasis on images, her clearest example of a disciple's complete conformity to God's will is seen in the Blessed Virgin Mary. She is so deified that she receives the same title "peaceful sea" that Catherine frequently calls God.[57] In a prayer preserved from the Feast of the Annunciation, Catherine prays to the Mother of God: "Oh Mary, vessel of humility! In you the light of true knowledge thrives and burns. By this light you rose above yourself, and so you were pleasing to the eternal Father, and he seized you and drew you to himself, loving you with a special love."[58] Catherine, like her Order, which came about through the prayers of the Virgin Mary, never tired of seeing God's most wonderful new creation, his most complete deification, in our Lady.

Conclusion

Blessed Jordan of Saxony, Saint Dominic's first successor as Master of the Order of Preachers, wrote of Dominic: "He had a special prayer

[54] Catherine of Siena, *Dialogue*, chap. 2, p. 27.
[55] Ibid., chap. 112, p. 211.
[56] Prayers 1 and 2, in Catherine of Siena, *Prayers*, 27.
[57] Prayer 18, in ibid., 186.
[58] Ibid.

which he often made to God, that God would grant him true charity, which would be effective in caring for and winning the salvation of men; he thought he would only really be a member of Christ's Body when he could spend himself utterly with all his strength in the winning of souls, just as the Lord Jesus Christ, the Savior of us all, gave himself up entirely for our salvation."[59] In various ways, the three Dominican Doctors of the Church have continued Dominic's prayer and labor to be true members of Christ in charity, being like the Savior who gave himself utterly for all. They, like their spiritual father, were deified through the charism of preaching and the salvation of souls. Stepping back from the teachings on deification from these three Dominican Doctors, we see how they themselves are examples of being conformed to the Lord. Their lives are examples of the deification that they sought to pass on to others. The philosopher, scientist, mystic, theologian, and all-around polymath Albert is "the Great", a title derivative from the One who alone is good (cf. Mk 10:18). Albert's prized pupil, *Divus* Thomas, became the teacher par excellence, radiant with godlike wisdom. Catherine is so utterly transformed into the Bridegroom of the Church that this pure virgin received his heart and his wounds in the fire of his love. All three are faithful children of Dominic, who both in his life and in his Order shines true to the deification signified by his own lordly name.

Readings for Further Study

Noffke, Suzanne, O.P. *Catherine of Siena: Vision through a Distant Eye*. Collegeville, Minn.: Liturgical Press, 1996.

Torrell, Jean-Pierre, O.P. *Saint Thomas Aquinas*. 2 vols. Translated by Robert Royal. Washington, D.C.: Catholic University of America Press, 1996–2005.

Tugwell, Simon, O.P., trans. *Albert and Thomas: Selected Writings*. Classics of Western Spirituality. New York: Paulist Press, 1988.

[59] Jordan of Saxony, *On the Beginnings of the Order of Preachers*, trans. Simon Tugwell, O.P., Dominican Sources: New Editions in English (Dublin: Dominican Publications, 1982), no. 13, p. 3 (translation slightly altered).

Chapter Six

LIKE ANOTHER CHRIST: THE FRANCISCAN THEOLOGY OF DEIFICATION

Sister M. Regina van den Berg

Saint Francis of Assisi (1181/1182–1226) gave grace such free rein in his life that, being transformed *by* Christ and *into* Christ, he could echo the words of Saint Paul: "I have been crucified with Christ; it is no longer I who live, but Christ who lives in me" (Gal 2:20). The likeness of Christ Crucified was imprinted on the body of Saint Francis even in a physical manner. The early writings about the saint already speak of him as being "like another Christ given to the world for the people's salvation".[1] Pope Pius XI, in his Encyclical Letter *Rite expiatis*, written on the occasion of the seventh centenary of the transitus of Saint Francis, does not hesitate to affirm that

> there has never been anyone in whom the image of Jesus Christ and the evangelical manner of life shone forth more lifelike and strikingly than in St. Francis. He who called himself the "Herald of the Great King" was also rightly spoken of as "another Jesus Christ," appearing to his contemporaries and to future generations almost as if he were the Risen Christ. He has always lived as such in the eyes of men and so will continue to live for all future time.[2]

Saint Francis did not reflect in a systematic manner on what it means to be deified, to become like unto Christ, although both by his example and by his writings the saint showed his followers how to

[1] Francis of Assisi, *The Little Flowers of Saint Francis*, chap. 7, in *Francis of Assisi: Early Documents*, vol. 3, *The Prophet*, ed. Regis J. Armstrong, O.F.M. Cap., J.A. Wayne Hellmann, O.F.M., Conv., and William J. Short, O.F.M. (New York: New City Press, 2001), 578.

[2] Pope Pius XI, Encyclical Letter *Rite expiatis*, April 30, 1926, no. 2.

attain to such likeness. It was probably not long after the saint's death that a mother prayed through his intercession to obtain a cure for her sick boy. The boy was cured, later entered the Order of the Friars Minor, became the Father General, was elevated to the College of Cardinals of the Holy Roman Church, and, after his death, was canonized and declared a Doctor of the Church, the Seraphic Doctor: Saint Bonaventure (1221–1274). Saint Bonaventure himself writes about the miraculous cure obtained through the intercession of Saint Francis in his *Major Legend*: "For when I was a boy, as I still vividly remember, I was snatched from the jaws of death by his invocation and merits."[3] Saint Bonaventure gave theological expression to the spirituality of his father in religion. The present chapter is accordingly divided into two parts: the first examines the notion of deification as it becomes visible in both the life and writings of Saint Francis; the second provides an overview of Saint Bonaventure's theological study of deification. The second part of the chapter will provide some theological insight into the spirituality expressed in the first part.

Saint Francis

Saint Francis' life, after his conversion, was marked from the outset by his filial adherence to God the Father, and by his profound love for the triune God, for the Blessed Mother, and for the sacraments of the Church. Although Saint Francis does not use the word "deification", his life is a testimony to the power of God's grace to transform men into his likeness, and his writings reveal that the sources of Saint

[3] Bonaventure, *The Major Legend of Saint Francis*, in *Francis of Assisi: Early Documents*, vol. 2, *The Founder*, ed. Regis J. Armstrong, O.F.M. Cap., J. A. Wayne Hellmann, O.F.M., Conv., and William J. Short, O.F.M. (New York: New City Press, 2000), 528. Cf. Bonaventure, *The Minor Legend of Saint Francis*, chap. 7, lesson 8, in *Francis of Assisi*, vol. 2, *Founder*, 717: "When I was just a child and very seriously ill, my mother made a vow on my behalf to the blessed father Francis. I was snatched from the very jaws of death and restored to the vigor of a healthy life. Since I hold this vividly in my memory, I now publicly proclaim it as true, lest keeping silent about such a benefit I would be accused of being ungrateful. Accept, therefore, blessed father, my thanks however meager and unequal to your merits and benefits." According to J. Guy Bougerol, O.F.M., in *Introduction to the Works of Bonaventure*, trans. José de Vinck (Paterson, N.J.: St. Anthony Guild Press, 1964), 3–4, it is most probable that the cure took place after the death of Saint Francis, not during the saint's lifetime (Saint Francis died when Saint Bonaventure was about five years old).

Francis' transformation into Christ were the sacraments and meditation on the mysteries of the faith.

One of the first things Saint Francis did after his conversion was to give away as alms money belonging to his father and money from the sale of his father's horse. Saint Francis tried to give the proceeds from the sale of the horse to the priest of the Church of San Damiano, but the priest refused to receive it, so Saint Francis threw the money on the windowsill of the church. When Saint Francis' father learned of his son's actions, he demanded the restitution of his money, taking the matter first to the magistrates and then to the bishop. The *Legend of the Three Companions* relates that Saint Francis exclaimed, in the presence of the bishop, his father, and the townspeople: "Listen to me, all of you, and understand. Until now I have called Pietro di Bernardone my father. But, because I have proposed to serve God, I return to him the money on account of which he was so upset, and also all the clothing which is his, wanting to say from now on: '*Our Father who are in heaven,*' and not, 'My father, Pietro di Bernardone'."[4] The event is symbolic of the saint's transformation into a "second Christ": he strips himself of all that is his own in order to allow Christ to transform him into himself. Henceforth, he lives as a child of God, casting all his cares on the Lord with full confidence in his providence (cf. Ps 55:22; 1 Pet 5:7), with the Blessed Virgin Mary as his Mother and Jesus as his brother. Speaking of the sweetness of belonging wholly to God the Father, Saint Francis exclaims:

> O how glorious it is to have a holy and great Father in heaven! O how holy, consoling to have such a beautiful and wonderful Spouse! O how holy and how loving, gratifying, humbling, peace-giving, sweet, worthy of love, and, above all things, desirable: to have such a Brother and such a Son, our Lord Jesus Christ, Who laid down His life for His sheep.[5]

[4] *Legend of the Three Companions*, chap. 6, in *Francis of Assisi*, vol. 2, *Founder*, 80.

[5] Francis of Assisi, *Earlier Exhortation to the Brothers and Sisters of Penance (The First Version of the Letter to the Faithful) (1209–1215)*, in *Francis of Assisi: Early Documents*, vol. 1, *The Saint*, ed. Regis J. Armstrong, O.F.M. Cap., J.A. Wayne Hellmann, O.F.M., Conv., and William J. Short, O.F.M. (New York: New City Press, 1999), 42. Cf. ibid., 41–42: "All those who love the Lord *with their whole heart, and their whole soul and mind, with their whole strength* and love their neighbors as themselves ... are children of the heavenly Father Whose works they do, and they are spouses, brothers, and mothers of our Lord Jesus Christ" (emphasis in original).

The Poverello lived what he exhorted others to do: "Hold back nothing of yourselves for yourselves, that He Who gives Himself totally to you may receive you totally."[6]

Saint Francis meditated upon God and the things of God, especially on the mystery of the Incarnation and of the prolongation of the Incarnation in the Blessed Sacrament,[7] with faith, reverence, and love; and it was in that way that God's grace was able to transform him into a reflection of God himself. Faith, reverence, and love are not only necessary for allowing God's grace to effect a transformation, but they are also the fruit of the selfsame transformation.[8] It is not surprising, then, that the writings of Saint Francis overflow with expressions of faith, reverence, and love.

Saint Francis had an abiding reverence for God's presence in churches and in the most Blessed Sacrament. The saint himself explains: "And the Lord gave me such faith in churches that I would pray with all simplicity in this way and say, 'We adore You, Lord Jesus Christ, in all Your churches throughout the whole world and we bless You because by Your holy cross You have redeemed the world'."[9] Thomas Celano describes that the friars, surely following the example of their Father, Saint Francis, repeated these words while "prostrate on the ground, bowing inwardly and outwardly".[10]

The Holy Eucharist, as the *Catechism of the Catholic Church*, quoting the words of *Eucharisticum mysterium*, reminds us, "is the efficacious sign and sublime cause of ... communion in the divine life ...

[6] Francis of Assisi, *Letter to the Entire Order (1225–1226)*, in *Francis of Assisi*, vol. 1, *Saint*, 118.

[7] Cf. Pope Leo XIII, Encyclical Letter *Mirae caritatis*, May 28, 1902, no. 7: "The Eucharist, according to the testimony of the holy Fathers, should be regarded as in a manner a continuation and extension of the Incarnation. For in and by it the substance of the incarnate Word is united with individual men, and the supreme Sacrifice offered on Calvary is in a wondrous manner renewed."

[8] Columba Marmion, O.S.B., notes that these three qualities are necessary for us to meditate fruitfully upon the mysteries of the life of Christ. Cf. Columba Marmion, *The Mysteries of the Life of Christ*, 10th ed. (Saint Louis: B. Herder, 1939). Although the present volume does not include a study of the notion of deification in the Benedictine tradition, the whole of the *corpus* of Blessed Columba Marmion, O.S.B., speaks about our status as adopted children of God and makes it, in fact, the basis for the spiritual life. He writes, too, of our becoming like unto God by living as children of God. As just one among other places, cf. *Mysteries of Christ*, pts. 1 and 2.

[9] Francis of Assisi, *The Testament*, in *Francis of Assisi*, vol. 1, *Saint*, 124–25.

[10] Thomas of Celano, *The Life of Saint Francis*, bk. 1, chap. 17, in *Francis of Assisi*, vol. 1, *Saint*, 222.

the culmination both of God's action sanctifying the world in Christ and of the worship men offer to Christ and through him to the Father in the Holy Spirit."[11] The Holy Eucharist gives us God himself and it is therefore the means par excellence for our deification. Saint Francis was caught up in the most reverent and loving devotion to the Blessed Sacrament. He exclaimed: "Behold, each day He humbles Himself as when He came *from the royal throne* into the Virgin's womb; each day He Himself comes to us, appearing humbly; each day He comes down *from the bosom of the Father* upon the altar in the hands of a priest."[12] We note, in the words just cited, also his tender devotion to the Blessed Virgin Mary, as the one who gave us God's Son in the Incarnation and who continues to give us her Son in the Holy Eucharist. The Saint of Assisi begged all his followers:

> Let everyone be struck with fear, let the whole world tremble, and let the heavens exult when Christ, the Son of the living God, is present on the altar in the hands of a priest! O wonderful loftiness and stupendous dignity! O sublime humility! O humble sublimity! The Lord of the universe, God and the Son of God, so humbles Himself that for our salvation He hides Himself under an ordinary piece of bread![13]

Since Jesus comes upon the altar daily only through the hands of a priest, Saint Francis revered all priests without condition. He explains:

> The Lord gave me, and gives me still, such faith in priests who live according to the rite of the holy Roman Church because of their orders that, were they to persecute me, I would still want to have recourse to them. And if I had as much *wisdom as Solomon* and found impoverished priests of this world, I would not preach in their parishes against their will. And I desire to respect, love and honor them and all others as my lords. And I do not want to consider any sin in them because I discern the Son in God in them and they are my lords.

[11] Sacred Congregation of Rites, Instruction *Eucharisticum mysterium*, May 25, 1967, no. 6, quoted in *CCC* 1325.

[12] Francis of Assisi, *The Admonitions*, admonition 1, in *Francis of Assisi*, vol. 1, *Saint*, 129 (emphasis in original).

[13] Francis of Assisi, *A Letter to the Entire Order (1225–1226)*, in *Francis of Assisi*, vol. 1, *Saint*, 118.

> And I act in this way because, in this world, I see nothing corporally of the most high Son of God except His most holy Body and Blood which they receive and they alone administer to others.[14]

When the Most High Son of God comes *from his royal throne* upon our altars and into our churches, he should receive a fitting welcome. Saint Francis repeatedly admonished his friars to see to it that churches and all appointments, especially the sacred linens, be clean and fitting. He writes to the custodians:

> With all that is in me and more I beg you that, when it is fitting and you judge it expedient, you humbly beg the clergy to revere above all else the most holy Body and Blood of our Lord Jesus Christ and His holy names and the written words that sanctify His Body. They should hold as precious the chalices, corporals, appointments of the altar, and everything that pertains to the sacrifice. If the most holy Body of the Lord is very poorly reserved in any place, let It be placed and locked up in a precious place according to the command of the Church. Let it be carried about with great reverence and administered to others with discernment. Let the names and written words of the Lord, whenever they are found in dirty places, be also gathered up and kept in a becoming place.[15]

[14] Francis of Assisi, *The Testament*, in *Francis of Assisi*, vol. 1, *Saint*, 125. See also *Later Admonition and Exhortation to the Brothers and Sisters of Penance (Second Version of the Letter to the Faithful) (1220?)*, in ibid., 47–48 (emphasis in original).

[15] Francis of Assisi, *The First Letter to the Custodians (1220)*, in *Francis of Asssi*, vol. 1, *Saint*, 56–57. We find many instances of similar exhortations in the writings of Saint Francis. Cf. *The Testament*, in ibid., 125; *Letter to the Entire Order (1225–1226)*, in ibid., 117ff; *Exhortations to the Clergy (Letter to the Clergy) (Later Edition 1220)*, in ibid., 54ff. Saint Francis and his early followers even carried brooms, so as to be able to clean churches they found in a dirty state. Cf. *The Assisi Compilation*, no. 60, in *Francis of Assisi*, vol. 2, *Founder*, 162–63. Cf. also *The Assisi Compilation*, no. 108, in ibid., 214ff., especially the interesting note on page 215: "He also wanted to send other brothers throughout every region with good and beautiful wafer irons for making hosts."

In *The Legend and Writings of Saint Clare of Assisi* (New York: Franciscan Institute, 1953), Thomas of Celano recounts that Saint Clare, like her spiritual father Saint Francis, had a deep devotion to the Blessed Sacrament and that "during the severe illness which confined her to bed, she had herself raised up and supported by props, and sitting thus she would spin the finest linens. From these she made more than fifty sets of corporals and enclosed them in silken or purple cases, and then had them sent to the different churches of the plains and mountains of Assisi" (38). It is touching to think that Saint Clare, in this way, helped to alleviate the situation of the dirty and unbecoming altar linens that Saint Francis lamented repeatedly.

It is reverent love for Christ truly present in the Holy Eucharist that makes Saint Francis so anxious that he receive a fitting welcome. Just as the churches must be fitting to receive the Great King, so each person must make his soul a fitting dwelling place for the Lord. Saint Francis says, "I beg all my brothers ... to serve, love, honor and adore the Lord God with a clean heart and a pure mind.... Let us always make a home and a dwelling place there for Him Who is the Lord God Almighty, Father, Son and Holy Spirit."[16] Saint Francis did, indeed, make a spacious home in his soul for the Lord whom he received and adored in the Blessed Sacrament, and he was thus transformed into the Christ he received.

Three years before his death, Saint Francis expressed the desire, as he explained it, "to enact the memory of that babe *who was born in Bethlehem*: to see as much as is possible with my own bodily eyes the discomfort of his infant needs, how he *lay in a manger*, and how, with an ox and an ass standing by, he rested on hay."[17] When the manger had been fashioned and the Holy Mass was offered there on Christmas Night, Thomas of Celano recounts that a man had a wondrous vision of a child lying lifeless in the manger and of Saint Francis awakening it. Thomas of Celano then remarks: "Nor is this vision unfitting, since in the hearts of many the child Jesus had been *given over to oblivion*. Now he is awakened and impressed on their loving memory by His own grace through His holy servant Francis."[18] In representing the reality of the God-Man by the building of the crèche in Greccio, Saint Francis sought to awaken the divine life in the faithful—he sought to deify them.

In addition to the mystery of the Incarnation, Saint Francis was devoted especially to the Passion of Christ. The *Legend of the Three Companions* remarks that, from the time Christ Crucified spoke to him, "his heart was wounded and it melted when remembering the Lord's passion. While he lived, he always carried the wounds of the Lord Jesus in his heart."[19] At the end of his life, then, he was so transformed into Christ that he was given the gift of the stigmata. In

[16] Francis of Assisi, *The Earlier Rule*, chap. 22, in *Francis of Assisi*, vol. 1, *Saint*, 80.

[17] Thomas of Celano, *Life of Saint Francis*, bk. 1, in *Francis of Assisi*, vol. 1, *Saint*, 255 (emphasis in original).

[18] Ibid., 256 (emphasis in original).

[19] *Legend of the Three Companions*, chap. 5, in *Francis of Assisi*, vol. 2, *Founder*, 76.

the words of Saint Bonaventure, our Lord himself gave "the irrefutable testimony of truth that *the seal of the likeness* of the living God, that is, of *Christ crucified*, was imprinted on his body, not by natural forces or human skill, but by the wondrous power *of the Spirit of the living God.*"[20]

Saint Francis recognized everywhere God's work, not only in the sacraments, in the mysteries of the life of Christ, and in the Church, but also in all creation. He loved and extolled animals and all created things, not for their own sakes, but because he recognized in them the work of God. Thomas of Celano remarks, "Who could ever express the deep affection he bore for all things *that belong to God*? *Or who would be able to tell* of the sweet tenderness he enjoyed while contemplating in creatures the wisdom, power, and goodness of the Creator?"[21]

When the physician named Good John from Arezzo came to visit Saint Francis in his final illness, the saint entreated him to tell him his true condition, encouraging the doctor with these words: "Tell me the truth. How does it look to you? Do not be afraid, for, by the grace of God, I am not a coward who fears death. With the Lord's help, by His mercy and grace, I am so united and joined with my Lord that I am equally as happy to die as I am to live."[22] He was so transformed into Christ that it was no longer Saint Francis who lived, but Christ who lived in him: "He was always with Jesus: Jesus in his heart, Jesus in his mouth, Jesus in his ears, Jesus in his eyes, Jesus in his hands, he bore Jesus always in his whole body."[23]

One can hardly speak about Saint Francis without thinking immediately of another saint of Assisi: Saint Clare, who referred to herself as the "little plant of the most Blessed Father Francis".[24] Saint Clare, too, speaks of our becoming like unto God, but does so in a typically

[20] Bonaventure, *Major Legend of Saint Francis*, prologue, in *Francis of Assisi*, vol. 2, *Founder*, 527–28 (emphasis in original).

[21] Thomas of Celano, *Life of Saint Francis*, bk. 1, chap. 29, in *Francis of Assisi*, vol. 1, *Saint*, 250 (emphasis in original). See also Julian of Speyer, *The Life of Saint Francis*, in ibid., 399: "The mind of Blessed Francis was filled with such great sweetness of divine love that, because he saw the marvelous work of the Creator in all things, he abounded in the greatest tenderness of pity towards all creatures."

[22] "The Assisi Compilation", in *Francis of Assisi*, vol. 2, *Founder*, 100, 203.

[23] Thomas of Celano, *Life of Saint Francis*, bk. 2, chap. 9, in *Francis of Assisi*, vol. 1, *Saint*, 283.

[24] Clare of Assisi, *The Rule and Life of the Poor Sisters of the Strict Enclosure*, chap. 1, no. 3, in Celano, *Legend and Writings of Saint Clare of Assisi*, 66.

feminine way, and we wish to say at least a few brief words about her. Consecrated to Christ, the Poor Ladies of San Damiano were not only adopted daughters of God the Father, but also spouses of Christ. Saint Clare reminded Saint Agnes of Prague that "you are ... held fast in the embrace of Him whose power is stronger, whose nobility is more exalted, whose countenance is more engaging, whose love is sweeter and whose graciousness is more elegant than that of any other."[25] In a subsequent letter to Saint Agnes, Saint Clare encourages her to allow herself to be wholly transformed into the image of God, writing:

> Stand your mind before the mirror of eternity, and set your soul down in the brightness of glory. Place your heart within this image of the divine substance, and through this contemplation transform yourself completely into the image of Divinity itself so that you yourself will experience what [h]is friends feel in tasting the hidden sweetness which God has reserved from the beginning for those who love Him.[26]

The Blessed Virgin Mary carried Christ corporally in her womb, and Saint Clare explains to her Poor Clare daughter that she, too, can carry Christ in her body by following the Blessed Virgin Mary's example of humility and poverty. Writing again to Saint Agnes, she declares, "Yes, you can bear within yourself Him who indeed bears all that is, possessing Him more assuredly than you could possess all the other transitory possessions of this world."[27]

Saint Bonaventure

Saint Bonaventure, who shares with Saint Anthony of Padua the distinction of being a Franciscan Doctor of the Church, writes explicitly about deification, especially in his theological exposition on grace. Once humanity had been deprived of grace through its fall, only

[25] Clare of Assisi, First Letter, in *Dance for Exultation: Letters of St. Clare to St. Agnes of Prague*, trans. Mother Mary Francis, P.C.C. (Roswell, N.Mex.: Poor Clare Monastery of Our Lady of Guadalupe, 1997), 1–2.

[26] Ibid., Third Letter, 9.

[27] Ibid., 10.

the Incarnation of the second Person of the Trinity would make it possible for man to share in the life of God. This grace is dispensed through the sacraments and allows man to share in the charity that characterizes the life of the Blessed Trinity. Grace, therefore, is the principle of our sanctification and of our deification.

Saint Bonaventure explains that original sin, which entered the world through the Fall of our first parents and is transmitted to all humanity, deprived man of natural justice and imparts to him "a fourfold penalty: weakness, ignorance, malice, and concupiscence".[28] In addition, fallen humanity suffers physical afflictions such as fatigue and illness, is subject to the penalty of death, and is shut out from the beatitude of heaven. Actual sin has its origin in each person's free will. Following Saint Augustine, Saint Bonaventure holds that every actual sin is in some way an imitation of the first sin.[29]

The Incarnation of the Word is the means used by God to restore fallen mankind to his friendship. God could have saved the human race in some other manner, but Saint Bonaventure shows that the Incarnation of the second Person of the Most Blessed Trinity was the most fitting and appropriate way. He summarizes some of his reasons by pointing to the incarnate Son's role in making us like unto God, conforming us to him and making us God's adopted children:

> No one is more suitable to lead humanity back to a knowledge of God than the Word, by whom the Father expresses himself, a Word that has the potential to be united to the flesh, as a [human] word has to its utterance. No one is more suitable to lead humankind back to a divine conformity than the one who is the image of the Father. No one can more fittingly restore human beings to their status as God's adopted children than the one who is God's son by nature. Hence no one is more suitable to become Son of Man than the Son of God himself.[30]

By his Passion, death, and Resurrection, Christ Jesus destroyed sin, restored mankind to grace, and merited for his Church all the graces that she dispenses by means of the sacraments, in order to allow the

[28] Bonaventure, *Breviloquium*, pt. 3, chap. 5, no. 2, in *Works of St. Bonaventure*, vol. 9, ed. Dominic V. Monti, O.F.M. (New York: Franciscan Institute, 2005), 109.

[29] Cf. ibid., pt. 3, chap. 8, no. 6, p. 121.

[30] Ibid., pt. 4, chap. 2, no. 6, p. 138.

Blessed Trinity to dwell in souls. The entire mission of the sending of the second Person of the Blessed Trinity *ad extra* in the Incarnation, as Father Peter Damin M. Fehlner notes, has as its end "the inhabitation of the divine persons in the souls of the just, as in a temple, in such a wise that the just is said to possess God and to be possessed by God, i.e. by the divine persons dwelling in him".[31]

The incarnate Word, who is wholly God and wholly man, has the fullness of spiritual gifts. Since God would restore mankind to himself through grace, "it necessarily follows that in our restorative principle, Christ the Lord, there was the fullness of every grace."[32] Christ possesses the grace of a particular Person, the grace of headship, and the grace of union. The grace of the particular Person made him immune from all sin; the grace of union made him worthy of the adoration due to God.[33] By "the grace of headship ... the Incarnate Word forms the Church, his body ... and sanctifies her members, i.e. makes them capable of a divine life in all its ramifications."[34] Like unto the members of the Church in his human nature, Christ is able to form and perfect the Church through the grace of headship.

Christ's restoration of man to God "embraced those *in heaven, on earth, and under the earth.* Through Christ, those in the nether world were released, those on earth restored, and those in heaven replenished. The first deed was accomplished through pardon, the second by grace, and the third by glory."[35] Grace is the principle of our deification, "for truly, together with grace and in it, we receive the Holy Spirit", and, at the same time

> grace is a gift by which the soul is perfected and becomes the bride of Christ, the daughter of the eternal Father, and the temple of the Holy

[31] Peter D. Fehlner, O.F.M. Conv., *The Role of Charity in the Ecclesiology of St. Bonaventure, Selecta Seraphica* 2 (Rome: Editrice "Miscellanea Francescana", 1965), 48. See also p. 48: "Every other mission is ordered in various ways to the inhabitation of the divine persons in the just, so that the just might enjoy God and be present to God as God enjoys and is present to himself."

[32] Bonaventure, *Breviloquium*, pt. 4, chap. 5, no. 2, p. 147.

[33] Cf. ibid.: "By virtue of the grace given to his own person, he was immune from all sin—both in act and in possibility—because he neither sinned nor was capable of sinning. By virtue of the grace of union, he was worthy not only of the bliss of glory, but the adoration of *latria*, which is that worship of reverence due to God alone."

[34] Fehlner, *Role of Charity*, 58.

[35] Bonaventure, *Breviloquium*, pt. 4, chap. 10, no. 3, p. 165 (emphasis in original).

> Spirit. This could in no way happen except by the ennobling condescension and condescending nobility of the eternal Majesty through the gift of his own grace. Finally, grace is a gift that purifies, illumines, and perfects the soul; that vivifies, reforms, and strengthens it; that elevates it, likens it, and joins it to God, and thereby makes it acceptable to God. This is a gift of such a kind that it is rightly and properly called "the grace that makes pleasing" [*gratia gratum faciens*].[36]

Saint Bonaventure explains that grace "flows from God generously and transforms human beings into God's own likeness".[37] Grace, then, is the principle that makes man godlike: it is the "influence that renders the soul dei-form".[38] It "comes from God, conforms us to God, and leads us to God as our end",[39] so much so that "whoever possesses it possesses God's own self."[40]

The one who possesses God through grace is, at the same time, also possessed by him. The Seraphic Doctor explains the effect of being so possessed by God—namely, that one becomes a child of God:

> And no one is loved in this way without being adopted as a child entitled to an eternal inheritance. Therefore, the "grace which makes pleasing" makes the soul the temple of God, the bride of Christ, and the daughter of the Eternal Father. And since this cannot occur except through a supremely gracious condescension of the part of God, it could not be caused by some naturally implanted habit, but only by a free gift divinely infused.[41]

The principle of our deification is normally dispensed by means of the sacraments: "God has decreed that we are to draw the grace of our healing from Christ, the supreme Physician in and through these sensible signs, 'although God has not restricted his power to the

[36] Ibid., pt. 5, chap. 1, no. 2, pp. 169–70.

[37] Ibid., pt. 4, chap. 5, no. 3, p. 147.

[38] Ibid., pt. 5, chap. 1, no. 3, p. 171.

[39] Ibid.

[40] Ibid., 172. Cf. pt. 5, chap. 1, no. 6, p. 173: Grace is "not only ... given freely by God, it also conforms to God and leads to God as an end, so that the work that came from God might return to God".

[41] Ibid., pt. 5, chap. 1, no. 5, p. 172. Cf. pt. 1, chap. 5, no. 2, p. 43: "'To indwell' indicates a spiritual effect and the acceptance of it; such is the effect of grace making us pleasing to God, which is God-conformed, leads to God, and makes God possess us and be possessed by us, and thus, 'to dwell' within us."

sacraments.' "[42] Christ continues his mission in an invisible manner in the sacraments, while he continues his mission in a visible manner through the apostolic hierarchy. Father Peter Damien M. Fehlner explains that "the jurisdiction of the apostolic hierarchy serves as the visible guarantee of the proper form of communicating the divine life sacramentally, by explaining authoritatively the doctrine of Christ, and regulating properly the life of the faithful and the administration of the sacraments by which the mystical body of Christ is formed and perfected."[43] The bishops and priests, and especially the Roman Pontiff, "make the head of the Church visibly present with his body, the bridegroom with the bride, in this way contributing to the continuance of the mission of the second person in a visible manner".[44]

Saint Bonaventure explains that the sacrament of the Eucharist is the most powerful means of increasing in us the divine life that was first granted in baptism:

> This sacrament contains Christ's true body and immaculate flesh in such a way that it penetrates our very being, unites us to one another, and transforms us into him. It does so by virtue of that burning love through which Christ gave himself to us, offered himself up for us, and now gives himself back to us, so that he might remain with us until the end of the world.[45]

Although grace is essential for man's restoration to God, it is not poured into the soul of the adult human person without his free consent.[46] Christ will transform man into himself through the sacraments, especially the sacrament of the Holy Eucharist, according to his faith.

> Therefore, if any are to approach this sacrament worthily, they must feed on Christ spiritually by chewing it by means of the recognition of faith and receiving it with the devotion of love. In this way they will not be transforming Christ into themselves, but instead will be taken

[42] Ibid., pt. 6, chap. 1, no. 5, pp. 213–14.

[43] Fehlner, *Role of Charity*, 64.

[44] Ibid.

[45] Bonaventure, *Breviloquium*, pt. 6, chap. 9, no. 3, p. 241.

[46] "God grants this grace to free will in a such a way that grace does not force it, but leaves the will free to consent" (ibid., pt. 5, chap. 3, no. 4, p. 180). Cf. *CCC* 2002.

> up into the mystical body of Christ. Clearly, then, those who receive it with lukewarm, irreverent and unthinking hearts *eat and drink judgment against themselves*, because they insult so great a sacrament.[47]
>
> This is why it has been prescribed that this sacrament be celebrated with particular solemnity in regard to the place, the time, the words and prayers, and even the vestments used in the celebration of Masses. In this way both the celebrating priests and the communicants might realize the gift of grace through which they are cleansed, enlightened, perfected, restored, vivified, and most ardently born[e] up into Christ himself through a most burning love.[48]

In his biography of Saint Francis, Saint Bonaventure notes that the saint "received Communion frequently and so devoutly that he made others devout".[49] Received with faith and deep reverence, the grace of the sacrament was most effective in deifying Saint Francis.

The Seraphic Doctor, himself so named for his ardent charity, noted that he was hardly competent to describe "the burning charity with which Francis, *the friend of the Bridegroom* was aflame."[50] The divine indwelling reveals itself in a burning charity which unites individuals to the source of all grace and also to one another. Saint Bonaventure explains that "all who are bound to him in faith and who, through an inpouring of grace, become *members of Christ* and *temples of the Holy Spirit*, and thus *children of God* the Father [are] joined to one another by the unbreakable bond of love."[51] Becoming like unto Christ always includes being bound more closely also to the members of the Mystical Body. As Christ "loved his own" and "loved them to the end" (Jn 13:1), so the individual transformed into him will share in his charity. Those who abide in Christ and, through him, in the Father abide also in his love and share in his love for all (cf. Jn 15:9).

Charity is the gift of the Holy Spirit to those who dwell in Christ. Father Peter Damien M. Fehlner observes that, just "as the unity of the Father and the Son is consummated in the procession of the Holy Spirit, so that unity of the adopted sons of God with the Father is

[47] Ibid., pt. 6, chap. 9, no. 6, p. 244 (emphasis in original).

[48] Ibid., pt. 6, chap. 9, no. 7, pp. 244–45.

[49] Bonaventure, *Major Legend of Saint Francis*, chap. 9, in *Francis of Assisi*, vol. 2, *Founder*, 598.

[50] Ibid., 596 (emphasis in original).

[51] Bonaventure, *Breviloquium*, pt. 4, chap. 5, no. 6, p. 149 (emphasis in original).

consummated in the mission of the Holy Spirit, a mission of charity."[52] The charity that is the gift of the Holy Spirit is a participation in the very life of God himself.[53]

Charity makes us most like unto God, for "God is love" (1 Jn 4:8). "That this love [of the Spirit] is deifying," says Saint Bonaventure, "is symbolized for us in the Virgin bearing God."[54] The Incarnation came about through and in the most Blessed Virgin Mary, who "believed, was willing, and consented", and "that is why she is called the Mother of God and the sweetest Virgin Mary."[55] Not only is the Blessed Virgin Mary the model of the deifying power of grace, but she is also the mediatrix of all these graces. Saint Bonaventure notes that the passage from the prophet Isaiah—"Can a woman forget her infant so as not to have pity on the son of her womb?"—is said of Christ, but that it can also "be understood to mean that the whole Christian people is begotten from the womb of the glorious Virgin".[56]

The Blessed Virgin Mary's union with God is the most intimate possible. Father Peter Damien M. Fehlner remarks that "so intimate is this union [with God] in the case of the Blessed Virgin that she is set above all other creatures in her relations with God, [and] is made worthy to be the Mother of God in a singular and miraculous fashion."[57] Her union with God is essentially a union of charity, and since she shares so profoundly in the Good that is diffusive of itself, "her sanctity, her virginity is unique, because it is also fecund."[58]

[52] Fehlner, *Role of Charity*, 92. Cf. 94: "What is begun by the Son through filial adoption is consummated and perfected by the Holy Spirit."

[53] Cf. ibid., 124: "The presence of the Holy Spirit in the soul as the uncreated gift of charity supposes in the soul a life whose exercise through acts of love (*dilectio*) involves a direct and immediate relation to or union with the life of charity as that is experienced by God himself. Because of this God is said to dwell in the just and the just in God—'Qui manet in caritate manet in Deo et Deus in eo.' So central is the uncreated gift of charity to the supernatural order that no one can be considered just before God unless he have those gifts of grace by which God does actually dwell in that person as in his temple."

[54] Bonaventure, *Collations on the Seven Gifts of the Holy Spirit*, trans. Zachary Hayes, O.F.M., conference 6, no. 11, *Works of St. Bonaventure*, vol. 14 (St. Bonaventure, N.Y.: Franciscan Institute Publications, 2008), 130.

[55] Bonaventure, *Breviloquium*, pt. 6, chap. 3, no. 1, p. 139.

[56] Bonaventure, *Collations on the Seven Gifts*, conference 6, no. 20, p. 136.

[57] Fehlner, *Role of Charity*, 78.

[58] Ibid., 79.

The fecundity of the Blessed Virgin Mary not only includes her conceiving the Son of God, but it is a perpetual fecundity and maternity that extends to all the members of the Body of Christ in her role as mediatrix of all graces. It is most fitting, therefore, that Saint Francis both began and concluded his life consecrated to God at our Lady's feet in her chapel of Our Lady of the Angels.

It is through the free gift of grace, therefore, granted to man by means of the redemptive Incarnation, that Saint Bonaventure explains how we are made to be sharers in God's life and in the charity that characterizes the inner life of the Blessed Trinity. The Blessed Virgin Mary is both model and mediatrix for our transformation into Christ.

Conclusion

The foregoing study of the notion of deification in Franciscan spirituality provides, perforce, solely an indication of the first development of this spirituality. It seemed important to devote a significant portion of this chapter to Saint Francis, whose living in conformity with Christ Crucified is the basis of all Franciscan spirituality. Saint Bonaventure is one of the earliest Franciscan theologians, but other important figures that must at least be mentioned include Blessed John Duns Scotus and Saint Maximilian Mary Kolbe, both of whom further clarify the key role of the Blessed Virgin Mary in our deification. Blessed John Duns Scotus, through his explanation of the Immaculate Conception of the Blessed Virgin Mary, shows that God the Father has willed to unite us to himself through the one mediator Jesus Christ by the mediation of Mary. As he did in the Incarnation, so God the Father continues always the work of our deification through the mediation of the Blessed Virgin Mary. It is on the basis of the importance of the role of the Blessed Virgin Mary that Saint Maximilian Kolbe develops his theology of total consecration to Mary Immaculate. The Franciscan spirituality of deification, then, both in the life of Saint Francis, who "embraced the mother of the Lord Jesus with an inexpressible love",[59] and in subsequent theological reflections, includes a strong Marian element.

[59] Bonaventure, *Major Legend of Saint Francis*, chap. 9, in *Francis of Assisi*, vol. 2, *Founder*, 598.

The life of Saint Francis of Assisi, "another Christ" given to the world, is a font from which has sprung a rich theological tradition. Saint Bonaventure gives theological expression to the reality of our being born to divine life as members of Christ's Mystical Body through grace freely received, in order to participate in the very charity of the triune God. Blessed John Duns Scotus and Saint Maximilian Kolbe, whose contributions have merely been mentioned in the present chapter, contribute to the Franciscan spirituality of deification by making explicit the strong Marian element present in the life of Saint Francis. Through the maternal intercession of the Blessed Virgin Mary, man is restored to the grace that makes him a child of God the Father, conforms him to the Crucified One, and grants him a share in the charity that is the gift of the Holy Spirit.

Readings for Further Study

Bonaventure. "The Major Legend of Saint Francis". In *Francis of Assisi: Early Documents*. Vol. 2, *The Founder*, edited by Regis J. Armstrong, O.F.M. Cap., J. A. Wayne Hellmann, O.F.M., Conv., and William J. Short, O.F.M., 525–683. New York: New City Press, 2000.

Fehlner, Peter D. *The Role of Charity in the Ecclesiology of St. Bonaventure. Selecta Seraphica* 2. Rome: Editrice "Miscellanea Francescana", 1965.

Francis of Assisi. *Francis of Assisi: Early Documents*. Edited by Regis J. Armstrong, O.F.M. Cap., J. A. Wayne Hellmann, O.F.M., Conv., and William J. Short, O.F.M. Vol. 1, *The Saint*. New York: New City Press, 1999.

Chapter Seven

DEIFICATION AT TRENT AND IN THE COUNTER-REFORMATION

Chris Burgwald

Introduction

The doctrine of justification was the tinder that sparked the Reformation. As Father Louis Bouyer put it, justification—specifically the *sola fide* (by faith alone) formulation coined by Martin Luther—was the material principle of the Reformation, the heart of the "matter" between the Magisterium and the Reformers.[1] And while other doctrinal issues arose as successive generations of Reformers increasingly split from the Catholic Church, justification remained among the central issues in contention. Even today, while ecumenical dialogue has seemingly resolved a number of differences on the issue, at least between Catholics and Lutherans,[2] this doctrine remains a central point of contention between Protestantism tout court and Catholicism.

Given the central role that this doctrine played as the Reformation unfolded, it is no surprise that at the ecumenical Council of Trent—in session intermittently from 1545 until 1563—the Catholic Church addressed her teaching on justification as she took up both moral and

[1] Bouyer described *sola Scriptura* as the formal principle of the Reformation. Cf. Louis Bouyer, *The Spirit and Forms of Protestantism* (Westminster, Md.: Newman Press, 1956), 14.

[2] The Joint Declaration on the Doctrine of Justification—signed in 1999 by authorized representatives of Pope Saint John Paul II and of the Lutheran World Federation—found that the differences between Lutheran and Catholic formulations of the doctrine of justification are not "church-dividing". The upshot of this is that the Catholic Church sees the Lutheran doctrine of justification—at least as articulated in the Joint Declaration—as compatible with Catholic teaching. (It should be noted that both Lutheran and Catholic theologians have challenged the Joint Declaration's claim that the church-dividing issues have been resolved; see Christopher J. Malloy, *Engrafted into Christ: A Critique of the Joint Declaration* [New York: Peter Lang Publishing, 2005] as one Catholic example.)

legal reforms within the Church as well as the doctrinal challenges posed by Luther and the other Reformers. Hence, one of the early sessions of the council—the sixth, in January of 1547—addressed the doctrine of justification in a formal decree and associated canons.

The typical theological examination of the Reformation-era disputes over justification tends to focus on the (broadly Protestant) notion of forensic justification as opposed to what some scholars describe as the "transformationist" account of justification articulated by the Catholic Church. In essence, the forensic account of justification claims that the justified sinner is *declared* just by God because of the grace and merits of Jesus Christ, while the Catholic "transformationist" account states that the justified sinner is actually *made* just (that is, transformed) by the grace and merits of Jesus Christ. It is certainly true that neither the Tridentine decree nor its canons speak of justification in the context of deification or divinization, and following Trent, neither did the theologians of the Counter-Reformation era. Nonetheless, we will see that—whatever the particular terms employed—the *concept* of justification as divinization or deification is most certainly present within the Tridentine formulations.

Martin Luther's Theology of Justification

This essay focuses on Trent's decree. But in order to understand Trent more fully, it is essential to understand its historical and theological context—that is, as a response to the Protestant position(s). We begin, then, by looking at Luther's account of justification. Whatever one's evaluation of the conclusions drawn by contemporary ecumenical dialogue, the fact remains that scholars today have found lesser-known details of Luther's understanding of justification containing significant parallels with Catholic teaching, even including language more typically associated with deification and divinization.

Luther, unlike John Calvin and other Reformers, did not offer a systematic account of justification as he understood it. And even among Lutherans, it isn't so much Luther himself as it is the Lutheran confessional documents as found in the Book of Concord that present

[3] There is a difference, in other words, between *Luther's* account of justification and the *Lutheran* account of justification, as will be seen shortly.

the Lutheran understanding of justification.[3] However, Luther's account was the genesis of the broadly Protestant account of justification, whatever the differences between his writings and later accounts. Regardless of the variations, all Protestants hold to justification *sola fide*, and Luther was the Reformer who first presented an account of justification *sola fide*.

Even more relevant is that in his articulation of justification, Luther employed not only forensic terminology, but also a conception of justification as union with Christ and—even more surprisingly—as deification. This is not to say that Luther's understanding and usage of the term is identical to that found within the Catholic tradition, but his use of the term and concept of deification is obviously relevant to both this chapter and the entire volume, and it serves as an important backdrop for an evaluation of deification as expressed in Trent's teaching on justification.

The contemporary "discovery" of Luther's use of deification is due largely, but not exclusively, to the Finnish school of Luther research, owing its name to its founder, the Finnish Lutheran theologian Tuomo Mannermaa and his former students. In examining Luther's writings in the context of the philosophy and theology of his era, Mannermaa and his colleagues found that, whatever the *Lutheran* account of justification might be, *Luther's* account was not exclusively forensic in nature, but also included transformationist aspects. According to the Finnish school, Luther conceived of justification as a real participation in Christ, in which God's righteousness, which we receive (by faith) at justification, is a real and true participation in the life of God. Consider, for example, the following excerpt from Luther's 1514 Christmas sermon: "Just as the word of God became flesh, so it is certainly also necessary that the flesh may become word. In other words: God becomes man so that man may become God."[4]

Similar statements can be found throughout Luther's writings, both before and after his public break with the Church in 1520. Theologian Bruce Marshall has shown how Luther used both the vocabulary

[4] As cited in Tuomo Mannermaa, "Why Is Luther So Fascinating?" in *Union with Christ: The New Finnish Interpretation of Luther*, ed. Carl E. Braaten and Robert W. Jenson (Grand Rapids, Mich.: Eerdmans, 1998), 11. The final statement in this citation—"God becomes man so that man may become God"—echoes almost verbatim statements made by Saints Irenaeus, Athanasius, and Thomas Aquinas, which are in turn quoted in the *Catechism of the Catholic Church* in no. 460, part of the *Catechism*'s section on the reasons for the Incarnation.

and conceptual framework of deification in his articulation of the doctrine of justification.[5] For example, Marshall cites a 1526 sermon of Luther's on the third chapter of Saint Matthew's Gospel, in which Luther wrote that God "pours out Christ his dear Son upon us and pours himself into us and draws us into himself, so that he is entirely humanized and we are entirely divinized ... and all with one another are one reality—God, Christ, and you."[6]

Other passages could be presented, but this suffices to give a sense of Luther's own theology of justification—particularly as he employs the concept of deification. This is not to argue that Luther's position was actually Catholic or even compatible with Catholic teaching; while some theologians do make that argument, the purpose here is merely to show that in addition to the forensic dimensions of Luther's theology of justification, we also find a transformationist dimension, with explicit reference to divinization and deification.

The Council of Trent's Decree on Justification

Considering the place of the doctrine of justification in the origins of the Reformation, Trent's decree is relatively brief, made up of less than forty-five hundred words.[7] The decree consists of an introduction and sixteen chapters—most of which are a single paragraph in length—each devoted to a particular point concerning the doctrine of justification. It concludes with thirty-three canons that present a distillation of the teachings of the preceding chapters in the form of an anathema, a condemnation of an erroneous teaching.[8]

[5] Bruce Marshall, "Justification as Declaration and Deification", *International Journal of Systematic Theology* 4, no. 1 (March 2002): 3–26. On a biographical note, Marshall himself entered into full communion with the Catholic Church a few years after this article was published.

[6] Cited in ibid., 7.

[7] That is, in the official Latin text of the decree. As with texts from other ecumenical councils, there are (thus far) no official English translations released by the Holy See, but unofficial translations of these texts—including Trent's decree on justification—can be found in print and online in abundance. Unless otherwise indicated, the text and English translation used in this essay comes from Heinrich Denzinger, *Compendium of Creeds, Definitions, and Declarations on Matters of Faith and Morals*, ed. Peter Hünermann et al., 43rd ed. (San Francisco: Ignatius Press, 2012). References to this text will be in the form of "DH", where the number refers to the paragraph, not the page.

[8] It is worth noting that care must be taken in attempting to formulate what the Church teaches on the basis of an anathema, in that an anathema merely asserts what is *not* Catholic doctrine.

The decree focuses on points of Catholic teaching concerning justification that were being called into question or even denied by the Reformers, either in fact or at least in appearance.[9] In addition, it affirmed certain truths which, generally speaking, were and are held in common by both Catholics and Protestants.

In summary, the decree affirms the following points:

- Man is unable to justify himself, to free himself from the yoke of sin (chapter 1).
- God sent his Son to redeem and justify us and to adopt us as his sons and daughters (chapter 2).
- While Jesus died for all men, that does not mean that all will necessarily be saved: his grace and redemption must be received (chapter 3).
- Justification is the transition from a state of sin (a child of the first Adam) to a state of grace (through the power of the Second Adam, Jesus Christ), which requires sanctifying grace (chapter 4).
- Man must be disposed by God to be justified, a divine action with which we cooperate (chapter 5).
- That preparatory disposition entails an acknowledgement and rejection of sin and a turn toward God and a desire to live a new life in Christ (chapter 6).
- Justification itself consists of the forgiveness of sins and renewal of the inner man, a point to which we will return (chapter 7).
- Faith is the first stage and foundation of justification, and justification is a free gift from God, completely unmerited by us (chapter 8).
- Forgiveness of sins does not occur simply because of our certainty that we are forgiven, because we cannot know with

[9] The infallible nature of Church teaching does not include its evaluation regarding what specific views were held by what specific individuals. For example, the decree on justification refers to heretical views on this doctrine. However, it may be that no specific individual (e.g., Luther, Calvin, and so forth) actually held the heretical views being condemned. To be clear, I am not asserting that this is in fact the case in this instance; it certainly seems that at least a number of the views condemned by Trent were held by the Reformers. I am simply noting that we cannot presume that specific individuals held views condemned by the Church.

the certainty of faith that we have received the justifying grace of God (chapter 9).

- Through our works of love, we can grow in justification (chapter 10).
- Living God's commandments is both necessary and possible (chapter 11).
- We cannot presume that we are among the predestined (chapter 12).
- Hence we must likewise persevere to the end and pray for the gift of final perseverance (chapter 13).
- If we should fall and sin (particularly mortally) after baptism, it is possible for us to be "rejustified" through the sacrament of reconciliation (chapter 14).
- Even though faith is lost only through the sin of apostasy, the grace of justification is lost whenever we commit any mortal sin (chapter 15).
- Finally, insofar as we cooperate with the grace of God and grow in justification, we will receive the crown of righteousness for our good works and merits (chapter 16).

These and the related points addressed in the canons are all aimed at positions held, or apparently held, by the Reformers, although not even the Council Fathers believed that all of the Reformers held all of the errors condemned, or that any one of them held all of these errors. Rather, the decree simply presents—in the words of the introduction—"for all the faithful of Christ the true and sound doctrine on justification", which was taught by Christ, handed down by the apostles, and retained by the Church under the guidance of the Holy Spirit,[10] at the same time condemning errors found at the time among a number of the Reformers.

The decree simultaneously presents a positive exposition of the Catholic doctrine on justification while condemning a number of erroneous views about the doctrine. In both cases, the context is the challenges that have been brought forward by the Reformers. Even the positive exposition, then, is contextualized by the Reformers' doctrines. This means Trent's decree cannot be regarded as the last word on the Catholic understanding of justification, or even

[10] DH 1520.

more, as a comprehensive treatment of the Catholic understanding of justification. It is important to recognize that Trent's definitive teaching comes in a specific historical and theological context—the Reformation and its theologies of justification—which means that points made by Trent and the language in which it does so reflect that context.

More broadly, Trent speaks in the language of Western theology and hence does not use the more Eastern language of divinization, deification, theosis, and so forth. Yet, "underneath" the language, the concepts remain the same. Pope Saint John XXIII, in the address given at the opening of the Second Vatican Council in 1962, expressed this truth succinctly: "What is needed is that this certain and immutable doctrine, to which the faithful owe obedience, be studied afresh and reformulated in contemporary terms. *For this deposit of faith, or truths which are contained in our time-honored teaching is one thing; the manner in which these truths are set forth (with their meaning preserved intact) is something else.*"[11] The deposit of faith, the teachings of Christ handed down by the apostles and their successors (the popes and the bishops in union with them), is one thing; the manner, the way, in which these teachings are presented is another thing. Even though care must be taken to ensure that the "translation" from one theological language to another is accurate and nothing essential is "lost in translation", the same doctrines can nonetheless be expressed in numerous ways, and in fact this variety enhances the richness of doctrine. The possibility of expressing beliefs in various theological languages reflects both the truth and the beauty of that deposit of faith referred to by Good Pope John in his address.

With this in mind, how does the theological language in which Trent spoke refer to the same realities as do terms like "divinization", "deification", and "theosis"? To answer that question, we turn to chapter 7 of the decree, which discusses the nature and causes of justification. Having set forth the teaching on the need for and nature of preparation for justification in the preceding chapters, chapter 7 focuses more precisely on what justification is and how it is caused. The opening sentence of the chapter states that justification "is not

[11] Pope John XXIII, "Gaudete Mater Ecclesia", October 11, 1962. English translation found at http://www.thedivinemercy.org/news/Pope-John-XXIIIs-Opening-Address-of-Vatican-Council-II-5666 accessed January 1, 2016 (emphasis added).

only the remission of sins but the sanctification and renewal of the interior man through the voluntary reception of grace and of the gifts, whereby from unjust man becomes just, and from enemy a friend, that he may be 'an heir in hope of eternal life'."[12] Justification is more than just the forgiveness of sins, contrary to what seemed to be the teaching of Luther and his followers. While justification certainly entails the forgiveness of sins, that is just one of several effects of justification. In addition to forgiveness, Trent affirms that justification entails the sanctification and renewal of the inner man. When we are justified, we are not only forgiven, but also renewed and made holy. There is, in other words, an inner transformation that occurs when we are justified. God not only pronounces us innocent of sin (forgiveness), but he also *makes* us innocent of sin (transformation). Whatever Luther's real or intended teaching on justification, the fact remains that for the vast majority of Lutheran and other Protestant theologians—and hence for the members of their traditions—in the sixteenth century and ever since, the emphasis has been on the declarative aspect of justification: God *declares* us innocent; he announces a verdict of innocence, akin to a court judge. Again, Trent agrees: justification *does* entail the forgiveness of sins. But it is much more than that: because God's word is *effective*, what he declares is what happens. Consider the creation accounts of the Book of Genesis (chapters 1–2). They state repeatedly, "God said"—and what he said *happened*. There is reference to the same truth in the Book of the Prophet Isaiah, where Isaiah proclaims that just as the rain and snow come down from heaven and do not return to heaven but instead water the earth, so too shall God's word go forth from his mouth and shall not return to him empty but shall accomplish his purpose and shall do that for which he sent it (see Is 55:10–11).

Just so with the justification of the sinner: God *declares* the sinner just, and as a result the sinner is *made* just, is *made* holy (sanctified), is *renewed* in the interior, spiritual life. When we are justified, we become just; we become a friend of God and even more, an heir—that is, a child!—of the heavenly Father. Trent employs the Aristotelian-Scholastic language of causality in its analysis of what justification is and how it occurs. Chapter 7 states that the *final cause*

[12] DH 1528.

(the purpose or goal) of justification is the glory of God and of Jesus Christ and eternal life, that the *efficient cause* (the thing that causes justification to happen) is the merciful God who freely washes and sanctifies us, that the *meritorious cause* (the thing that merits the justification of the sinner) is Jesus Christ and in particular his Passion, that the *instrumental cause* (the means by which God justifies us) is baptism, the sacrament of faith, and the single *formal cause* is the justice of God by which he makes us just. It is the final mode of causality that particularly concerns us here.

The decree states,

> Finally, the single formal cause is "the justice of God, not by which he himself is just, but by which he makes us just," namely, the justice that we have as a gift from him and by which we are spiritually renewed. Thus, not only are we considered just, but we are truly called just and we are just, each one receiving within himself his own justice, according to the measure that "the Holy Spirit apportions to each one individually as he wills" and according to each one's personal disposition and cooperation. For although no one can be just unless the merits of the Passion of our Lord Jesus Christ are imparted to him, still this communication takes place in the justification of the sinner, when by the merit of the same most holy Passion, "God's love is poured through the Holy Spirit into the hearts" of those who are being justified and inheres in them. Hence, in the very act of justification, together with the remission of sins, man receives through Jesus Christ, into whom he is inserted, the gifts of faith, hope, and charity, all infused at the same time.[13]

The first sentence quotes Saint Augustine and states that we are justified not by that justice of God's which is his alone, but rather by that justice of God's which he freely gives to us and which spiritually renews us. The justice that justifies us truly is ours—that is, we are truly just, we are really just, as the next sentence in the citation indicates. Again, God does not just pronounce or consider us just, but he gives us that justice by which we actually become just.

The decree reiterates the importance of the meritorious cause: we cannot be justified apart from the merits of the Passion of Jesus Christ.

[13] DH 1529–30.

Nonetheless, those merits are really, actually, and truly imparted, as well as given and communicated: those who are being justified receive those merits into their hearts, and those merits truly inhere or dwell in them. The exposition of the formal cause of justification reaffirms the reality that justification involves a real spiritual transformation of the sinner: the sinner is truly made just, and the justice of God truly dwells in him when he is justified. These teachings found in chapter 7 are reiterated in canons 10 and 11 of the decree, which read as follows,

> Can. 10. If anyone says that men are justified without the justice of Christ, by which he gained merit for us, or that they are formally just by his justice itself, let him be anathema.[14]

Canon 10 states almost verbatim what is expressed in chapter 7: it is false to hold that we are justified by the justice of God that is his alone. Again, the truth is that God gives us his justice, which truly makes us just. Canon 11 reiterates that justification is not *only* the remission of sins, but includes the reception and inhering of grace and charity in the sinner:

> Can. 11. If anyone says that men are justified either by the imputation of Christ's justice alone or by the remission of sins alone, excluding grace and charity that is poured into their hearts by the Holy Spirit and inheres in them, or also that the grace that justifies us is only the favor of God, let him be anathema.[15]

The Decree on Justification is a clear affirmation of the doctrine of justification always held by the Church: when we are justified, we are truly made just, we are really made righteous, we are really made holy, we are actually renewed in spirit. Justification is not merely the juridical forgiveness of our sins, let alone a legal fiction by which God "pretends" that we are just when we are in fact unjust. No: in justification, God's word accomplishes its purpose—we are actually made righteous. "The grace of the Holy Spirit," states the *Catechism of the Catholic Church*, "has the power to justify us, that is, to cleanse us from our sins and to communicate to us 'the righteousness of God

[14] DH 1560.
[15] DH 1561.

through faith in Jesus Christ' (Rom 3:22; cf. 6:3–4) and through Baptism" (*CCC* 1987).

The intimate connection with deification, divinization, or theosis should be clear. Again, the content of a doctrine is one thing; the mode or language in which that content is expressed is another. Although Trent's Decree on Justification does not employ the terminology of divinization, deification, or theosis, the realities expressed by those terms is identical with the realities expressed by Trent's decree. The Eastern terms all refer to the fact that the Christian is made like God: that we are deified or divinized. We are made—in the words of Saint Peter—"partakers of the divine nature" (2 Pet 1:4).

To partake of the divine nature indicates that by virtue of our baptism we come to share in God's being. And to share in his way of being means to share in his attributes, including the attribute of justice. Here we see a close connection between the Western language of justification and the Eastern language of deification and divinization. To receive the justice of God means to share in God's justice, as we've seen. But to say that we share in God's justice entails a broader sharing of being, a partaking of nature—it entails divinization and deification.

There is also a connection between justification and theosis in Trent's description of the nature of justification. In the previous citation from chapter 7 of the decree, Trent speaks of the reception of faith, hope, and charity that occurs in justification, stating that "man receives through Jesus Christ, *into whom he is inserted*, the gifts of faith, hope and charity."[16] In justification, we are inserted into Jesus Christ or—in the words of another translation—grafted into him.[17] In justification, we are joined to Jesus Christ, inserted into him, grafted into him. And what happens when one plant is grafted into another? The new plant shares in the life of that into which it is grafted!

After Trent

By and large, the Counter-Reformation Magisterium and theologians took up the language found in the Tridentine decree, and

[16] DH 1530 (emphasis added).

[17] The Latin word here is *inseritur*.

hence what we have already examined above applies to much of the Counter-Reformation thought on justification as well. There is one text, however, worth mentioning in this context: the *Roman Catechism*, or the *Catechism of the Council of Trent*, published in 1566, three years after the close of the Council of Trent.

Regarding the sacraments, the *Roman Catechism* speaks of justifying grace as the first of the principal effects of the sacraments. Even more relevant to our topic is the *Catechism*'s teaching on the effects of the sacrament of baptism, specifically its teaching on the third effect of baptism, the grace of regeneration. As with the Counter-Reformation theology in general, much of this section echoes Trent's decree, but there is one particularly relevant phrase in this section: by baptism, "our souls are replenished with divine grace, by which we are rendered just and children of God and are made heirs to eternal salvation."[18] By baptism, we are rendered just and heirs to eternal salvation, as Trent also stated. But we are likewise made sons and daughters of God. Interestingly, this reality of being adopted sons and daughters of God by baptism—divine filiation—is not referred to explicitly in Trent's Decree on Justification nor in its decree regarding baptism. Nonetheless, this teaching is found throughout the Western theological tradition, and its inclusion in the *Roman Catechism* is notable, stating that by virtue of our justification—which occurs first at our baptism—we are really and truly made children as God, and, precisely as a child, we partake in the nature of our Father. In fact, this point is reiterated in the section of the *Roman Catechism* that discusses the Our Father:

> Accordingly the pastor should instruct his spiritual children and constantly recall to their minds the surpassing love of God for us, so that they may be fully alive to the fact that having been redeemed in a wonderful manner they are thereby made the sons of god. To them, says St. John, "he gave power to be made the sons of God" ... and "they are born of God." This is why Baptism, the first pledge and token of our redemption, is called the Sacrament of regeneration; for it is by Baptism that we are born children of God.... By reason of this redemption we have received the Holy Ghost and have been

[18] *Catechism of the Council of Trent for Parish Priests*, trans. John A. McHugh, O.P., and Charles J. Callan, O.P. (Rockford, Ill.: Tan Books and Publishers, 1982), 188.

> made worthy of the grace of God. As a consequence of this gift we are the adopted sons of God, as the Apostle Paul wrote to the Romans.... The force and efficacy of this adoption are thus set forth by St. John: "Behold what manner of charity the Father hath bestowed upon us, that we should be called, and should be the sons of God."[19]

We should be called—because we are—sons of God. What love indeed.

Readings for Further Study

Bouyer, Louis. *The Spirit and Forms of Protestantism.* Westminster, Md.: Newman Press, 1956.

Denzinger, Heinrich. "Decree on Justification". In *Compendium of Creeds, Definitions, and Declarations on Matters of Faith and Morals*, 43rd ed., edited by Peter Hünermann et al., 374–88. San Francisco: Ignatius Press, 2012.

Malloy, Christopher J. *Engrafted into Christ: A Critique of the Joint Declaration.* New York: Peter Lang Publishing, 2005.

McGrath, Alister. *Iustitia Dei: A History of the Christian Doctrine of Justification.* 2nd ed. Cambridge: Cambridge University Press, 1998.

O'Callaghan, Father Paul. *Fides Christi: The Justification Debate.* Dublin: Four Courts Press, 1997.

[19] Ibid., 506.

Chapter Eight

DIVINE EXCESS AND HIDDEN GRANDEUR: DIVINIZATION IN THE FRENCH SCHOOL OF SPIRITUALITY

Michon M. Matthiesen

Seventeenth-century France, often called *le grand siècle*, was an era indeed *grand* in terms of political power and economic opulence, as the reign of Louis XIV, the great Sun King, so amply gives witness. It was a century dedicated to perfecting the classical form of drama and poetry and prose, and one in which the *salon* and *academie* became the center of court life and French culture. Yet, even as political and cultural life was moving quickly toward a grandness that spilled over into excess and decadence, it is likewise true that this century was *grand* in terms of religious reform and renewal. No period in French history has been either as rich in spiritual treatises or as abundant in the formation of religious orders and societies. One could say that even in the realm of the spirit, this century tended toward excess.

Such "excess" was certainly the case with two religious movements, Jansenism and Quietism, which both stretched beyond the boundaries of sound Roman Catholic teaching and were declared, at least in part, heterodox. Jansenism, in its desire for rigorous religious *mores* and practice, exaggerated both the depravity of man and the stern justice of God. Few Christians were accounted worthy of salvation; few were deemed pure enough to receive and profit from the Church's healing sacraments. The heterodoxy of Quietism, by contrast, was located in its radical passivity and its doctrine of "pure love". The spiritual teaching of Quietism suggested that the believer need not avail himself of devotional practices, of religious and domestic duties, and of the Church's sacramental economy: all that truly mattered was a will lovingly passive to God.[1]

What we now name the Seventeenth-Century French School of Spirituality avoids such extremes, while remarkably providing a *grand* vision of the potential of ordinary believers to participate in the divine life of Christ in their earthly existence. This chapter explores the teaching of key seventeenth-century figures who, in their prodigious efforts to inaugurate the reforms of Trent, proffered a rich spiritual doctrine—and did so courageously under the eyes of a French national government suspicious of all signs of loyalty to Rome. They announced a teaching of intimate union to the divine life of Jesus, proclaiming that a share in the triune life was not only accessible to but also incumbent upon laity and clergy alike. Our treatment of this School shall be bookended by acknowledging the two saints whose doctrines provide what I understand to be the significant prelude and coda to the French School of Spirituality—namely, Francis de Sales and the Carmelite Thérèse of Lisieux. Three critical leaders and evangelizers of the School in the seventeenth century shall occupy our primary attention: Pierre Cardinal de Bérulle (1575–1629), who may justly be called the father of the School, and whose Christocentric vision of the spiritual life establishes its platform; Jean-Jacques Olier (1608–1657), for whom a share in Christ's life is decidedly sacrificial; and John Eudes (1601–1680), who, more than his predecessors, underscored the call of each Christian life to be a *continuation* of the life of the God-Man. Jesuit Jean-Pierre de Caussade, who wrote his treatise *L'abandonment à la divine providence* in the 1740s, marks the apex of the French School.[2]

Briefly, and in anticipation, I want to identify the distinctive features of the School's vision of the spiritual life and its optimism about a real sharing in the divine life. First and foremost, the French School places before us the awe-inspiring reality of the Incarnation: the Son became man in such a full and complete way that the humanity of Jesus became united inseparably to the Divinity. It is from this

[1] Madame Guyon, a woman born into the wealth of the court of Louis XIV, was (perhaps unfairly) accused and imprisoned at various times in her life for expressing and living a Quietist spirituality.

[2] Hans Urs von Balthasar has written that de Caussade's work is the culmination of the French School—its best, most accurate, balanced, and eloquent expression. See *The Glory of the Lord*, vol. 5 (San Francisco: Ignatius Press, 1991), 48–140.

hypostatic reality, this *state* of the incarnate God, that the spiritual life and deification flows. Second, the divinization of the believer follows from a union to Christ, a union that occurs through participating in Jesus' earthly life, sharing in his dispositions and in his acts of adoration, abnegation, sacrifice, and annihilation of the will—all of which are to be carried out *in* the *love* Jesus exhibited to his Father and to man. It is true that the French School underscores an awareness of human depravity, for such abasement stands as the gateway to participating in the states of Jesus. The third distinctive feature of the French School is its particular emphasis upon baptism and the Eucharist, through which every Christian gains access to sharing in the priesthood of Christ. Finally, we can remark that the French School's path to holiness and divinization appears neither flashy nor eccentric. Rather, it is a hidden, ordinary spiritual path. The "grandness" of the French School has nothing in common with the external display and ostentation of the court life in seventeenth-century France.

Saint Francis de Sales (1567–1622): *Vive Jésus!*

The life of Francis de Sales straddles the sixteenth and seventeenth centuries, and in many ways his thought inaugurates the emergence of the humanistic French School. Francis held out the possibility of perfection in the spiritual life to those who lived in the secular world. He instructed people living in cities with family duties, he advised those who were lawyers at court, and he wrote for soldiers in the army. Francis encourages those who love God to place themselves in God's presence continually during the day—through prayer, through acts of charity, through lifting the heart to God, through quick "ejaculations" of love and praise, and through a simple recognition of one's poverty or nothingness before the divine. Such devout actions not only honor God, but they place the believer in his presence and at his disposal, thereby making ordinary souls receptive to whatever "heavenly dew" might fall upon them.[3] Francis does not promote aiming at the great raptures of contemplative prayer; rather, he urges a preference for experiencing an "*ecstasy of life*", by which he means

[3] See particularly *Francis de Sales, Jane de Chantal: Letters of Spiritual Direction*, trans. Péronne Marie Thibert, selected and introduced by Wendy Wright and Joseph M. Power (New York: Paulist Press, 1988), 100–101.

a life no longer lived by the natural, old self, but a self-sacrificing life devoted to God, a hidden life in Christ. This new life is a "supernatural ecstatic" existence of love; it brings with it newfound vigor.[4]

The devout life, which is the way to union with God, largely focused on the will. Spiritual perfection comprised a practical doctrine of intimacy with Jesus that reaches beyond simple imitation to a union of wills and life. The possibility of deification is largely embedded in the language of the soul or will "going beyond" the limits of its natural life. Francis' profound teaching about this union of wills and about living in the *permissive will* of God establishes a keystone in the French School of Spirituality. As we shall see later, de Caussade's thought on self-abandonment to divine providence clearly depends upon Francis' treatment of the will. In the devout life, the will must *die* to itself, no longer choosing according to its own desires and cares. Through such a self-obliteration,[5] the will "departs" from the "limits" of its natural life, thereby being transformed into "the divine".[6] The believer's will can so participate in the divine will that those "tiny, ordinary things of life" done with love are, as it were, done by God.[7] Francis brings his *Treatise on the Love of God* to a close with passionate words that identify his call to all believers to *live Jesus*, and to live him with immense love.[8] This *vive Jésus* is the surest way to union with him, and therefore to a union with the Father. Such fervent language of loving and living Jesus is a constant echo in the spiritual school of *le grand siècle* and is sounded again most distinctively by that nineteenth-century daughter of the French School, Thérèse of Lisieux.

Pierre Cardinal de Bérulle (1575–1629)

Pierre Cardinal de Bérulle justly can be named *the* theologian of the French School. Like Francis, Bérulle emphasizes the Christocentric

[4] Francis de Sales, *The Love of God, A Treatise*, trans. Vincent Kerns (Westminster, M.D.: Newman Press, 1962), 7.7, 290–91.

[5] To clarify, Francis describes this obliteration with care, comparing it to the star that disappears into the sun's greater light when the sun ascends. The will is not "entirely lost" but, rather, "swallowed up" in the divine will, so that there are no traces of its own intending and choosing. See ibid., 9.13, 389.

[6] Ibid., 9.13, 387–88.

[7] Ibid., 12.9, 539.

[8] Ibid., 12.13, 545.

nature of the spiritual life, but he does so through an adaptation of Denys the Areopagite's metaphysical vision. Bérulle is fascinated by Denys' contemplation of God's ecstatic desire to go outside of himself in creation—and particularly in the Incarnation[9]—in order to call mankind to a share in the divine nature and unity. In Bérulle's *Discourse on the State and Grandeurs of Jesus*, he claims that God's masterwork is the Incarnation, the God-Man, in whom God has completely, ineffably, and "unspeakably" communicated himself. Jesus uniquely possesses the complete divine essence.[10] The order of grace emanates from Jesus' perfection and is thereby a "living portrait" and a "*formal participation*" in the divine coming forth of the Son from the Father. This means that the grace by which believers are transformed into a divine likeness has a "singular rapport" with the incarnate Word—and, as we shall see, with the Eucharist.[11]

Bérulle's *Grandeurs* is an extended meditation on the wonder of the Incarnation, a meditation that often breaks out in praise and exaltation of this great mystery—"O deified humanity, O humanized divinity!... Oh, abundance! Oh, abyss!"[12] It is likewise a work that relishes in employing analogies to consider this hypostatic union, analogies that are suggestive of how Christians might themselves come to participate in Jesus' life. For instance, Bérulle draws a comparison between the Incarnation and a gardener who grafts a new plant from an existing trunk. In the Incarnation, the "divine cultivator" split open human nature with its sinful flesh and "substituted" a "heavenly graft, the divine subsistence, the very person of the Son" for the human subsistence. This plant, therefore, "bears different fruits", fruits that do not belong to it. In fact, "its actions no longer flow from it nor belong to it" but rather are attributed to the nature of the graft. There is, of course, one striking

[9] "You [Jesus] are the Center, the Circle, the Circumference of all the outer emanations of God! You are the masterpiece of God. As he moved outside himself you became the work in which he exhausted his greatness, power and goodness and in which he enclosed himself so as to become part of his handiwork ... thus dignifying and deifying you through his very being" (Pierre de Bérulle, *Discourse on the State and Grandeurs of Jesus* 2.5, trans. Lowell H. Glendon, S.S., in *Bérulle and the French School: Selected Writings*, ed. William Thompson [New York: Paulist Press, 1989], 117). All works by Bérulle, Olier, and Eudes are cited in this Paulist Press edition of selected writings from the French school.

[10] Ibid., 1.6, 111–12.

[11] Ibid., 2.5, 119 (emphasis added).

[12] Ibid., 118.

difference between the gardener's graft and God's grafting in the hypostatic union: it is the graft—not the trunk—that comes to sustain the *entire* plant; it is the Word that sustains the human nature in Jesus.[13] Bérulle also provides the analogy of a man who has lost his liberty and become slave to another. Such a person no longer has power over his own possessions and actions. Similarly, the human nature in Jesus has become the "fortunate slave" of the divine power and love. With both of these illustrations of the hypostatic union, Bérulle suggests that the goal of Christian existence is to be similarly ingrafted by the divine nature, to be similarly enslaved to Christ—with the distinction, naturally, that the believer's participation in Christ's nature is never the personal, substantial union that obtains in the Incarnation.

It is not only the state of hypostatic union that Bérulle exalts in his *Grandeurs*; he envisions that believers can participate in many of the "states" of Jesus. These states—or permanent conditions and aspects of Jesus' life—are "available" to the believer for "adoration" and "communion". For example, the Christian can participate in Jesus' perfect adoration of the Father, in Jesus' humility and abasement, and in Jesus' obedience and renunciation of his will. The way to union with God, likeness to God, is through a sharing in these "stable" states or dispositions of Jesus. Two of those states seem to be quintessentially Bérullian: Jesus' love and adoration for the Father, and concomitantly, his contemplation of the Father. Our participation in these states comes by way of imitation: we love, adore, and contemplate the Son, as he did (does) the Father.

> Our gaze toward [Christ] should be a gaze of the greatest honor, the most powerful love and total and absolute dependence. We should wish that ... we could be completely occupied and given over to this spiritual and divine contemplation of the new source and principle of our being.[14]

Contemplation and adoration of Jesus, an imitation of the God-Man's own *interior* life, leads to a transformative sharing in his divine life. The more we adore and contemplate Christ, the more our relation toward him is purified and he can alter the "substance of our

[13] Ibid., 2.10, 122–23.
[14] Ibid., 5.9, 136–37.

being".[15] Bérulle does not hesitate to name Jesus the "Father of the world to come": just as the eternal Word proceeds in his divine being from the Father, we "proceed in our supernatural being", though differently, from Jesus the Son.[16] The contemplation and adoration of Jesus creates in the believer an interior likeness to Jesus, through which divinization may be worked.

If Jesus' earthly action and regard revealed his unceasing love of the divine Father, Bérulle also draws our attention to the Son's powerful and transformative love *for* mankind. This love deprived him of his heavenly glory and bade him accept the humility of a weak humanity. This love, strong enough to exercise "its power over and its discipline on the very Person of God" is capable also of overwhelming human hearts: "There is a crucifying love, which crucifies a God. Let it not be less powerful toward men." Indeed, this same love can divinize the individual soul. Even as this love transported the Son out of his divine homeland, love "transports us out of ourselves into him"; "what is more, it makes us like he is in himself, by divinizing and transforming us into God."[17]

Jesus' love for mankind is also manifest in the Eucharist. The Eucharist, like the exchange of substantial, indwelling life in the Trinity and the Incarnation, works *substantial* change in the individual person. For Bérulle, the great mystery of the Eucharist (third after the Trinity and the Incarnation) effects a "substantial and bodily indwelling of the living and glorious body of the Son of God in our earthly and mortal bodies".[18] Just as Jesus speaks of his unity with the Father in John's Gospel, the one who receives the Eucharist lives a "holy and divine life" in Christ. The body that Jesus deigned to take from humanity in the Incarnation is "returned" to us like a "sacred deposit"—and with interest. For through the Eucharist the believer is imprinted with the Son's divinity, his Spirit, and his grace, the human substance thereby receiving a dispositive power to the resurrection and a "new and supernatural privilege".[19] In other words, the Eucharist is both the operating power of divinization and the earthly beginning of supernatural and resurrected life.

[15] Ibid., 137.
[16] Ibid., 136.
[17] Ibid., 8.10, 145, and 9.1, 148.
[18] Ibid., 6.4, 139.
[19] Ibid., 6.1, 138–39.

Bérulle thus establishes for the French School of Spirituality a rich and sophisticated vision of the centrality of the Incarnation for spiritual life and deification. His singular theological contribution about *participating in the states* of Christ provided later seventeenth-century writers with a strong orientation toward a spirituality centered on Jesus' incarnate life. Jean-Jacques Olier frames his spiritual teaching predominantly around a participation in Christ's abnegation and sacrifice, with the Eucharist and Holy Spirit figuring prominently in his understanding of deification.

Jean-Jacques Olier (1608–1657)

With Jean-Jacques Olier, the founder of the Sulpician religious society dedicated to the formation of educated and holy priests, emerges the fervent teaching that all Christians (not simply the clergy) are called to be "living hosts" to God. The path to deification for Olier is decidedly sacrificial, and his language about this transformation is layered with images of altar, host, and victim-consummation. Like Bérulle, Olier speaks to the goals of true adoration and *religion*. How are such goals to be achieved? Most directly, the demands of authentic religion are met by becoming a host-victim to the Father, joining one's own sacrifice to that perfect oblation of Jesus. This oblative act of the Christian depends upon a prior abnegation, which serves to clear a path to union with Jesus in his own kenosis. Jesus not only stripped himself of the divine glory properly his own, but he also willingly sacrificed his life out of reverence and love for God.[20] Among the seventeenth-century theologians of this distinct School, Olier's language is most austere on this point of abnegation or annihilation (*anéatissement*). This abnegation, however, is a requisite preparation to the believer's gradual consummation into the very life of God.

Jesus wishes to "*dilate* (*dilater*) his holy religion toward God", and he does this in a twofold way at the Holy Mass. First, Jesus stays present to his earthly followers as a "host of praise" at the Eucharistic altar, so that believers might commune with the spirit of the host-victim, praising him and inwardly uniting to him in the "sentiments"

[20] Jean-Jacques Olier, *Introduction to the Christian Life and Virtues*, chap. 1, in Thompson, *Bérulle and the French School*, 217.

of his religion. Jesus thus comes to us in the Eucharist to "anoint" the soul and fashion us anew, that we might possess that which makes for true religion.[21] In a second manner, Jesus draws the worshipper to "communicate in his state of host-victim so as to be a victim with him" "in truth" and "in reality". This communication demands that the believer willingly sacrifice all that is not God, annihilating all idols and things of the flesh.[22] This mortification, this abnegation, is an interior *consuming* that occurs with Jesus Christ, the host-victim consumed on the altar. It is the "fire" of Jesus' intimate presence within the Christian that "devours" and consumes, making possible a share in that perfect host-victim state. Communing in this state with Jesus, the Christian is consumed for God's glory *and* participates in that glory: "Such a host no longer lives through its own life and the life of the flesh, but lives totally through the divine life and the life of one consumed in God."[23]

Olier speaks of being consumed into divine life within the context of the Eucharistic sacrifice and the perfect host-victim, Jesus. But his writing likewise underscores that this "dilation" and transformation occurs through the agency of the Holy Spirit. In one of his meditations upon the "wondrous" and "holy" vocation of Christians to share in the divine nature, Olier explains that the operations of the Holy Spirit within us are "participations in the immanent operations of God in himself", operations that God desires to make "tangible" in the interior life of Christians.[24] Olier's God is profoundly generous, willing to externalize through the Spirit his own inner life for the benefit of human participation. The Spirit leads believers to detachment and to the virtues, "dilating" the dispositions and loves and actions of Christ in the hearts of believers, all to the end of uniting the believer to Jesus and to the Father. The Spirit teaches the soul how to imitate the states of Jesus, which need to be taken in their proper order; that is, no one participates in the ascension of Christ who does not first pass through Jesus' abnegation,

[21] Ibid., 219.

[22] "It is a true sign of our religion to offer everything in sacrifice to God and this to testify how vile and despicable all things are in his presence. In this way we value and respect nothing other than him alone" (ibid.).

[23] Ibid., 220.

[24] Olier, "Upon Hearing the Birds Sing", from *The Christian Day*, in Thompson, *Bérulle and the French School*, 286.

suffering, humiliation, Cross, and his "death to everything".[25] After this spiritual death, the Christian may participate in the resurrected life of Christ. This risen life, effected by the Spirit, is a life hidden in God, in which the soul is engulfed, absorbed, and annihilated by God, who hides the soul in himself.[26] Sharing in this state, all the earthy crudeness of the soul disintegrates into the fire of God's light; the soul places itself entirely at the service of God, loving God alone and hardly concerned with its own flesh:

> [The soul] is in such a breathless pursuit of God that only a very small part of it actually enlivens the flesh. For this reason the soul's least concern is to give life to the body, which is half-dead and without energy, since the soul has been caught up in God and only lives for him. The soul *borrows the qualities of God and his being*. It is much more appropriate that God should consume us than enliven us, since he is ablaze in himself.[27]

This remarkable description of divinization, here considered as a "resurrection" in the Spirit, asserts that the soul can borrow divine power, and, more, that such a state is somehow fitting—given the nature of God and the capacity of the soul for intimate union with him.

As we have seen, Olier amplifies Bérulle's understanding of the Christian life as a communion in the states of Christ, with a particular emphasis upon the state of Jesus as host-victim. This sacrificial state shapes Olier's depiction of the spiritual life, leading to an understanding of divinization centered upon the consumption of the host-victim in God, in and through the workings of the Spirit in the interior life. As we move to the thought of John Eudes, such sacrificial language shifts to a much greater emphasis on the practical imitation of Jesus' life and a theology of the common priesthood of the baptized.

Saint John Eudes (1601–1680)

For John Eudes, the Bérullian vision of participating in the states of Jesus' life is replaced by a simpler, realistic portrayal of the Christian

[25] Olier, *Introduction to the Christian Life*, chap. 1, in Thompson, *Bérulle and the French School*, 218–19.

[26] Ibid., chap. 2, 223.

[27] Ibid. (emphasis added).

life as a *continuation* of that most holy life which Jesus lived on earth.[28] This continuity depends upon an intimate union between Jesus and the believer, a union that Eudes compares to the Johannine vision of the unity of life between the Father and the Son. If rooted in the Gospel of John, Eudes' teaching on sharing in the divine life is also distinctively Pauline in its dependence upon an ecclesial-sacramental understanding of Christ's Body. John's Gospel portrays Jesus as *in* the Father and as living the life that the Father communicates to him. Jesus in turn tells the Christian believer that "you are also in me living my life and I am in you, communicating that very life to you."[29] Such mutual indwelling indicates the actual continuation of Jesus' holy life in his followers. Eudes points to several other New Testament passages (for example, Col 3:3–4; Eph 2:5; 2 Cor 4:10–11; Gal 2:20; 2 Thess 2:11–12)[30] that insist upon this intimacy between Christ and his disciples: this scriptural witness leaves believers no choice but to conclude that "Jesus Christ should be living in us and that we should live only in him ... that our life should be a continuation and expression of his life."[31] In fact, we have "no right" to live any other life on earth but his. In short, the baptized Christian should aim for nothing short of being "other Jesus Christs on earth". This "basic truth" of Christianity reflects the will of Jesus, whose union to us makes such an existence possible.[32]

Significantly, Eudes portrays this *alter Christus* capacity in terms of the gift of faith, of the life and power of the sacraments, and of the ecclesial body of the Church. For Eudes, union with Christ must be understood both *spiritually* and *bodily*. The believer is united spiritually to Jesus through the faith we are given in the waters of baptism. Faith is a "communication" of the "divine light" infused into the soul of Jesus at the Incarnation; it is a participation in that "inaccessible eternal light" from the countenance of God. By sharing in this divine truth and light, the believer is not only safe from

[28] See John Eudes, *The Life and Kingdom of Jesus in Christian Souls: A Treatise on Christian Perfection for Use by Clergy or Laity*, translated by a Trappist of Gethsemani, introduction by Fulton J. Sheen (New York: P.J. Kenedy and Sons, 1946), 2, i.

[29] Ibid., in Thompson, *Bérulle and the French School*, 294.

[30] Ibid., 294–95.

[31] Ibid., 295.

[32] Ibid., 2, ii, 295–96.

the "darkness" and deception of human *scientia*, but he is enabled also to carry out and *fulfill* the submission and docility of the earthly Jesus to the truth of his eternal Father. The Christian's subjection to Christ, and to all that he teaches through the Church, is a participation in the voluntary and perfect submission of Jesus via the very light that Jesus has "drawn from the bosom of the Father".[33] When we see the world and ourselves in this shared light of faith, we are looking with the eyes of Christ. Sounding much like Bérulle and Olier, Eudes stipulates that this divinized vision grants a twofold knowledge: we know the infinite worth of God, and we are aware keenly of the world's smoky "vanity" and of our own "nothingness, sin and abomination".[34]

If faith unites us spiritually to Christ, the Eucharist and the Church effect a *bodily* intimacy. The Eucharist expresses Jesus' "burning desire" to dwell within our hearts and bodies: "He wants to be within you."[35] Jesus' divine life operates within the believer who has received his "sacred body" in faith and love. If Jesus is within us, he is our animating spirit, even as the members of our bodies are animated by the "spirit" of our souls. This means that we "live and walk in his ways", that we are "clothed" with his "sentiments", and that we act with his dispositions, intentions.[36] The same conclusion obtains when Eudes reflects on the tight bond between Christ and the members of his Body, the Church. Jesus Christ may be said to possess two bodies and two lives: the body he received from the Virgin Mary at his birth and the life he lived in that body which concluded at his death on the Cross; and his Mystical Body, the life he continues to live through "those authentic Christians who are members of this body".[37] Though Eudes speaks of two bodies and two lives, he understands that the body and life of the Church is the "same" body and life in which Christ lived and died on earth. His Mystical Body is the continuation of Jesus' incarnate life, so "much so that the temporal, vulnerable life that Jesus has in his Mystical Body has not yet reached its fulfillment, but is fulfilled day by day

[33] Ibid., 2, i, 294, iv, 299.
[34] Ibid., 2, iv, 299.
[35] Ibid., 6, xxiv, 324.
[36] Ibid., 2, i, 294.
[37] Ibid., 2, ii, 295.

in every true Christian."[38] Bodily united to Jesus in the Eucharist and the Church, the believer thus perpetuates and brings to completion the bodily life of the Lord.

As should be evident by now, the French School attends with remarkable care to the spiritual life of the laity. John Eudes, in particular, shows himself to be quite ahead of his time, anticipating by three centuries the Second Vatican Council teaching on the common priesthood of all the baptized, and on the active participation of the laity in the offering of the Eucharistic sacrifice.[39] Eudes articulates that the laity are not simply to attend Mass in order "to assist or to see". Rather, the Christian worshipper at Mass *performs an action*—"the most important thing you have to do in the world". Again, because of the ecclesial intimacy between Jesus and his members, all Christians are "one with Jesus Christ, who is the high priest".[40] Because this is so, the laity ought to "exercise this quality" to offer to God, "with the priest and Jesus Christ himself the sacrifice of his body and blood offered in the holy Mass". Moreover, this offering ought to be made sharing in the "same dispositions"—humility, purity, detachment—as Jesus Christ when he offers it: "Oh, with what holy and divine dispositions it is offered to [God] by his Son Jesus! Unite yourself in desire and intention with these dispositions of Jesus. Pray that he will engrave them within you."[41] Eudes joins Olier in also urging the laity to offer *themselves* as hosts and victims:

> You should pray that Jesus Christ come within you and that he draw you within himself, that he unite himself to you and that he unite and incorporate you with him as host, in order to sacrifice you with him to the glory of his Father.[42]

For Eudes, then, the Mass itself is an occasion for the Christian to *continue* the holy life of Jesus, to perform the action of the God-Man

[38] Ibid.

[39] See the following Vatican Council II documents: Dogmatic Constitution on the Church, *Lumen gentium*, November 21, 1964, no. 10, and Constitution on the Sacred Liturgy, *Sacrosanctum concilium*, December 4, 1963, nos. 11, 14.

[40] Eudes, *Life and Kingdom*, 6, xxiv, in Thompson, *Bérulle and the French School*, 322.

[41] Ibid., 323.

[42] Ibid., 324.

as priest and victim. Such an action is genuinely possible because of Christ's desire to be one with his members, to share his life, and to incorporate his members into his divine activity.

These three towering figures of the French School in the seventeenth century bestow a doctrine of deification that focuses upon an intimate sharing in the life and states of the God-Man. As we have seen, Bérulle and Olier shape their understanding of the spiritual life upon the Christian's authentic participation in the states of Jesus' life—from the Incarnation to the Resurrection. This sharing in the stable aspects and dispositions of Jesus' life comes by way of contemplation, imitation, and communion. Believers unite themselves to the states of Jesus with adoration and love, through a prior kenosis and self-abnegation, and in and through the working of the Spirit (Olier). With John Eudes, the possibility of deification is specifically and practically oriented to *continuing* Jesus' life through a union that is spiritual and bodily, sacramental and ecclesial. In all three figures, there is palpable optimism that sharing in the divine life of Jesus is possible for Christians who live in the world. If John Eudes appears more accessible, less esoteric, than Bérulle and Olier, all three stand in appreciation of Francis de Sales' foundational intuition about the universality of the devout, holy Christian life.

Jean-Pierre de Caussade (1675–1751) and Thérèse of Lisieux (1873–1897)

The French School stretched beyond the seventeenth century proper, reaching its fulfillment, one could argue, in the writings of de Caussade and Thérèse. Both of these later figures discover the possibility of deification in loving abandonment to the providential will of the Father.[43] De Caussade and Thérèse understand that this abandonment—simple and complete—means that Jesus Christ becomes the source of action within the believer. In language more dramatic and youthful than de

[43] Although we have no evidence that Thérèse knew the work of de Caussade or read any of the French School theologians, it is nonetheless likely that she knew well this tradition of spirituality, especially as the seventeenth-century French Carmelite Madeleine de Saint-Joseph was a disciple and close spiritual confidant of Cardinal Bérulle.

Caussade, Thérèse speaks of God entirely taking over one's desire, will, and actions. For both of these spiritual writers, the universality of their spiritual teaching—its hidden, sacrificial way—epitomizes the *vive Jésus* that animates the entire School.

De Caussade sees holy abandonment as the short and easy way to union with God; he preaches that this way is open to all. In this spirituality, the secular—the "wholly worldly"—and the "religious" are held to a single demand, to one necessary thing: "Nothing in the spiritual life is easier and ... within everybody's reach"; simply "let God act and do all he wishes."[44] In this surrender to *ce qui arrive* (whatever may happen) is found the perfection of the believer, for the soul's perfection lies only within *God's design* for the "new self", the self that enjoys a share in the divine life. De Caussade puts it this way: "God desires to be the unique cause of all that is holy in us, so all that comes from us is very little. In God's sight there can be nothing great in us—with one exception: our total receptivity to his will."[45] While it is true that de Caussade's thought on the abandonment of the will depends largely on Francis de Sales, whom he quotes frequently in his letters of spiritual direction to the Visitation Sisters at Nancy, it is likewise the case that Bérulle's influence emerges in de Caussade's depiction of *abandon* as a permanent state or disposition. De Caussade does speak of many discreet punctual acts of sacrifice that manifest self-abandonment; but he also addresses abandonment as a kind of continuous or habitual act.[46] Formal acts of turning one's will over to God are gradually replaced by a steady disposition of heart, a readiness to will what God wills in every moment and circumstance. This surrender thus becomes a kind of perpetual state, one that shares in Jesus' continual *fiat voluntas tua* (thy will be done). Perhaps most accurately, we could say that abandonment is a more general *fiat* that contains a multiplicity of individual acts of surrender. De Caussade speaks of these acts as more or less unconscious;

[44] In this essay I am using John Beevers' new translation (New York: Doubleday Publishing, 1975) of Henri Ramière's edited volume of de Caussade's *Abandonment to Divine Providence* (10th ed.). See pages 26, 85.

[45] Ibid., 91.

[46] De Caussade's letters can be found in Henri Ramière's collection of letters in the 10th edition of *Abandonment to Divine Providence*, trans. E.J. Strickland (Saint Louis: Herder, 1921). See especially 126, 106, 120.

that is to say, they may leave little or no "trace" upon the spirit, so that the will does not recognize the act as its own—which is, in fact, the ideal, for then it is God acting through the human will without resistance of any kind. At this point, what God wills and what the believer desires is one.[47] When such a unity of wills obtains, the believer is participating not only in God's design, but in God's life.

Like the seventeenth-century writers in the French School, de Caussade connects this abandonment to true worship, true religion. God "has a right" to expect our voluntary abandonment—a rendering to God of all that one has received and shall receive. This is due worship, and not the self-flattery of a false attempt to appropriate what does not belong to us. Significantly, abandonment participates in a kind of economy of sacrifice (*do et des*), wherein the surrender received by God from his creatures allows God to pour out his abundant goodness and a share in his divine gifts. At the heart of abandonment, one finds not an abyss of emptiness, but rather infinite riches: "What an exchange of the divine liberality! What ingenuity of divine wisdom! What a contrivance and surprise of the divine goodness!"[48] Still, we should clarify that this homage duly expected by God is possible only because God gives the power to offer it to him, "by giving us the thought, the desire, the will" to do so. In other words, God gives the grace of *abandon*.

De Caussade also underscores the French School confidence in the power of love to achieve a unity with God. Love accompanies abandonment: "The whole business of self-abandonment is only the business of loving, and love achieves everything."[49] God cannot deny the soul's love, and it is this love which allows God to act in and take control of the soul: "When he finds such a heart, he takes possession of it, controls all its responses, and so uses it that it finds in everything, no matter what, something which is invaluable in its progress to holiness."[50] The soul that longs for God and to give over its will

[47] De Caussade draws attention to Mary, Joseph, and Jesus as examples of those who acted with little awareness of their abandonment: "Because of the continual submission of their hearts, this (divine) will gives complete self-mastery. Whether they co-operate consciously with it or obey it without even noticing they are doing so, is all one. God uses them to help other souls." Beevers, *Abandonment to Divine Providence*, 77.

[48] "Letters", in Ramière, *Abandonment to Divine Providence*, 115–16.

[49] Beevers, *Abandonment*, 113.

[50] Ibid.

to God shall "enjoy him and all his gifts".[51] If, as some scholars have noted, de Caussade's work appears spare in its extended reflections on Jesus and his earthly life, he is nonetheless clear that the path of abandonment, the path to holiness, is an imitation of the Jesus of the Gospels and a continuation of his divine activity:

> If we wish to live according to the Gospel, we must abandon ourselves simply and completely to the action of God.... The life of each saint is the life of Christ. It is a new gospel.... They are happy, for their part, to do what is proper to their state. To let God act and obey his demands on us: *that is the gospel and the whole scripture and law.*[52]

De Caussade eloquently articulates the *vive Jésus* and Eudes' firm assertion that Christians continue in their daily lives that holy and divine life of Jesus. His particular contribution is to locate this participation in a union (by way of surrender) of the human will to the divine will.

In Thérèse of Lisieux, at the end of the nineteenth century, the French School of spirituality finds a dramatic coda to its teachings. The autobiographical writings of this young Carmelite, who dies of tuberculosis at the age of twenty-four, take up the themes of democratic holiness, living Jesus, abandonment, love of God, consummation, and divinization, and raise them to a sublime strain. For Thérèse, the divine possession and transformation of souls is not restricted to a few extraordinary spiritual seekers. Rather, it is a vital possibility for all the baptized who desire it with childlike confidence, and for all who practice complete abandonment to God. If Thérèse of Lisieux's path to holiness was that of a cloistered Carmelite nun, her spirituality of the Little Way applies to believers in every walk of life. The French School calls for an abnegation of the self, and Thérèse echoes this, insisting upon our becoming nothing—"a poor little thing, nothing at all"[53]—before God. In this "little way"—the "very straight, very short" way to holiness and union with God—the soul places itself before the divine activity of Jesus, the "elevator" to heaven and

[51] Ibid., 114.

[52] Ibid., 84 (emphasis in original).

[53] Thérèse of Lisieux, *Story of a Soul: The Autobiography of St. Thérèse of Lisieux*, 3rd ed., trans. John Clarke, O.C.D. (Washington, D.C.: ICS Publications, 1996), 206.

purity.[54] The "elevator" is always prepared to arrive, but only for the one who has become little and weak.

Thérèse employs a similar image when reflecting upon the Eucharistic Host—the Eagle. Thérèse envisions herself as a tiny weak bird, who in her "folly" of great love longs to fly "toward the Sun Itself", and with the "*Divine Eagle's own wings*". A prey to the Eagle's love, Thérèse petitions to be so transformed by Jesus' divine substance in the Eucharist that she might ascend to the very Furnace of Love in the Trinity.[55] It is the work of divinization to lift up and consume the soul, but Thérèse avers that such divine operation is effective only in one who becomes nothing: the smaller one is, the wider the vessel one presents to God to fill with himself. Abandonment of the self, abandonment of the will to God's desire, should be the Christian's only "compass".[56] Such abnegation allows God to be working through the soul so that every act is love.[57]

In language reminiscent of Olier, Thérèse discovers her own particular mission and vocation: to be a holocaust to God's mercy and love, through an insight about God as a living furnace of divine mercy (not judgment). God longs to spread his consuming flame of mercy into many souls, he longs to be loved, and Thérèse prays to be a "happy victim" of this consuming fire of Divine Love. Like the French School of which she gives the soprano performance, Thérèse does not hesitate to imagine herself doing Christ's work, being an *alter Christus*. In her childlike audaciousness, Thérèse writes herself into Jesus' sacerdotal prayer in John 17. She cites this passage, making it her own, and only then pauses to wonder if she has been too bold, desiring to share in Jesus' own words to the Father. Her response

[54] Ibid., 209.

[55] Ibid., 199–200 (emphasis in original).

[56] Ibid., 178.

[57] Thérèse describes this divine overtaking of her actions through a stanza from John of the Cross' *Spiritual Canticle*:

> After I have known it
> LOVE works so in me
> that whether things go well or badly
> love turns them to one sweetness
> transforming the soul in ITSELF.

(Quoted by Thérèse in *Story of a Soul*, 179.)

excuses any potential transgression: "Perhaps this is boldness? No, for a long time You permitted me to be bold with You. You have said to me as the father of the prodigal son said to his older son: 'EVERYTHING *that is mine is yours.*'"[58] Thérèse, in a manner more strikingly direct than Francis de Sales and John Eudes, teaches that the believer who lovingly makes herself nothing before the will of God does indeed become a *continuation* of the life of Christ and a daring sharer in his divine powers. The divine and prodigal excess of the Father finds a receptacle in the soul's *abandon*.

Such is the legacy of that *grand siècle*, which bestows on the Catholic tradition of deification a confident and optimistic belief in the capacity of the Christian to *vive Jésus*—accomplished through an intimate union to Jesus and accompanied by what can only be described as an immense, godlike love. In fact, these French theologians know that the love by which they are united to God is a *borrowed* one—a participation in the state of adoration and love of the incarnate God-Man. That grand potential of believers to participate in the divine nature of Jesus through love is itself his gift, given to those whose souls have emptied themselves before the divine. We shall let Thérèse sum up for the whole French School the source and work of this transforming love: "Your Love has gone before me, and it has grown within me, and now it is an abyss whose depths I cannot fathom. Love attracts love, and, my Jesus, my love leaps towards Yours.... For me to love You as You love me, I would have to borrow Your own Love."[59]

Readings for Further Study

Bérulle, Pierre de. *Bérulle and the French School: Selected Writings*. Edited with an introduction by William M. Thompson. Translation by Lowell M. Glendon, S.S. New York: Paulist Press, 1989.

Bremond, Henri. *A Literary History of Religious Thought in France*. Vol. 3, *The Triumph of Mysticism*. London: SPCK, 1936.

Caussade, Jean-Pierre de. *Abandonment to Divine Providence*. Translated by John Beevers. New York: Doubleday Publishing Group, 1975.

[58] Ibid., 255–56 (emphasis in original).
[59] Ibid., 256.

______. *Abandonment to Divine Providence.* Edited by J. Ramière. Translated by E.J. Strickland. From the 10th complete French ed. Saint Louis: B. Herder, 1921.

______. *A Treatise on Prayer from the Heart.* Translated by Robert McKeon. Saint Louis: Institute of Jesuit Sources, 1998.

Eudes, John. *The Life and Kingdom of Jesus in Christian Souls: A Treatise on Christian Perfection for Use by Clergy or Laity.* Translated by a Trappist of Gethsemani. Introduction by Fulton J. Sheen. New York: P.J. Kenedy and Sons, 1946.

Francis de Sales. *Francis de Sales: Finding God Wherever You Are; Selected Spiritual Writings.* Introduced and edited by Joseph F. Powers, O.S.F.S. Hyde Park: New City Press, 1993.

______. *Francis de Sales, Jane de Chantal: Letters of Spiritual Direction.* Translated by Péronne Marie Thibert. Selected and introduced by Wendy Wright and Joseph M. Power. New York: Paulist Press, 1988.

______. *Introduction to the Devout Life.* Translated by John K. Ryan. New York: Doubleday, 1989.

______. *The Love of God, a Treatise.* Translated by Vincent Kerns. Westminster, Md.: Newman Press, 1962.

Marie-Eugene of the Child Jesus. *Under the Torrent of His Love: Thérèse of Lisieux, a Spiritual Genius.* Translated by Mary Thomas Noble, O.P. New York: St Paul's, 1994.

Thérèse of Lisieux. *St. Thérèse of Lisieux: Her Last Conversations.* Translated by John Clarke, O.C.D. Washington, D.C.: ICS Publications, 1977.

______. *Story of a Soul: The Autobiography of St. Thérèse of Lisieux.* 3rd ed. Translated by John Clarke, O.C.D. Washington, D.C.: ICS Publications, 1996.

Chapter Nine

"STRANGE IMMODERATION OF THE THINGS OF GOD": DEIFICATION AND MYSTICAL UNION IN NEO-THOMISM

John Saward

Reginald Garrigou-Lagrange died at dawn on February 15, 1964, just a few days before his eighty-seventh birthday. For the preceding four years, his mind, which shone so brilliantly in the high summer of the Thomistic revival, had been clouded by the infirmities of old age. He could no longer read his Breviary, or even recite the Rosary, the inseparable companion of his Dominican and Christian life. As he entered the darkness, a confrere found him one day weeping, his head in his hands. "My final years will be terrible. Lord, I have become like a beast before you, *ut iumentum factus sum apud te* [Ps 72:23]."[1] Jacques Maritain, writing in his journal, regarded the death of his old friend and mentor as a "deliverance": "What a black night he has passed through! He must have gone straight to Heaven. *Strange immoderation of the things of God.*"[2]

Maritain's description of Père Garrigou's last years of suffering is a fitting summary of the spiritual doctrine of his entire career. *Strange immoderation of the things of God*: Garrigou made the bold and seemingly immoderate claim that mystical intimacy with Christ and the Blessed Trinity is not an extraordinary grace, but rather the normal, albeit uncommon consummation of the life of sanctifying grace, the grace that is conferred, restored, and increased by the Church's

[1] M.R. Gagnebet, O.P., "L'oeuvre du P. Garrigou-Lagrange: itinéraire intellectuel et spirituel vers Dieu", *Angelicum* 42 (1965): 31.

[2] *Journet-Maritain Correspondance*, vol. 5, *1958–1964* (Fribourg: Éditions Saint-Augustin, 2006), no. 667 (emphasis on *immoderation* is the original author's; emphasis on the other words added).

sacraments, the grace that makes us "partakers of the divine nature" (2 Pet 1:4).[3] All the baptized are called, at least remotely and sufficiently, to the mystical life. Through the perfection of the Holy Spirit's gift of wisdom, infused with the other gifts into every soul in God's grace and friendship, we attain a kind of experimental knowledge of God; in the words of the Areopagite, we "undergo the things of God".[4] *Strange immoderation of the things of God*, indeed, for to reach this goal of transforming union with the Trinity, beyond nature's claims and powers, the soul must be plunged into Christ's Passion, be purged in nights of sense and spirit, beyond nature's unaided powers of endurance.[5] The Living Flame of Love burns in order to heal. These truths, which Père Garrigou taught in the lecture halls of the Angelicum, he lived out in the nursing home on the via della Camilluccia. What he had once preached, about self-giving love and abandonment to divine providence, he now practised; in moments of lucidity he renewed the surrender of himself to the wise and loving will of the heavenly Father: "It is good for me to be like this, because it is what God wills. On earth there is only one thing necessary, to love God, and in my present state I can still love God."[6] For adults, he had written, there is no heaven without purgatory, "either in this life while meriting, or in the life to come without meriting".[7] Père

[3] "Since sanctifying grace is the beginning of eternal life, and since every just soul enjoys habitual union with the Blessed Trinity dwelling in it, the mystical union, or the actual, intimate, and almost continual union with God, such as is found here on earth in holy souls, appears as the culminating point on earth of the development of the grace of the virtues and Gifts, and as the normal, even though rather infrequent, prelude to the life of Heaven. This mystical union belongs, in fact, to the order of sanctifying grace; it proceeds essentially from 'the grace of the virtues and of the Gifts,' and not from graces *gratis datae* [extraordinary graces], which are transitory and in a sense exterior (as miracles and prophecy), and which may accompany it. The mystical life is Christian life, which has, so to speak, become conscious of itself" (Reginald Garrigou-Lagrange, O.P., *Christian Perfection and Contemplation according to St. Thomas Aquinas and St. John of the Cross*, trans. Sister M. Timothea Doyle, O.P. [Saint Louis and London: Herder, 1949], 127f. [hereafter *CPC*]). On the general call to the mystical life, see *CPC* 337ff.

[4] *STh* Ia, q. 1, a. 6 ad 3; IIa–IIae, q. 45, a. 2; *CPC* 271ff.

[5] Cf. Reginald Garrigou-Lagrange, *L'amour de Dieu et la Croix de Jésus: Étude de théologie mystique sur le problème de l'amour et les purifications passives d'après les principes de saint Thomas d'Aquin et la doctrine de saint Jean de la Croix*, vol. 2 (Paris: Cerf, 1929), 458–545 (the night of the senses) and 549–631 (the night of the spirit).

[6] Gagnebet, "L'oeuvre", 31.

[7] Cf. *CPC* 357.

Garrigou had a purgatory on earth, and, so far as any man living can judge, a purgatory of very great merit.

In what follows, I shall try to show how the mystical life, as expounded by the greatest neo-Thomist of them all, has its fundamental principle in the deification of the soul that is sanctifying grace. What is "immoderate" about a general call to the mystical life is but one expression of what is immoderate about God's free and infinitely generous bestowal upon us of a supernatural final end, "to the praise of his glorious grace which he freely bestowed on us in the Beloved [Son]" (Eph 1:6).

The Apologetics of Deification

In 1909 the Master General of the Order of Preachers asked Reginald Garrigou-Lagrange to take up a teaching post at the Collegio Angelico. There he made the acquaintance of a Spanish friar, the Servant of God Juan González Arintero (1860–1928). The two men shared only a year together in Rome before the Spaniard, seventeen years older than the Frenchman, returned to his homeland. But the conversations of that time were a turning point in Père Garrigou's intellectual development and confirmed him in the spiritual doctrine he would defend to the end: "We agree with ... Father Arintero OP that the supernatural life has its full development in this life only in the transforming union, such as it is described by St. John of the Cross and by St. Teresa."[8] In his book *The Mystical Evolution* Arintero argued that the life of the Christian, incorporated into the incarnate Son of God and receiving grace from his fullness, is meant to develop ("evolve"), under the action of the gifts of the Holy Spirit, toward mystical union with the incarnate Word, and, in him, with the triune God. Arintero was trained in physics, chemistry, and biology, and had been absorbed for many years with apologetics and the demonstration of the harmony of science and faith, but as he grew older, he became convinced that a clear presentation of the divine and supernatural beauty of sanctifying grace was the best way to motivate the faithful to pursue the path of holiness, and even had the power under God to enlighten and attract the minds of unbelievers:

[8] *CPC* 368f.; cf. 34f.

> The apologetic method most universal, most efficacious, most facile, and most in harmony with the systems of present-day thought is a positive exposition, vital and pulsating with the mysteries of the Christian life and the whole process of the deification of souls. Such a method will demonstrate in a practical way that the supernatural does not come to us as an exterior and violent imposition, oppressing us and depriving us of our nature, but as an increase of life, freely accepted, liberating and ennobling us. It does not destroy our humanity; it makes us superhuman, sons of God, gods by participation.... The living and true God, the God of infinite goodness, does not come to us to kill or paralyze, but to deify us, to make us participants in His own life, virtue, dignity, happiness, and absolute power and sovereignty. By communicating His Spirit to us He gives us the only true autonomy and liberty, the glorious liberty of the sons of God. "Where the Spirit of the Lord is, there is liberty" (Cf. 2 Cor 3:17).[9]

What Padre Arintero expresses with the exuberance of a poet is essentially the same thesis that Père Garrigou defended in the plain prose of the professor. It is the common spiritual wisdom of the Dominican neo-Thomists, and, as is clear from the text just quoted, it rests upon the dogma of the transfiguring, deifying effects of sanctifying grace. By grace we are caught up into the life of the Blessed Trinity, and the Trinity dwells within us: what else can the mystical life be than the living out to perfection of the divinely strange immoderation of the life of grace?

The Metaphysics of Deification: Deification according to the Fathers and Saint Thomas

As the earlier chapters of this book demonstrated, the doctrine of deification, though it is the evident predilection of the Greek Fathers, is not their exclusive property; on the contrary, it is the common teaching of all the Fathers and Doctors of the Church. Now, as Pope Leo XIII says in his encyclical *Aeterni Patris*, quoting Cajetan, Saint Thomas Aquinas, since "he most venerated the ancient doctors of the Church, in a certain way seems to have inherited the intellect

[9] John G. Arintero, O.P., *The Mystical Evolution*, vol. 1, trans. Jordan Aumann, O.P. (Rockford, Ill.: Tan Books, 1978), 7.

of all."[10] We should therefore expect to find in Saint Thomas a most perfect exposition of the doctrine of deifying grace that he received from the Fathers and earlier Doctors; and indeed we do:

> The gift of grace [says Saint Thomas in the treatise on grace in the *Summa*] surpasses every capacity of created nature, since it is nothing short of a partaking of the divine nature, which exceeds every other nature. Thus it is impossible for any creature to cause grace. For *it is as necessary that God alone should deify, bestowing a sharing of the divine nature by a participated likeness, as it is impossible that anything except fire should enkindle.*[11]

The habitual grace that overflows from Christ as Head of the Church,[12] the grace he merited for us in his Passion[13] and confers in the sacraments of his Church,[14] is nothing less than "a participation in the divine nature" (cf. 2 Pet 1:4).[15] This deification of man is the great goal freely and lovingly willed by God from before the foundation of the world and accomplished after Adam's fall through the Incarnation, Death, and Resurrection of God the Son: "The only-begotten Son of God, wanting to make us sharers of His divinity, assumed our nature, so that He, made man, might make men gods."[16]

Deification according to Père Garrigou

What Saint Thomas taught in continuity with the Fathers, Père Garrigou affirmed in fidelity to Saint Thomas: "Grace is really and formally a participation in the divine nature precisely insofar as it is divine, a participation in the Deity, in that which makes God God, in His intimate life.... Grace not only vivifies and spiritualizes us, but

[10] Cajetan's commentary on *STh* IIa–IIae, quoted in Pope Leo XIII, Encyclical Letter *Aeterni Patris*, August 4, 1879, no. 17.

[11] *STh* Ia–IIae, q. 112, a. 1 (emphasis added); see also, Humbert-Thomas Conus, O.P., "Divinisation: Saint Thomas", *Dictionnaire de spiritualité* 3 (Paris: Beauchesne, 1957), 1426–32.

[12] Cf. *STh* IIIa, q. 8.

[13] Cf. *STh Super Sent.*, lib. 3, d. 13, q. 3, a. 2, qc. 2 ad 5.

[14] Cf. *STh* IIIa, q. 62.

[15] Cf. *STh* Ia–IIae, q. 112, a. 1.

[16] Thomas Aquinas, *Officium de festo Corporis Christi*, pars 3, n. 3.

also *deifies* us."[17] Now, in his treatise *De gratia*, originally delivered as lectures at the Angelicum, Garrigou protects deification by grace from misunderstanding, whether through underrating its nature or exaggerating its effects. "Sanctifying grace is a participation in the divine nature that is not only moral but physical, not only virtual but formal, and yet is analogical, imperfectly imitating as an accident what in God is substance."[18]

Deification: Avoiding a Deficient Understanding

"Deification" is not a mere metaphor, as we might say in our enthusiasm at the opera house that a soprano's voice is "divine". Such a deficient doctrine of grace was proposed by the Nominalists, for whom, as Garrigou says, "sanctifying grace is a moral participation [in the Godhead] consisting in rectitude of the will and imitation of God's holiness and justice, as those who imitate the faith of Abraham are called the sons of Abraham."[19] By contrast, according to the Fathers and Doctors, the sharing in the life of the Trinity that the Father's incarnate Son once merited for us in his saving mysteries, and that he now bestows upon us in his sacraments, is truly "physical" in the sense that it modifies our nature (*physis*) and transfigures the essence of our souls with new, supernatural, godlike life, so that we are not only called, but truly are, the "children of God" (1 Jn 3:1).

Garrigou's principal argument for the physical and formal, rather than simply moral and virtual, character of deification-by-grace is based on the relation of grace to glory, or more exactly on the way in which it prepares the soul for the face-to-face vision of God in heaven. He points out that the "divine nature" of which by grace we partake is "the radical principle of the divine operations by which God intuitively sees Himself and loves Himself". "Now sanctifying grace physically and formally imitates this radical principle of properly divine operations, since it radically disposes man to see God

[17] *CPC* 55–56.

[18] Reginald Garrigou-Lagrange, O.P., *De gratia: Commentarius in* Summam Theologicam *S. Thomae, 1ae2ae qq. 109–114* (Turin and Rome: Marietti, 1950), 104.

[19] Ibid., 103.

intuitively [in heaven], and to love Him with a beatific love." Garrigou concludes: "Therefore, sanctifying grace is a physical and formal participation in the divine nature."[20]

Garrigou shows us how grace causes in us a divine sonship that is more than merely moral. The grace of the Spirit of the Son, sent into our hearts, makes us the adopted sons of God, enabling us to cry, "Abba, Father" (Gal 4:6). Now this adoptive sonship, says Garrigou, repeating the teaching of Saint Thomas, is "a participated likeness of the sonship of the Word, for in natural sonship the whole indivisible nature as it is in the Father is communicated, as essence and substance [to the Son], while to us a participation of the divine nature is communicated by an accidental gift."[21] The adoption of a child by a human father is something external to the child, the outcome of a legal process and doubtless the fruit of his adoptive father's affection, but our adoption in Christ by the heavenly Father, who loves us in the Holy Spirit with an infinite love, brings about an internal transformation of our soul, for "the love of God infuses and creates goodness in things."[22]

In arguing that we are *not just* the children of God in a moral way, Garrigou is not suggesting that we are *not at all* the children of God in a moral way—that is, through exercising the Christian virtues. His point is simply that "this moral sonship does not exclude [the physical], but rather presupposes it":

> First God infuses the grace by which we are partakers of the divine nature, and become pleasing to God and his sons through a physical participation in His nature. Then man by meritorious acts becomes a son of God in a moral way, imitating the conduct of his Father.[23]

[20] Ibid., 105.

[21] Ibid. On our adoptive sonship as a participated likeness of the natural sonship of the Word, see *STh* IIIa, q. 23, and Luc-Thomas Somme, O.P., *Fils adoptifs de Dieu par Jésus Christ: la filiation divine par adoption dans la théologie de saint Thomas d'Aquin* (Paris: Vrin, 1997).

[22] "Since our will is not the cause of the goodness of things, but is moved by it as by its object, our love, by which we will good to anything, is not the cause of its goodness; but conversely its goodness, whether real or imaginary, calls forth our love, by which we will that it should preserve the good it has, and receive besides the good it has not, and to this end we direct our actions, whereas the love of God infuses and creates goodness in things" (*STh* Ia, q. 20, a. 2).

[23] Garrigou-Lagrange, *De gratia*, 106.

Deification: Avoiding Exaggeration

Some Christians shun the terms "deification" and "divinization" because of what they imagine to be the dangers of pantheism, as if this way of speaking implied that man, incorporated into Christ and indwelt by the Holy Spirit, were somehow absorbed into the Godhead, or made to be equal with God. Père Garrigou, like all the masters of sacred doctrine, by careful distinctions excludes such disfigurements of the beauty of deifying grace. Deifying grace does not destroy our human nature, but rather perfects it, and far from abolishing our personalities it ennobles and enriches them in the "glorious liberty of the children of God" (Rom 8:21). Our participation in the divine nature, as we have seen, is more than merely metaphorical, yet is not "univocal", as if per impossibile we became God in exactly the same way in which God is God. No, says Garrigou; we partake of the Godhead "by an *analogical* participation", for this participation is something created, an accidental, not a substantial change, of our nature; it confers a likeness to God more perfect than the image in which we were created, and yet, as Garrigou reminds us, quoting the Fourth Lateran Council, "however great the likeness that can be noted between Creator and creature, a greater unlikeness between them is to be noted."[24]

Deification by Participation

To guard against any misunderstanding of the phrase "participation in the divine nature", when applied to sanctifying grace, we must consider more exactly what is meant by "participation" in general.[25] Saint Thomas defines it as follows: "To participate (*participare*) is, as it were, to take a part (*partem capere*). Therefore, when something receives in a particular way what belongs to something else in a universal way, the former is said to 'participate' in the latter. So a man is

[24] Ibid., 107.

[25] The classic twentieth-century works on Saint Thomas' understanding of participation are L. B. Geiger, *La participation dans la philosophie de S. Thomas d'Aquin* (Paris: Vrin, 1942), and C. Fabro, *La nozione metafisica di partecipazione secondo S. Tommaso d'Aquino*, 2nd ed. (Turin: Società editrice internazionale, 1950).

said to participate in animality, because he does not possess animality in its totality; in the same sense, Socrates participates in humanity."[26] In its everyday meaning, "participation" (or "sharing", as we often say) applies first of all to the use of material things with parts, as when we share a cake by handing round slices. We also share in qualities, whether material such as the heat of the sun, or spiritual like the knowledge imparted by a teacher to his student.[27] Moreover, as Saint Thomas' examples indicate, we share a common nature with the other individuals of our species or genus. Now Saint Thomas uses "participation" to speak of creatures in relation to their Creator. Creatures possess certain perfections *by participation* (stones share in existence, plants and animals in life, man in intellectuality), but God possesses them *by essence*. His creatures are by analogy like him, whether by trace (*vestigium*, in nonrational creatures) or by image (in rational creatures);[28] their existence, life, or intellectuality, derived from him as Creator, is a likeness, a partial and finite sharing, of what in him is essential, complete, and infinite. Now the supernatural participation in the divine nature that is sanctifying grace surpasses beyond measure these natural participations, or sharings-by-likeness, of God's being, life, and intellectuality. Sanctifying grace, says Garrigou, gives us a share, not just in this or that divine perfection, but in the *Godhead* as it is in *itself*, as it subsists in the *three Divine Persons*:

> From all eternity God the Father has a Son, to whom He communicates the whole of His nature, without dividing or multiplying it; He begets necessarily a Son who is equal to Him; He gives to Him the gift of being God from God, Light from Light, true God from true God. Then, out of sheer goodness, *gratuitously*, He wanted to have other sons in time, adopted sons, in a sonship that is not only moral (by exterior declaration), but real and intimate (by the production of sanctifying grace, the effect of God's active love for us). He has loved us with a love that is not only creating and conserving, but also vivifying, which makes us *participate in the very principle of His inner life*, in the principle of the immediate vision He has of Himself, and that He communicates to His Son and to the Holy Spirit. Thus He "has

[26] Thomas Aquinas, *In De hebdomadibus*, lect 2.
[27] Cf. Garrigou-Lagrange, *De gratia*, 103.
[28] Cf. *STh* Ia, q. 93, a. 6.

> predestined us to be conformed to the image of His only Son, so that He might be the first-born among many brethren" (Rom 8:29). The just in this way belong to the family of God and enter into the cycle of the Blessed Trinity. Infused charity assimilates us to the Holy Spirit (personal love), the Beatific Vision will assimilate us to the Word, who will assimilate us to the Father, whose Image He is. Thus the Trinity, already within us as in a darkened temple, will be in us as in a luminous and living temple, wherein the Trinity will be seen without veil and loved with a love that cannot be lost.[29]

Père Garrigou's student Père Marie-Michel Labourdette, O.P., sums up the doctrine as follows: "For the just, the interiority of God is opened up. He is taken to the level of the inner life of God, His Trinitarian life; He enters, so to speak, into the family of the Divine Persons, not as a stranger, but as a son of the house."[30]

The Mysticism of Deification

The message of Garrigou-Lagrange in his spiritual writings resembles the exhortations of the Fathers in their Christmas sermons. Like Saint Leo the Great, he wants the baptized to wake up to their dignity as partakers, by grace, in the divinity of Christ, who humbled himself to partake of our humanity.[31] The "mystical life", leading to spiritual marriage with the Word-made-flesh, is, he proposed, the summit of this divinized life of sanctifying grace, the life communicated in the sacraments to all who place no obstacle. Now, as the man incorporated into Christ grows in the life of grace through devout reception of the sacraments and prayer and spiritual combat, the gifts of the Holy Spirit hold increasing sway, enabling him to live and act as a

[29] Garrigou-Lagrange, "La grace: Est-elle une participation de la Deite telle qu'elle est en soi?", *Revue thomiste* 19 (1946): 478 (emphasis in original); cf. *STh* IIa–IIae, q. 2, a. 3.

[30] Michel Labourdette, O.P., *Cours de théologie morale, De la grâce* (Ia–IIae, qq. 109–114), unpublished lectures (Toulouse: n.d.), 99.

[31] "Recognize, O Christian, your dignity, and, having been made a partaker of the divine nature, do not by conduct unworthy of your lineage return to the baseness of old. Remember of whose Body you are the member. Call to mind that you have been snatched from the power of darkness and transferred into the light and kingdom of God" (Pope Leo the Great, *In nativitate Domini, sermo* 1, no. 3; *Sources chrétiennes*, 22B, 72f.).

child of God in a more than human way, under the strong but gentle motion of the Paraclete.

> The basic principle of the mystical life is sanctifying grace, or "the grace of the virtues and the Gifts". It manifests itself in the interior ascetical life according to the human mode of the virtues; in the mystical life, according to the superhuman mode of the Gifts which predominates in it. These Gifts, as habitual dispositions rendering us docile to the inspirations of the Holy Ghost, grow, as do the infused virtues, with charity, which in this life ought always to develop, through our merits and Holy Communion, according to the requirements of the first precept of love, which has no limit. Therefore, the soul cannot possess charity in a high degree without having the Gifts, as habitual dispositions, in a corresponding degree. It follows that a truly generous and faithful soul will come more and more under the immediate direction of the Holy Ghost, and the human mode of its activity will be gradually subordinated to the divine mode of the inspirations of the interior Master. This mode should end by dominating, a condition which characterizes the mystical life.[32]

Père Garrigou's friend Padre Arintero likewise argues that in all the faithful, reborn in Christ as God's adopted sons and endowed by the Spirit with the grace of the virtues and gifts, the seeds of the mystical life are sown:

> By means of the Gifts, all the faithful who live in grace can sometimes work heroically and mystically. So, in the very dawn of the spiritual life, the mystical life is begun, although in a very remiss state. In reality, the mystical state comprises the whole development of the Christian life and the entire way of evangelical perfection, however much its principal manifestations are reserved for the unitive way.... When the soul habitually produces heroic acts of virtue, and, dead to self and offering no resistance, lets itself be moved by the impulses, touches, and breathings of the Spirit, who, as on a delicate musical instrument, strokes the soul at His pleasure and draws from it divine melodies (St. Gregory Nazianzen), then we can say that the soul is fully in the mystical state, although at times it must still descend to the ascetical state.[33]

[32] *CPC* 349f.

[33] Arintero, *Mystical Evolution*, 2:425–27.

Conclusion

When Père Garrigou died, it seemed as if Thomism itself were dying with him. The second session of the Second Vatican Council opened on Michaelmas Day 1963, and already the Swiss theologian Charles Journet sensed that anti-Thomism was in the air. In a letter to Jacques Maritain, written ten weeks into the session and eight weeks before Garrigou's death, he adds the postscript: "Poor St. Thomas. They tell me that in the second session his name was only mentioned twice, and then it was just to criticize him. Gagnebet [Dominican disciple of Garrigou] has written to me saying that Louvain and the Germans would like to delete his name from the Constitution on the seminaries and universities."[34]

The apparent death of Thomism mourned by Journet was part of that false "spirit of the Council" and "hermeneutic of discontinuity", which proved so destructive of the council's true fruits in the years following its closure.[35] Hostility to the Angelic Doctor was certainly alien to the mind of the Supreme Pontiff, Papa Montini, who was steeped in Thomism and counted the great Thomists Maritain and Journet among his friends; indeed, he made Journet a cardinal and a Father of the council. If further proof were needed, we could cite the pilgrimage Pope Paul made to Aquino in 1974, in which he made a statement about the Angelic Doctor's place in the life of the Church as vigorous as anything said on the same subject by his predecessors Leo XIII, Saint Pius X, and Pius XI: "*All of us* who are faithful sons of the Church can and *must*, at least in some measure, be his disciples."[36] Eighteen years after this address, thirty after the opening of the council, the *Catechism of the Catholic Church* showed that discipleship in action by making Saint Thomas its most quoted authority, after Saint Augustine, among the Doctors of the Church. Moreover, having reaffirmed with the Fathers that the grace received in baptism and the other sacraments is "*sanctifying* or *deifying*" (*CCC* 1999; emphasis in original), "a *participation in the life of God*", and "introduces us

[34] *Journet-Maritain Correspondence*, 653.

[35] On the necessity of a "hermeneutic of discontinuity" in understanding the teaching of the council, see Pope Benedict XVI, Address to the Roman Curia, December 22, 2005.

[36] Emphasis added. These words were repeated by Pope Benedict XVI in his General Audience address of June 23, 2010, which was one of three on Saint Thomas.

into the intimacy of Trinitarian life" (*CCC* 1997; emphasis in original), the *Catechism* gives magisterial authority to the understanding of the mystical life defended by Garrigou and the other Dominican neo-Thomists:

> Spiritual progress tends toward ever more intimate union with Christ. This union is called "mystical" because it participates in the mystery of Christ through the sacraments—"the holy mysteries"—and, in him, in the mystery of the Holy Trinity. God calls us all to this intimate union with him, even if the special graces or extraordinary signs of this mystical life are granted only to some for the sake of manifesting the gratuitous gift given to all. (*CCC* 2014)

Reginald Garrigou-Lagrange is dead, but, to the confounding of his critics, his theology of deification and the mystical life lives on in the teaching of the Church, indeed in the very catechism by which she instructs converts and educates the faithful. Such earthly immortality, in doctrine rather than reputation, is the only kind that Père Garrigou, servant of truth and son of Saint Dominic, would desire.

Readings for Further Study

Arintero, John G., O.P. *The Mystical Evolution.* 2 vols. Translated by Jordan Aumann, O.P. Rockford, Ill.: Tan Books, 1978.

Garrigou-Lagrange, Reginald, O.P. *Christian Perfection and Contemplation according to St. Thomas Aquinas and St. John of the Cross.* Translated by Sister M. Timothea Doyle, O.P. Saint Louis and London: B. Herder, 1949.

_____. *Grace: Commentary on the Summa Theologica of St. Thomas, Ia IIae, q. 109–14.* Translated by the Dominican Nuns, Corpus Christi Monastery, Menlo Park, Calif. Saint Louis: B. Herder, 1952.

Chapter Ten

JOHN HENRY NEWMAN ON DEIFICATION

Daniel J. Lattier

John Henry Newman's (1801–1890) conversion to the Roman Catholic Church followed an unusual path. He went from High Anglicanism to Roman Catholicism through primarily reading the Eastern Church Fathers. Newman began systematically reading the Fathers in 1828 and, over the years, focused his efforts on Eastern Fathers such as Ignatius of Antioch, Irenaeus, Origen, the Cappadocians (Basil and the two Gregories), Cyril of Alexandria, and Athanasius, "the great Saint in whose name and history years ago I began to write, and with whom I end".[1] Newman's theology remained heavily influenced by these Fathers even after his conversion to Rome, leading Charles Dessain to remark that Newman was "an embodiment of the Eastern Tradition ... an upholder in the West of the theology of the Eastern Fathers".[2]

Given the Eastern influence on Newman, it is unsurprising to find that he affirmed the doctrine of deification. Stephen Finlan and Vladimir Kharlamov have rightly pointed out that Eastern Christian theology by no means has a "copyright" on deification; one finds Western sources affirming the doctrine throughout Christian history.[3] But it is fair to say that deification is a much greater emphasis of Eastern theology and is more frequently referred to in Eastern

[1] John Henry Newman, *Select Treatises of St. Athanasius*, vol. 1 (London: Longmans, Green, 1903), ix. Citations from Newman's works, unless otherwise noted, are those from the Longmans, Green uniform edition provided by the National Institute for Newman Studies on www.newmanreader.org.

[2] Charles Dessain, "Cardinal Newman and the Eastern Tradition", *Downside Review* 94 (1976): 85.

[3] Stephen Finlan and Vladimir Kharlamov, eds., *Theosis: Deification in Christian Theology*, Princeton Theological Monograph Series 52 (Eugene, Ore.: Pickwick Publications, 2006), 9.

than Western patristic writings. Dessain has written that the doctrine of deification "lay at the foundation of [Newman's] religious life".[4] In this essay, I will show that it lay at the foundation of Newman's theological thought as well. Newman's main theological principles are embodied in his understanding of deification; and, vice versa, Newman's understanding of deification helps us to understand better his theological principles. In the conclusion, I wish to touch upon the ecumenical implications of Newman's doctrine of deification.

Sources of Newman's Doctrine of Deification

The Eastern character of Newman's doctrine of deification is not readily apparent. Modern Eastern Christian writers typically use the terms "deification" and "divinization", which are English translations of the Greek patristic terms *theosis* and *theopoiesis*. Newman, on the other hand, typically referred to the deified as those who have received the "divine indwelling", the "indwelling of Christ", the "indwelling of the Spirit", "divine adoption", "divine sonship", and been made "temples of the Holy Spirit".[5] In places, he even refers to the "new birth [by which] the Divine Shechinah is set up within [the Christian]".[6] These terms, of course, are scriptural (mainly Pauline) and give credence to Dessain's position that "the source of [Newman's] teaching on the indwelling of the Blessed Trinity was primarily Holy Scripture."[7]

But Dessain's position requires qualification. For one, most of Newman's allusions to deification are in works where scriptural language would have been the expected mode of discourse—namely, his *Parochial and Plain Sermons* and *Lectures on Justification*. The *Parochial and Plain Sermons* were extended reflections on each Sunday's Scripture readings, which the Anglican Newman delivered to the Oxford

[4] Charles Dessain, "Cardinal Newman and the Doctrine of Uncreated Grace", *Clergy Review* 47 (1962):207.

[5] For the most thorough account of Newman's references to deification, see ibid., 207–25, 269–88. See also John Connolly, "Newman's Notion of the Indwelling of the Holy Spirit in the *Parochial and Plain Sermons*", *Newman Studies Journal* 5, no. 1 (Spring 2008): 5–18.

[6] Newman, *Parochial and Plain Sermons*, 3:266.

[7] Charles Dessain, "The Biblical Basis of Newman's Ecumenical Theology", in *The Rediscovery of Newman: An Oxford Symposium*, ed. John Coulson and A. M. Allchin (London: Sheed and Ward, 1967), 104–5.

community at Saint Mary's from 1825 through 1843. The *Lectures on Justification* were directed at an ecumenical audience with an eye to providing a *via media* between limiting Lutheran and Roman Catholic understandings of the doctrine of justification. "Deification" was this *via media*. Writes Newman, "*This* is to be justified, to receive the Divine Presence within us, and be made a Temple of the Holy Ghost."[8]

Newman primarily used scriptural language in describing the divine indwelling. But as a translator of the works of the Fathers, he was well aware of the term "deification". He even writes a summary of the term in volume 2 of his *Select Treatises of St. Athanasius*.[9] And in his lengthy defense of Saint Cyril of Alexandria's *mia physis sesarkomene* (one nature [of the Word] made flesh) formula, Newman refers to the Greek terms *theosis* and *theopoiesis*: "Hence it was usual with Athanasius and other Fathers to call the incarnation a [*theōsis*] or [*theopoiēsis*] of the [*anthrōpinon*] ... from the great change which took place in its state, or rather difference in its state from human nature generally."[10]

Also, Newman's reflections on deification may very well have been largely the fruit of his reflection on Scripture, but they are not for that reason less patristic—quite the contrary, as the Fathers' writings were for the most part extended exegeses of Scripture. In fact, as Andrew Louth has argued, Newman and the other members of the Oxford Movement sought to return to the patristic method of engaging with the Bible, which was itself a deifying exercise:

> And so in dwelling on the Tractarian approach to the interpretation of Scripture—or better, the engagement with Scripture, or better still, our engagement with God himself in the Scriptures—we come to the very heart of the vision of the Oxford Movement: namely that God has given himself to us, utterly and entirely, and in that self-giving is drawing us into the very life of the blessed Trinity, so that we receive God, become God, are deified.[11]

[8] Newman, *Lectures on Justification*, 144 (emphasis in original).

[9] Newman, *Select Treatises of St. Athanasius*, 2:88–90.

[10] Newman, *Tracts Theological and Ecclesiastical*, 361. *Anthrōpinon* refers here to the human nature of Christ.

[11] Andrew Louth, "The Oxford Movement, the Fathers, and the Bible", *Sobornost* 6 (1984): 45.

Finally, for all his favoring of tradition over private judgment in interpreting Scripture, it would have been uncharacteristic for Newman to comment on Scripture without the aid of that tradition.[12] Newman not only inherited the works of the Fathers, but an Anglican tradition that had been both preserving and retrieving those Fathers for some time. In *Participation in God: A Forgotten Strand in Anglican Tradition*, Arthur Allchin shows that deification had a place in Anglican theology since the time of the Reformation, even if it was not always emphasized.[13] Most importantly, Newman's context provided plenty of patristic inspiration. He was part of the Oxford Movement, a renewal movement within the Anglican church that sought to once again make present that "fresh vigorous Power" of the patristic era.[14] His compatriots in the Movement, John Keble and Edward Pusey, were well versed in the Fathers, and deification was their "central conviction".[15]

Newman also possessed that fuller, patristic understanding of tradition as not only comprising those doctrines not found in Scripture, but the entirety of God's revelation received by the Church. This received revelation is "partly written, partly unwritten", and includes Scripture within it.[16] Like the Fathers, too, Newman understood tradition as including the "Rule of Faith", or the "ecclesiastical *phronema*". The "Rule of Faith" is the lens through which the members of the Church faithfully interpret revelation, the lens that "suppl[ies] for us the true sense of Scripture in doctrinal matters".[17] This "Rule" is received and cultivated by Christians through their participation in the life of Christ and his Church—in other words, through their deification. Therefore, as strange as it sounds, the primary source of Newman's teaching on the divine indwelling was really that divine indwelling itself.

[12] See, for instance, Newman, *Lectures on the Prophetical Office of the Church*, 1:239–65; *Essays Critical and Historical*, 1:102–37; 2:336–74.

[13] Arthur Allchin, *Participation in God: A Forgotten Strand in Anglican Tradition* (Wilton, Conn.: Morehouse-Barlow, 1988).

[14] John Henry Newman, *Apologia Pro Vita Sua*, ed. Ian Ker (London: Penguin Books, 1994), 47.

[15] Andrew Louth, "Manhood into God: The Oxford Movement, the Fathers and the Deification of Man", in *Essays Catholic and Radical*, ed. Kenneth Leech and Rowan D. Williams (London: Bowerdean Press, 1983), 74.

[16] Newman, *Lectures on the Prophetical Office of the Church*, 1:250.

[17] Newman, *Select Treatises of St. Athanasius*, 250.

Principles of Newman's Doctrine of Deification

Newman scholars like to point out that Newman was an occasional writer who wrote for the situations presented before him. But that does not mean that his writing was unsystematic. One is struck not only by the patristic character of Newman's thought, but also by its consistency. That is because Newman did indeed have a system: his life in Christ. He wrote that Christ, through his deifying presence, acts as "the one principle of life in all His servants", and that a proper system "buries itself in the absorbing vision of a present, an indwelling God".[18] Newman understood the divine indwelling to mean that Christ acted as the first principle of not only his life but also his thought. In fact, a separation between life and thought in Newman is terribly insufficient. Newman's thought is patristic not only because he was versed in the works of the Church Fathers, but because he incorporated their ethos through the intellectual and spiritual participation in the life of Christ he shared with them—both the Eastern *and* Western Fathers. "It was the Thought of Christ," writes Newman, "not a corporate body or a doctrine, which inspired that zeal [in the Fathers] which the historian so poorly comprehends."[19] Unless one understands this about Newman, one can perhaps grasp parts of his thought, but never the whole. It is the reality of deification, of Christ dwelling within him, that holds the key to unlocking Newman's genius.

The centrality of deification in Newman's thought is thus linked to the centrality of Christ in his thought. Newman described the Incarnation as the "central aspect of Christianity"[20] and "the article of a standing or a falling Church".[21] According to Newman, divine revelation is marked by a sacramental character whereby God progressively reveals himself in more concrete ways to his people. The Incarnation is God's sacrament par excellence and "establishes in the

[18] Newman, *Lectures on Justification*, 190, 195.

[19] Newman, *An Essay in Aid of a Grammar of Assent* (Notre Dame, Ind.: University of Notre Dame Press, 1979), 359. By "the historian", Newman is here referring to Edward Gibbon. But Newman's critique applies to all those who fail to interpret the actions of Christians without taking into account their animating principle of Christ. See also Brian Daley, "The Church Fathers", in *The Cambridge Companion to John Henry Newman*, ed. Ian Ker and Terrence Merrigan (Cambridge: Cambridge University Press, 2009), 36.

[20] Newman, *An Essay on the Development of Christian Doctrine*, 36.

[21] Newman, *Oxford University Sermons*, 35.

very idea of Christianity the *sacramental* principle as its characteristic".[22] Newman's focus on the person of Christ gave the whole of his theology a Christocentric character, leading Terrence Merrigan to describe it as "radically incarnational".[23]

This Christocentrism was also characteristic of patristic theology. The Orthodox theologian Georges Florovsky has written that "the main theme of Patristic theology was always the Mystery of Christ's Person."[24] For the Fathers, Christocentrism implied anthropocentrism, since Christ became incarnate for the sake of man's deification. Newman was well aware of Saint Athanasius' passage that so famously summarizes the Fathers' Christocentric anthropology: "God became man so that man might become God."[25] Indeed, Newman even entertained the idea of Fathers such as Saint Irenaeus and Saint Maximus the Confessor that the Incarnation was necessary for this deification and would have occurred regardless of original sin.[26]

But Newman's Christocentrism is no "Christomonism"—that term for a theology with an excessive focus on Christ to the exclusion of the other persons of the Trinity.[27] In speaking of the deifying presence within the Christian, Newman frequently invokes both Christ and the Spirit in the same breath. In his *Parochial and Plain Sermons*, he speaks of deification as "a present entrance into the next world, opened upon our souls through participation of the Word

[22] Newman, *Essay on the Development*, 325 (emphasis in original).

[23] Terrence Merrigan, "Revelation", in Kerr and Merrigan, *Cambridge Companion*, 56.

[24] Georges Florovsky, "Patristic Theology and the Ethos of the Orthodox Church", in *The Collected Works of Georges Florovsky*, vol. 4, *Aspects of Church History*, ed. Richard Haugh (Belmont, Mass.: Nordland Publishing, 1975), 24.

[25] Athanasius, *On the Incarnation* 54,3. Writes Newman, "The greatest and special gift is the actual presence, as well as the power within us of the Incarnate Son as a principle or [*archē*] of sanctification, or rather of deification. On this point Athan., especially dwells in too many passages to quote or name" (*Select Treatises of St. Athanasius*, 2:130). See also Newman, *Parochial and Plain Sermons*, 5:118.

[26] See Newman, *The Letters and Diaries of John Henry Newman*, vol. 13, ed. C. Stephen Dessain et al. (Oxford: Oxford University Press, 1961–2006), 335, and *Select Treatises of St. Athanasius*, 2:187–88. This position is most famously linked to Duns Scotus (1266–1308). Ultimately, Newman appears to recognize that the question of whether or not Christ would have become incarnate regardless of original sin is unanswerable and acknowledges that "it is the general teaching of the Fathers in accordance with Athan., that our Lord would not have been incarnate had not man sinned" (*Select Treatises of St. Athanasius*, 2:188).

[27] Donald Graham especially defends Newman on this point in his recent book, *From Eastertide to Ecclesia: John Henry Newman, the Holy Spirit, and the Church* (Milwaukee: Marquette University Press, 2011).

Incarnate, ministered to us by the Holy Ghost."[28] He writes in his *Oxford University Sermons* of "Christ being formed in us—dwelling in the heart—of the Holy Spirit making us His temple".[29] And in the *Lectures on Justification*, Newman maintains that "Christ then is our Righteousness by dwelling in us by the Spirit."[30]

In the *Lectures*, Newman elaborates on the difficulties of sharply distinguishing between the deifying presence of the Son and Spirit:

> It appears, moreover, that this inward presence is sometimes described as God's presence or indwelling; sometimes that of Father and Son; sometimes of the Holy Ghost; sometimes of Christ the Incarnate Mediator; sometimes "of God through the Spirit"; sometimes of Christ, of His Body and Blood, of his Body in "flesh and bones," and this through the Spirit. Different degrees or characteristics of the gift are perhaps denoted by these various terms, though to discriminate them is far beyond our powers.[31]

Elsewhere, Newman clarifies the theological reason behind this apparent confusion: the "circumincessio" (*perichoresis*) of the trinitarian Persons.[32] Newman affirms that the Father, Son, and Holy Spirit dwell within each other such that, in the economy of salvation, "God the Son and God the Holy Ghost have so acted together in their separate Persons, as to make it difficult for us creatures always to discriminate what belongs to each respectively."[33] Because of the *perichoresis* of the trinitarian Persons, Newman is also able to claim that we have "the indwelling in us of God the Father and the Word Incarnate through the Holy Ghost"—that is, the indwelling of the Trinity.[34] Yet, at the same time, Newman clarifies that the Persons of the Trinity are "really and eternally distinct from each other" and takes seriously their different characteristics revealed by their names Father, Son, and Holy Spirit.[35]

[28] Newman, *Parochial and Plain Sermons*, 3:263.

[29] Newman, *Oxford University Sermons*, 29.

[30] Newman, *Lectures on Justification*, 150.

[31] Ibid.

[32] See Newman, *Tracts Theological and Ecclesiastical*, 160–61; *Select Treatises of St. Athanasius*, 2:72–79.

[33] Newman, *Lectures on Justification*, 208.

[34] Ibid., 144.

[35] See Newman, *Tracts Theological and Ecclesiastical*, 161; *Select Treatises of St. Athanasius*, 2:72, 74; *Parochial and Plain Sermons*, 4:249; 6:58.

The above discussion illustrates that Newman had a theologically mature understanding of deification. The Church Fathers were unwavering in their belief that true participation in Christ required that one maintain "right teaching" about Christ—that orthopraxy was intimately linked with orthodoxy. In fact, the Fathers recognized that man's deification was at stake in the christological controversies of the first millennium. Dessain aptly summarizes this point in his article "Cardinal Newman and the Eastern Tradition": "One of the reasons why the Greek Fathers of the fourth century defended so firmly the divinity of Christ and the divinity of the Holy Spirit, was the connection of these truths with the divinization, the deification of the Christian."[36] If Jesus Christ was not truly God, then the human nature he assumed could not truly partake of the divine life. In his later years, Newman expressed humans' inability to participate in God through Christ as the "cardinal difference of doctrine between the Catholic and Arian".[37] Gregory Nazianzen's maxim "what is not assumed is not redeemed" also entails that what is not assumed by God is not deified.[38]

Newman considered himself more of an apologist or controversialist than a theologian in the traditional sense of the term.[39] Yet, he was remarkably able to combine a reputation as perhaps the greatest English prose writer with the theological precision of the Fathers.[40] He affirmed that the change the Christian undergoes in deification is not only a moral but an ontological change, "raising him in the

[36] Dessain, "Cardinal Newman and the Eastern Tradition", 95.

[37] Newman, *Select Treatises of St. Athanasius*, 2:424.

[38] Gregory of Nazianzus, *Epistle* 101, 32, from *Sources Chrétiennes* 208 (Paris: Éditions du Cerf, 1974), 50.

[39] In a letter of 1869 Newman writes, "Really and truly I am not a theologian. A theologian is one who has mastered theology—who can say how many opinions there are on every point, what authors have taken which, and which is the best—who can discriminate exactly between proposition and proposition, argument and argument, who can pronounce which are safe, which allowable, which dangerous—who can trace the history of doctrines in successive centuries, and apply the principles of former times to the conditions of the present. This is it to be a theologian—this and a hundred things besides. And this I am not, and never shall be" (*Letters and Diaries*, 24:212–13).

[40] The estimation that Newman was the greatest English prose writer was from none other than James Joyce (see Richard Ellmann, *James Joyce* [New York: Oxford University Press, 1959], 40).

scale of being".[41] The deified Christian, according to Newman, is brought intimately close to God, while at the same time God retains his otherness and mystery. With the Fathers, Newman holds "the great revealed principle [of] the incommunicable character and individuality of the Divine Essence".[42] Yet, we are able to share in the divine life through "participation"[43] by grace, whereas the Son shares in the life of the Father "*not by participating*, but *in* Himself".[44]

Newman's understanding of our participation in Christ also concurs with his consistent emphasis on growth and development. In his autobiography, the *Apologia Pro Vita Sua*, Newman wrote that Thomas Scott's maxim "growth the only evidence of life" served as a first principle in his thought since his undergraduate days at Oxford.[45] According to Newman, growth is a necessary characteristic of living, organic realities. Newman famously applied this characteristic to the Church's reception of revelation in history in his *Essay on the Development of Christian Doctrine*. In this work, Newman proposed that divine revelation is an "idea" received by the "mind of the Church". Like other ideas, the Church must continue to grow or develop in her understanding of revelation if she is to remain a living reality. This development sometimes results in "new" doctrinal definitions, which are only new in the sense that the Church has not previously defined them. They are not new revelations.[46]

Some think Newman's emphasis on organic growth was a fruit of the Enlightenment or Romanticism, as well as of the theory of evolution.[47] Others hold that "we can affirm without hesitation that

[41] Newman, *Parochial and Plain Sermons*, 2:222; 3:267.

[42] Newman, *Arians of the Fourth Century*, 189.

[43] See Newman, *Selected Treatises of St. Athanasius*, 2:40, 88, 424–25.

[44] Ibid., 2:40 (emphasis in original).

[45] Newman, *Apologia*, 26. Thomas Scott (1747–1821) was a famous preacher and convert from Unitarianism to Calvinist Christianity and is most known for his autobiography—*The Force of Truth*—and his commentaries on the Bible (see *Apologia*, 521, n. 16).

[46] See Newman, *Essay on the Development*, 3–75. Against the charge that Newman's theory promotes the idea of new revelation, see Ian Ker, "Newman's Theory—Development or Continuing Revelation?" in *Newman and Gladstone Centennial Essays*, ed. James D. Bastable (Dublin: Veritas Publications, 1978), 145–59.

[47] See Andrew Louth, "Is Development of Doctrine a Valid Category for Orthodox Theology?" in *Orthodoxy and Western Culture: A Collection of Essays Honoring Jaroslav Pelikan on His Eightieth Birthday*, ed. Valerie Hotchkiss and Patrick Henry (Crestwood, N.Y.: SVS Press, 2005), 45–63.

Newman derived the idea of development from no other source than his own mind."[48] But Newman's works also reveal a christological foundation to his emphasis on growth. He held the patristic belief that Christ progressively deified human nature throughout his entire life, and in support mentions the position of Saint Leo the Great, who "speaks of the whole course of redemption, i.e. incarnation, atonement, regeneration, justification, &c., as one sacrament, not drawing the line distinctly between the several agents, elements, or stages in it, but considering it to lie in the intercommunion of Christ's person and ours".[49] Christ's death and Resurrection were the crowning of this deification, rather than the isolated source of it.

Furthermore, Newman held that Christ continues this work of deification in history through the Church.[50] As both an Anglican and a Catholic, Newman had recourse to the organic, Pauline image of the Church as the true Body of Christ.[51] Newman even claims in a letter of 1846 that he was "the *first* writer to make *life the* mark of a true church".[52] As a sign of her life, the Body of Christ is progressively deified until the end of time. Newman's emphasis on the Church as the true Body of Christ shows that his Christocentrism implied a corresponding "ecclesiocentrism". As Andrew Louth recognizes, the members of the Oxford Movement held "that the doctrine of deification is essentially ecclesial, that it is through our life in the Church, through our participation in the sacraments, that we are deified".[53] Membership in the Body of Christ comes through

[48] H. A. Tristram, "J. A. Moehler et J. H. Newman et la renaissance catholique en Angleterre", *RSPhTh* 27 (1938): 196; quoted in Jan Walgrave, *Unfolding Revelation: The Nature of Doctrinal Development* (London: Hutchinson, 1972), 294.

[49] Newman, *Select Treatises of St. Athanasius*, 2:190. See also *Parochial and Plain Sermons*, 2:32: "Thus He came, selecting and setting apart for Himself the elements of body and soul; then, uniting them, to Himself from their first origin of existence, pervading them, hallowing them by His own Divinity, spiritualizing them, and filling them with light and purity, the while they continued to be human, and for a time mortal and exposed to infirmity. And, as they grew from day to day in their holy union, His Eternal Essence still was one with them, exalting them, acting in them, manifesting Itself through them, so that He was truly God and Man, One Person,—as we are soul and body, yet one man, so truly God and man are not two, but One Christ."

[50] See Newman, *Select Treatises of St. Athanasius*, 2:191.

[51] See Ker, "The Church as Communion", in Kerr and Merrigan, *Cambridge Companion*, 139.

[52] Newman, *Letters and Diaries*, 11:101; quoted in Nicholas Lash, *Newman on Development: The Search for an Explanation in History* (Shepherdstown, W.Va.: Patmos Press, 1975), 73 (emphasis in original).

[53] Louth, "Manhood into God", 75.

participation in the life of Christ, which is communicated through the sacraments. Newman specifies in his *Lectures on Justification* that "the Presence of Christ is ... first conveyed into us in Baptism, then more sacredly and mysteriously in the Eucharist", the regular celebration and reception of which continues the work of "reform[ing] and refashioning" the Church into Christ.[54]

Newman also held that growth is a necessary condition of each of the members of the Body of Christ. He writes, "The heart of every Christian ought to represent in miniature the Catholic Church, since one Spirit makes both the whole Church and every member of it to be His Temple."[55] Like the Church as a whole, each member must figuratively undergo Christ's progressive deification of our humanity: "Christ Himself vouchsafes to repeat in each of us in figure and mystery all that He did and suffered in the flesh. He is formed in us, born in us, suffers in us, rises again in us, lives in us.... We are ever receiving our birth, our justification, our renewal, ever dying to sin, ever rising to righteousness."[56] And, "in the life of a Saint, we have a microcosm, or whole work of God, a perfect work from beginning to end."[57] Newman wrote in his *Essay on Development* that "to live is to change, and to be perfect is to have changed often."[58] He truly felt that the Christian's life and salvation required continual growth in deification, on "being changed into his likeness from one degree of glory to another; for this comes from the Lord who is the Spirit" (2 Cor 3:18).[59]

According to Newman, the progressive growth and deification of the Church and its members involves both thought and life, word and deed, reason and faith. As George Dragas has also recognized, "This interrelationship of thought and life characteristic of Athanasius and of Patristic theology is impressively realised in Newman."[60] Usually, Newman's theory of doctrinal development is regarded as

[54] Newman, *Lectures on Justification*, 187, 193. Newman does not elaborate on the specific function of the sacrament of confirmation. He writes only that the Holy Spirit "communicates Himself... in another way in Confirmation" (Newman, *Letters and Diaries*, 6:80).

[55] Newman, *Sermons on Subjects of the Day*, 132.

[56] Newman, *Parochial and Plain Sermons*, 5:139.

[57] Newman, *Letters and Diaries*, 12:399.

[58] Newman, *Essay on the Development*, 40.

[59] This passage is the starting point of Newman's sermon "The Gift of the Spirit" (*Parochial and Plain Sermons*, 3:254–70).

[60] George Dragas, "Conscience and Tradition: Newman and Athanasios in the Greek-Orthodox Church", *Newman Studien* 11 (1980): 78.

something that principally takes place on the intellectual plane of the Church's life, where new doctrines come to be defined as a result of rational reflection on Christian revelation.

Indeed, Newman says as much. In the *Grammar of Assent*, Newman makes a famous distinction between "real" and "notional" knowledge, where the "real" refers to that which we know through personal experience, and the "notional" that which we know through rationally reflecting on that experience. In regard to the Catholic faith, real knowledge corresponds to our relationship with God and our participation in the life of Christ through his Church, whereas notional knowledge corresponds to our reflection on God: his revelation and our relationship with him. According to Newman, it is principally through this notional reflection on God that our knowledge of him develops.[61]

But Newman also maintained that real and notional knowledge must cooperate with one another if religion is to thrive. Without notional knowledge of God, writes Newman, "we should for ever [*sic*] pace round one small circle of knowledge." The Church would never refine her knowledge of God's revelation, would never be able to respond to new historical problems that present themselves, and would merely repeat the formulas of the past. Without real knowledge of God, however, "we shall waste ourselves in vague speculations", as so often happens today in those increasingly abstract reflections on religion that take place in secular academia. A purely notional theology is really no theology at all, since it becomes divorced from the object of theology, which is participation in the divine life. Newman implies that the Church's deification requires a growth in both real and notional knowledge.[62]

This growth in real and notional knowledge is a condition of deification not only for the Church as a whole, but also for each of her members. "Every religious man is to a certain extent a theologian", writes Newman, since all possess a reasoning intellect through which

[61] See Newman, *Grammar of Assent*, 47.

[62] Ibid. According to Friedrich von Hügel, Newman thought the greatest weakness of his *Grammar* was its lack of a test to distinguish between true and false certitudes (Ronald K. Brown, "Newman and von Hügel: A Record of an Early Meeting", *The Month* 212 [1961]: 28). However, I believe its greatest weakness to be that Newman did not further draw out the link between real and notional knowledge.

they come to understand revelation.[63] A reasoned reflection on revelation is part of each Christian's deification, as illustrated by the example of Mary, who "kept all these things, pondering them in her heart" (Lk 2:19). Newman sees a lesson in this passage for all Christians, as Mary "does not think it enough to accept [Divine Truth], she dwells upon it; not enough to possess, she uses it; not enough to assent, she developes [*sic*] it; not enough to submit the Reason, she reasons upon it."[64]

At the same time, each Christian must cultivate his "real knowledge" of God through his actions, for "life is for action",[65] and those "who cultivate the intellect without disciplining the heart" do not truly know God.[66] The divorce of thought from life (the life in Christ) was the very essence of rationalism for Newman. Instead, according to Newman, Christians must proceed in their deification with both "clear heads and holy hearts".[67] Development of doctrine requires the Church and her members to grow in both their real *and* notional knowledge of God. It is not an exaggeration, then, to say that "development of doctrine" is really for Newman a description of the Christian path of deification.[68]

Newman's emphasis on life as crucial to the Christian's, and the Church's, deification is most impressively on display in his *Parochial and Plain Sermons*, written and delivered as an Anglican. In these sermons, Newman sought to recover some of the patristic ascetical

[63] Newman, *Grammar of Assent*, 93.

[64] Newman, *Oxford University Sermons*, 313.

[65] Newman, *Discussions and Arguments*, 295.

[66] Newman, *Parochial and Plain Sermons*, 1:316–17.

[67] Newman, *Lectures on the Prophetical Office of the Church*, 1:lxxv. Terrence Merrigan uses this phrase for the title of his book—*Clear Heads and Holy Hearts: The Religious and Theological Ideal of John Henry Newman* (Louvain: Peeters Press, 1992)—which is perhaps the best systematic treatment of Newman's thought.

[68] George Dragas has also seen this implication in Newman's theory of doctrinal development: "Newman developed catholically and believed in catholic development.... Christians are catholics *in via*, in development and growth. They seek to integrate themselves with the whole world, because they know that all belongs to Him who makes, redeems from sin and gives the gift of eternal and blessed life. Christians know that He is constantly coming to make them whole in His wholeness and integrate the world with catholicity. This is what Newman has bequeathed to the modern Roman Church and through her to all the Christian churches everywhere—the catholic truth of the Risen Lord with all its implications for Christian life and growth in history" ("John Henry Newman: A Starting-Point for Rediscovering the Catholicity of the Fathers Today", *Greek Orthodox Theological Review* 25 [1980]: 281–82).

spirit that had "well-nigh faded away out of the land [of England]".[69] Fasting was among those ascetical practices that Newman frequently preached to his Anglican hearers, wishing to subject them, as he wrote in an 1835 letter, to "a continual Ash-wednesday".[70] According to Newman, fasting was one of those forms of self-denial needed in post-lapsarian times "to unlearn the love of this world" so that we may "learn to love things which we do not naturally love". Love of God cannot be gained "without a vigorous struggle, a persevering warfare against ourselves".[71] Newman undertook this struggle himself as indicated by the detailed notes he kept of his fasting in his diaries.[72]

Newman also sought to recover the ascetical practice of "watchfulness", "inner vigilance", or, as it is known in Greek, *nepsis*. The practice derives from Christ's repeated admonition in the Gospels to "watch" for his Second Coming. It involves maintaining a constant state of spiritual vigilance within—immediately cutting off the appearance of sinful passions—so that one may be prepared for Christ's coming without, either upon death or at the *eschaton*. The very first sermon Newman ever preached was on the subject of watchfulness, and it, like fasting, was a recurrent theme in his Anglican sermons.[73] He describes watchfulness as follows: "This then is to watch; to be detached from what is present, and to live in what is unseen; to live in the thought of Christ as He came once, and as He will come again; to desire His second coming, from our affectionate and grateful remembrance of His first." This "living in the thought of Christ", writes Newman, "cannot be acquired without much and constant vigilance, generally not without much pain and trouble."[74]

[69] Newman, *Apologia*, 57.

[70] Newman, *Letters and Diaries*, 7:417. For more on Newman's preaching of fasting, see my essays, "Newman's Theology and Practice of Fasting as an Anglican", *Newman Studies Journal* 5:2 (Fall 2008): 56–68, and "Newman's Silence on Fasting as a Roman Catholic", *Newman Studies Journal* 6:2 (Fall 2009): 38–48.

[71] Newman, *Parochial and Plain Sermons*, 7:86.

[72] See Newman, *Autobiographical Writings*, ed. Henry Tristram (New York: Sheed and Ward, 1957).

[73] Newman's first sermon is entitled "Waiting for the Lord" and was preached on June 23, 1824. See *John Henry Newman Sermons 1824–1843*, vol. 5, *Sermons Preached at St. Clement's, Oxford: 1824–1826 and Two Charity Sermons: 1827*, ed. Francis McGrath (Oxford: Oxford University Press, 2012), 5–16.

[74] Newman, *Parochial and Plain Sermons*, 1:75; 4:325.

For Newman, the principal motivation for these ascetical practices, and for living a moral life in general, was the divine indwelling that the Christian possessed. Modern Christian ethics has been plagued by a deontological impetus since the time of Kant, which primarily conceives of morality as following rules whose justification lies outside of the Christian faith.[75] Again, for Newman, such a conception of morality is a form of rationalism, "being nothing less than the attempt to subject Scripture to a previously-formed system".[76] Newman, however, is more consonant with the Church Fathers in maintaining that the Christian acts a certain way primarily because of the deifying gift he was given in baptism. The Christian holds within himself the very "Divine Shechinah", so much so "that in one sense He can be worshipped in us as being His temple or shrine."[77] According to Newman, it is this doctrine, rather than any generalized emphasis "on our responsibilities and duties", that "makes us more watchful and more obedient, while it comforts and elevates us".[78] Moreover, it takes the focus away from ourselves and directs it toward Christ, whose indwelling is the true foundation of the Christian's moral life.

Conclusion

Among Christians, the renewed interest in deification seems to hold ecumenical hope. For over a century, Roman Catholics have been engaged in a *ressourcement*—a "return to the sources" of the Christian faith represented by the writings of the Church Fathers. As the narrative goes, the West lost contact with some of these sources as time passed, and elements of their theologies went underemphasized. In particular, the West has sought a reengagement with the thought of the Eastern Church Fathers. This reengagement with the East is most famously represented in the work of Roman Catholic theologians Yves Congar, Louis Bouyer, Jean Daniélou, Henri de Lubac, and Hans Urs von Balthasar, and has been reiterated recently in *Orientale*

[75] See especially Alasdair MacIntyre, *After Virtue: A Study in Moral Theory* (Notre Dame, Ind.: University of Notre Dame Press, 1981).

[76] Newman, *Lectures on Justification*, 117.

[77] Newman, *Select Treatises of St. Athanasius*, 2:88.

[78] Newman, *Lectures on Justification*, 190.

lumen's call for Catholics "to deepen their knowledge of the spiritual traditions of the Fathers and Doctors of the Christian East".[79]

The East has also returned to its sources through what is commonly referred to as a "Neo-patristic synthesis"—a term and call initiated by Georges Florovsky. For the most part, it has involved a recovery of Eastern patristic sources, but is increasingly re-receiving Western authors.[80] It is hoped that this Eastern turn in the West, and perhaps vice versa, will result in healing the breach of 1054 through a gradual recovery of the (supposedly) unified mind of the first millennium. Then the Church, according to the well-known metaphor of Vyacheslav Ivanov, can once again "breathe with both lungs".

The renewed emphasis on deification is one of the first fruits of these recovery efforts, and serves a symbolic role because of its centrality in the Christian system of doctrine. Hence, one of the purposes of this present volume is to show that Roman Catholic theology has always affirmed the idea of deification, even if the doctrine was not always formally emphasized. John Henry Newman was both a forerunner and catalyst of the modern *ressourcement* movement in the West, which makes his understanding of deification particularly significant. Like the Fathers, he was a "prophet of great truths" who returned to the Eastern Fathers of the Church before it was en vogue.[81] His appropriation of the Eastern Fathers, and the centrality of deification in their thought, led him to the Roman Catholic Church, which he saw as "the nearest approximation in fact to the Church of the Fathers".[82] The Eastern character of Newman's thought began to influence the shape of Catholic theology in the years leading up to the Second Vatican Council, leading some to term Newman the "Father of the Second Vatican Council".

But the ecumenical value of Newman's recourse to deification goes even deeper. As he demonstrated in his own life, the indwelling of Christ was not only a doctrine for Christians to affirm, but the

[79] Pope John Paul II, Apostolic Letter *Orientale lumen*, May 2, 1995, no. 24.

[80] Two recent examples of this renewed Eastern reception of Western sources are *Orthodox Readings of Augustine*, ed. George Demacopolous and Aristotle Papanikolaou (Crestwood, N.Y.: SVS Press, 2008), and Marcus Plested's *Orthodox Readings of Aquinas* (Oxford: Oxford University Press, 2012).

[81] Newman, *Essays Critical and Historical*, 2:371.

[82] Newman, *Essay on the Development*, 97.

very principle of their life, thought, and action. No one has recognized this as well as George Dragas. He showed that Newman's thought was patristic primarily because he sought to "appropriate the vision and mind of the Orthodox Fathers", which was rooted in their shared participation in Christ's life.[83] Such was the true goal of the Oxford Movement and is the true meaning of what is variously referred to as *ressourcement* and "Neo-patristic synthesis".[84] It cuts across the distinction between East and West. Furthermore, Dragas writes, "Newman like Athanasius demonstrates (*contra mundum*) that the real appropriation of the catholic conscience in every single person in The Church is the basis for the historical solution of schism and heresy."[85] What Newman teaches us, too, is that the reunion of Christians will depend upon each of them living out and developing his union with Christ.

Readings for Further Study

Dessain, Charles. "Cardinal Newman and the Doctrine of Uncreated Grace". *Clergy Review* 47 (1962): 207–25, 269–88.

______. "Cardinal Newman and the Eastern Tradition". *Downside Review* 94 (1976): 83–98.

Dragas, George. "Conscience and Tradition: Newman and Athanasios in the Greek-Orthodox Church". *Newman Studien* 11 (1980): 73–84.

Louth, Andrew. "Manhood into God: The Oxford Movement, the Fathers and the Deification of Man". In *Essays Catholic and Radical*, edited by Kenneth Leech and Rowan D. Williams, 70–80. London: Bowerdean Press, 1983.

[83] Dragas, "Conscience and Tradition", 74.

[84] See also Louth, "Manhood into God", 79: "In the Oxford Movement we could indeed say that we find not so much recourse to the Fathers, as a rediscovery of the patristic tradition, in that in the lives and writings of those whom we may well call the Oxford Fathers we rediscover that 'immediacy of contact with spiritual realities,' which is the hallmark of the Fathers."

[85] Dragas, "Conscience and Tradition", 79. Dragas here is influenced by Georges Florovsky, whose call for a "Neo-patristic synthesis" was precisely a call for a return to the "existential theology" of the Fathers (see Florovsky, "Patristic Theology and the Ethos of the Orthodox Church").

Chapter Eleven

"AN ACTIVITY OF SPECIAL, SUPERNATURAL, AND EXTRAORDINARY BENEFICENCE AND LOVE": MATTHIAS SCHEEBEN'S THEOLOGY OF DEIFICATION

Timothy Kelly

One of the great Catholic minds to have illumined the mystery of Christian deification belonged to a great but relatively unappreciated Rhineland theologian: Matthias Joseph Scheeben (1835–1888). His particular theological vocation, shaped by both the challenges of the nineteenth century as well as his own native skills and character, equipped him to this theme certainly more than any other theologian since Saint Thomas Aquinas, and probably since the patristic era. Scheeben's most recent commentator has described him as, "*above all*", a theologian "of human deification".[1] But his special interest in the elevating and deifying effects of sanctifying grace was not an independent curiosity, but one of the most prized fruits of the dominant theme of all Scheeben's theology: the supernatural character of Christianity. This preoccupation with the supernatural order—"the leading idea of his life"[2]—is a feature shared by Scheeben's neo-Scholastic contemporaries. But Scheeben's place in that era is unique, his theological status incontestably higher than any of that distinguished generation, and his theology of deification correspondingly luminous and distinctive.

How Scheeben relates to his time, and the important formative and methodological differences between him and his theological mentors

[1] Aidan Nichols, O.P., *Romance and System: The Theological Synthesis of Matthias Joseph Scheeben* (Denver: Augustine Institute, 2010), 287 (emphasis added).

[2] Cyril Vollert, S.J., "Matthias Joseph Scheeben and the Revival of Theology", *Theological Studies* 6 (1945): 461.

and peers, is a good place to start in order to appreciate this distinctiveness of his treatment of deification. If he is placed among the neo-Thomists of the late nineteenth century, then he was, unquestionably, "the fairest flower of the spring of Neo-Scholasticism",[3] but he goes beyond the movement too; as another put it, "Like a brilliantly-hued spring blossom he grows above all the great theologians of his century."[4] Martin Grabmann considered him to be "the greatest dogmatic theologian of the nineteenth century"[5] and his *Mysteries of Christianity* a "masterpiece of independent creative genius".[6] Michael Schmaus regarded that same work an "immortal, monumental masterpiece" and "scarcely surpassable",[7] while no less than Pope Pius XI proclaimed Scheeben "a man of genius".[8] It is hardly surprising, then, that the victory of the sense of the supernatural over Enlightenment naturalism and rationalism is identified with Scheeben more than with any neo-Scholastic theologian. His "greatest contribution to neo-scholasticism", writes one commentator, lies in his "bringing the supernatural, in all its purity and beauty, back to the center of theological thought".[9] If neo-Scholasticism represents a revival of theology as the science of the supernatural, in Scheeben a climax is reached: "The ascent from the icy regions of rationalism ... is at length reached with Scheeben."[10]

But Scheeben, like all the great theologians, cannot be explained in terms of a "school", or even classified in any one. Like his master Saint Thomas Aquinas, a deep and broad catholicity characterizes his theological work. He was "at home with the Councils, Scripture, the Fathers, the Scholastics—in a word, with the whole Christian tradition".[11] As Grabmann writes admiringly, "I am aware of no

[3] Karl Eschweiler, *Die zwei Wege der neueren Theologie* (Augsburg: Benno Filser, 1926), 25.

[4] H.J. Brosch, "Das Werden des Jungen M.J. Scheeben", *Stimmen der Zeit* 123 (1932): 395.

[5] Martin Grabmann, "Theological Synthesis", in W. Meyer et al., *The Pastoral Care of Souls* (Saint Louis: Herder, 1944), 97.

[6] Ibid., 94.

[7] Michael Schmaus, "Die Stellung M.J. Scheebens in der Theologie des 19. Jahrhunderts", in *Matthias Joseph Scheeben, der Erneuerer katholischer Glaubenswissenschaft* (Mainz: Matthias Grünewald, 1935), 38.

[8] Reported in *L'Osservatore Romano*, March 11–12, 1935.

[9] Vollert, "Scheeben and the Revival of Theology", 473.

[10] Brosch, "Das Werden des Jungen M.J. Scheeben", 395.

[11] Vollert, "Scheeben and the Revival of Theology", 479.

theologian of modern times who possesses so extensive a knowledge of the whole theological tradition as Scheeben."[12] How does one explain this?

He both was, and was not, a typical product of the Roman theology of the 1850s. As a student of such neo-Scholastic theologians as Joseph Kleutgen,[13] Clemens Schraader, and Johann Baptist Franzelin, Scheeben was amply exposed to the Thomistic revival of mid-nineteenth-century Rome,[14] and always celebrated it.[15] Yet, this was a formation not entirely neo-Scholastic in spirit, for he was also drawn to the patristic leanings of Carlo Passaglia, and to the theological method of Giovanni Perrone, whose particular aspiration was, like Scheeben's would later be, "to arrange biblical, scholastic, and patristic approaches into a synthesis".[16] Though Scheeben was principally a disciple of Thomas, and championed the revival of his doctrine, it is said that he thought "like no other neo-scholastic".[17]

[12] Martin Grabmann, "Matthias Joseph Scheebens Auffassung vom Wesen und Wert der theologischen Wissenschaft", in *Matthias Joseph Scheeben, der Erneuerer katholischer*, 58.

[13] Kleutgen (1811–1883) never taught Scheeben formally, though certainly influenced him by his work and his correspondence. "Kleutgen was not a teacher of Scheeben—he was never professor at the Gregorianum—but [Kleutgen's] *Theologie der Vorzeit* was a guide for the young Scheeben, and later the theologian used it as a resource" (H. Schauf, "Vorwort", to Scheeben, *Handbuch der katholischen Dogmatik* 6 [Freiburg: Herder, 1957], xv). For the correspondence between them, see E. Paul, *Denkweg und Denkform der Theologie von Matthias Joseph Scheeben* (Munich: M. Hueber, 1970), 8ff.

[14] For more on Scheeben's Roman formation, see A. Kerkvoorde, "La formation théologique de M.J. Scheeben à Rome (1852–1859)", *Ephemerides theologicae Lovanienses* 22 (1946): 174ff.; H.J. Brosch, "Das Werden des jungen M.J. Scheeben", *Stimmen der Zeit* 123 (1932): 395ff. On this "Roman School" in general, see W. Kasper, *Die Lehre von der Tradition in der Römischen Schule* (Freiburg: Herder, 1962).

[15] As Scheeben wrote, "Kleutgen was the first who twelve years ago undertook to rehabilitate scientifically the 'Theology and Philosophy of the Past' which had been neglected for a century. He did it with a vast and profound erudition, with clarity and peace.... No one will brand the author with the slogan 'neoscholastic' as a member of a dark and closed direction, for Kleutgen showed that he stands on the height of our age and knows its ideas and performances well—he does not want a repristination but a regeneration" (*Literarischer Handweiser* 28 [1864]: 323). Translation provided by T.F. O'Meara, O.P., in *Church and Culture: German Catholic Theology, 1860–1914* (Notre Dame, Ind.: University of Notre Dame Press, 1991), 222.

[16] See O'Meara, *Church and Culture: German Catholic Theology*, 53. As Vollert writes, "He tried to bring together in the focus of his own mind the beams of light emanating from the most brilliant theologians of the patristic, medieval, and modern eras" ("Scheeben and the Revival of Theology", 471).

[17] K. Eschweiler, *Die zwei Wege der neueren Theologie: G. Hermes—M.J. Scheeben* (Augsburg: Verlegt bei Benno Filser, 1926), 183. Kleutgen himself was troubled by Scheeben's unconventional brand of Thomism, insisting "it will confuse more heads than it will illumine"

There are two features of his work that account for this independence. The first concerns Scheeben's adherence to the actual writings of Thomas rather than to any subsequent commentarial tradition, and the second concerns the enormous influence of the Fathers, who were said to "live anew in him".[18] Regarding the former characteristic, one might describe Scheeben as a *ressourcement* Thomist, for his intention was always to "reach back to theological sources, to pass beyond scholasticism to Thomas Aquinas" himself.[19] Consequently, he "did not come to Aquinas through Suarez, Molina, De Lugo, or Bañez" but sought to engage with Thomas directly, acquiring "a broad knowledge of Aquinas' [actual] writings".[20] As Vollert put it simply, "he desired to know Thomas through St Thomas himself."[21] Allied to his esteem for the Fathers (Athanasius and Saint Cyril of Alexandria in particular) what emerged from this was not only a Thomism forged through close adherence to Thomas' writings, but a Thomism contrived "in the spirit of the Greek Fathers",[22] in the spirit therefore of Thomas' own theological sources. Scheeben's acquaintance with the Fathers is not merely competent for a Thomist but "astonishes all who read him",[23] allowing him to be considered both "a scholastic *and* a patristic theologian",[24] and in some senses he "invites comparison with the Fathers rather than with the Scholastics".[25] So, though indisputability a disciple of Saint Thomas, he nevertheless eludes the easy categories, winning acclaim and sympathy from theologians as diverse as Réginald Garrigou-Lagrange and Hans Urs von Balthasar.[26] This patristic-Scholasticism is what lends Scheeben's Thomism such vibrancy and freshness, as though in him

(J. Kleutgen, *Briefe aus Rom* [Münster: Verlag Theissing, 1865], 130ff. [Sept. 4, 1892]) and, with his fellow neo-Scholastic Franzelin, he ultimately advised the Roman Curia against recommending his *Handbuch der katholischen Dogmatik* (See H. Schauf, A. Eröss, *M.J. Scheeben, Briefe nach Rom* [Freiburg: Herder, 1939], 132. See also Paul, *Denkweg und Denkform*, 32ff.).

[18] Brosch, "Werden des jungen M.J. Scheeben", 404.

[19] O'Meara, *Church and Culture: German Catholic Theology*, 54.

[20] Ibid., 55.

[21] Vollert, "Scheeben and the Revival of Theology", 468.

[22] Hans Urs von Balthasar, *The Glory of the Lord, A Theological Aesthetics*, vol. 1, *Seeing the Form*, trans. Erasmo Leiva-Merikakis (San Francisco: Ignatius Press, 1998), 116.

[23] Vollert, "Scheeben and the Revival of Theology", 468.

[24] O'Meara, *Church and Culture: German Catholic Theology*, 54 (emphasis in original).

[25] Vollert, "Scheeben and the Revival of Theology", 468.

[26] See Nichols, *Romance and System*, 19.

"changeless Scholasticism had won a new form."[27] Such splendid catholicity of theological influences shapes and determines his theology of deification in important ways. Let us see how.

Christ and the Christian: "One Single Son of the Father in the Son and with the Son"

The first observation we wish to make about Scheeben's treatment of Christian deification is a general one, but it allows us to illustrate the points we have been making about the range of his theological sources, and it also serves to make clear his fundamental understanding of what the process of deification involves. When reading Scheeben on the effects of sanctifying grace, the reader is immediately struck by our author's combination of lofty, audacious terminology and metaphysical care. The former characteristic owes itself to Scheeben's fidelity to the Fathers, and the manner in which they articulated doctrine, whilst the latter is a consequence of Scheeben's debt to Saint Thomas. We can see this in a number of ways. First of all, Scheeben's theology of deification is built upon the great Pauline and patristic axiom of the *admirabile commercium*, the "wonderful exchange" of divine riches and human poverty established at the Incarnation (cf. 2 Cor 8:9). The Fathers' consistent assertion that "God has become man so that man might become gods" is repeated, asserted, and reasserted by Scheeben to such an extent that the reader is left in no doubt as to the seriousness with which this disconcerting doctrine is to be understood.[28] If the divinising effects which this maxim implies were understood as a pious, devotional metaphor, an excusable but metaphysically unintelligible exaggeration found within ancient homiletic Christian literature,[29] not only would

[27] Brosch, "Werden des jungen M.J. Scheeben", 404.

[28] On the doctrine of the *admirabile commercium*, Scheeben lists dozens of patristic citations. See *The Mysteries of Christianity*, trans. Cyril Vollert, S.J. (Saint Louis: Herder, 1951), 378–82.

[29] The rationalists who deny the communication of the divine nature to man, writes Scheeben, "regard the beautiful expressions and teachings of Sacred Scripture [on our divine sonship] as exaggerations and vivid figures" (*Nature and Grace*, trans. Cyril Vollert, S.J. [Saint Louis: Herder, 1954], 117). In their hands, "all the noble and exalted teaching of the Fathers and Scripture degenerates into a pretentious bombast that has little or no meaning" (ibid., 136).

we be gravely underestimating and misunderstanding the nature and extent of Christian sanctification, thinks Scheeben, but we would miss the entire reason for the Incarnation. "For if the Son of God becomes man," insists Scheeben, "He does so only for the purpose of deifying man."[30]

But in what does this "deifying" consist? According to Scheeben, we gain some first indication of the meaning and extent of this sanctifying process by the scriptural application of the term "Son of God" not only to Christ, but also to the Christian (1 Jn 3:1; Eph 1:5; Rom 8:19). As it is for the Fathers, Scheeben sees a very precise ontological category indicated by the term "son", a category which sinners supernaturally reborn in time truly share with the eternally and only begotten One.[31] According to Scheeben, the Christian sonship of which Scripture speaks, and which the Fathers expound, is not meant, he says, "by simple analogy or resemblance" with the eternal Sonship of the second Person of the Trinity, but in "literal truth".[32] This is an astonishing claim. By "literal truth", Scheeben does not mean to abolish the personal distinction between the natural Son of the Father and the adoptive sons of God, but rather to emphasise the point that the predication "son of God" for the Christian is, somehow, warranted ontologically. Our sonship is not meant, he insists, "in some vague way",[33] but insofar as "the most important relations existing between a son and a father are present in our relations of sonship to God."[34]

Above all else, this involves the real imparting of the divine nature to man—a finite communication of that same nature infinitely communicated to the eternal Son. Now, if the Son is one with the Father (cf. Jn 10:30), he is so "because He has the same nature" as he; likewise, insists Scheeben, "we too are one with God, like Him and conformable to Him in nature", because we "receive, so to speak,

[30] Scheeben, *Mysteries*, 378 (emphasis added).

[31] On this, see Scheeben, *Nature and Grace*, 116–49.

[32] Scheeben, *Mysteries*, 383. Scheeben consistently adjusts his language for the sake of emphasis. Elsewhere, for example, he moderates his words on this question: as he says, "grace confers on [man] only an analogous, not a literal, relationship of son to the Father" (ibid., 397).

[33] Scheeben, *Nature and Grace*, 117.

[34] Ibid., 149.

the same nature, to the extent that we are capable of it".[35] Moreover, this is a new, divinely filial status, neither extrinsically realised nor imputed by decree, but procured by means of the real communication of a new life, effecting in the sinner's very essence "a new internal goodness and beauty".[36]And though the Fathers speak of an "adoption", they mean by this no "mere juridical adoption",[37] for what is communicated to us is a "new existence and life by an act that implies a kind of generation".[38]

But recognising the infinite differences between the two cases is vital if we are to understand the extent of the sanctified creature's privileges. Whilst the Son possesses the "fullness of the divine nature substantially and in numerical identity", the Christian does not, and cannot, possess the divine nature in this way, "but only participate in it".[39] Furthermore, in this elevation to divine sonship, the Christian does not, of course, become God, but remains who he is; though he has undergone a true, supernatural regeneration,[40] he remains himself—what has been communicated is not a new "substance but a new quality, modifying his own substance".[41] The divine nature exists in the sanctified soul not to replace or abolish it but, rather, to elevate it, to ennoble it supernaturally and enrich it.

Scheeben show us, then, that to speak of the divine "sonship" of the Christian involves neither a "sacrilegious encroachment"[42] on the unique privileges of the natural Son, nor any "pretentious

[35] Ibid., 134.

[36] Ibid., 127.

[37] Ibid., 131. Scheeben makes the point that adoption by God "differs greatly from adoption among men. When we are adopted by God we are not only called but actually are His children. We are not only morally elevated but in a certain sense are reborn and receive a kind of new nature and new life. We acquire not only an external right to an inheritance, but are interiorly equipped and empowered to receive it, since the inheritance does not consist in external goods but is a most exalted life of knowledge and love of God" (ibid., 126).

[38] Ibid., 131. Scheeben seeks, in his words, "to verify the analogy of generation as fully as possible" (ibid., 128). As he explains, for "generation, in effect, is the origin of a living being from a living being in similarity and likeness of nature" (*generatio est origo viventis a vivente in similitudinem naturae*). Scheeben goes on to show how this is realized in the case of Christian sanctification. See ibid., 128–31.

[39] Ibid., 127.

[40] Ibid., 128.

[41] Ibid., 130.

[42] Ibid., 123.

bombast",[43] nor the "exaggerations" of pious metaphor.[44] What the Spirit of the Son effects in us is, in Cyril's words, a "participation in the true Son",[45] causing there to be, Scheeben puts it, "something of the natural sonship of Christ" in us.[46] As he repeats with the Fathers, we become by grace what the Son is by nature, and hence we are invited to call "the Father of the Word *our* Father" not because, in the domain of love, we are permitted a degree of exaggeration, but because "in actual fact He is such."[47] Through considering this status of sonship we can come to an understanding of what deification involves, thinks Scheeben. Let us proceed, then, to consider how Scheeben understands this trinitarian basis of the mystery.

The Divine Processions: The "Basis of Possibility" for Deification

According to our author, the chief motivating factor behind God's revelation of his inner life, the disclosure of the hidden names and relations of the Divine Persons, was, paradoxically, to reveal something about us. "Nothing is truer than this," he insists, and "we need feel no misgiving in maintaining [it]."[48] The revelation of the Blessed Trinity has "for its very purpose", Scheeben says, our own enlightenment concerning our supernatural relationship to Him.[49] By admitting man into a certain knowledge of the mystery of the Father's eternal generation of the Son and their own eternal spiration of the Holy Spirit, God reveals the coherence and intelligibility of the related mystery of Christian sanctification, man's own filial adoption and deification. By nature we did not know the Father and, indeed,

[43] Ibid., 136.

[44] Ibid., 117.

[45] Scheeben, *Mysteries*, 380.

[46] Ibid., 383. "What the Father's love has destined for us and the Son's love has gained for us, is applied to us by the Holy Spirit ;.. by Him the Father has raised us to the condition of His adopted children; and therefore He is called pre-eminently the Spirit of sonship (the Spirit of the Son is also the Spirit of the adoption of sons)" (Scheeben, *Nature and Grace*, 125).

[47] Scheeben, *Mysteries*, 383.

[48] Ibid., 142.

[49] Ibid.

could not know him, "because He dwells in inaccessible light".[50] Indeed, before Christ, we had no idea of a *Father* in the "proper and higher sense of the term", and therefore had no notion "that we ourselves could be made children of God in a proper sense and thus see Him face to face".[51] The revelation of the Trinity changes this for us. In Scheeben's view this supreme dogma of the faith is not only the root of deification, but also the "key to the understanding of our elevation",[52] that which "helps us to understand it".[53]

Now the first feature of the intra-trinitarian life that strikes Scheeben as pertinent to the doctrine of deification lies in the beautiful and humanly resonant notion of loving donation; in the Father's generation of the Son, he appears to us in the "absolute surrender and communication of His entire essence".[54] Like Bonaventure before him,[55] Scheeben pauses to admire the splendour of this revelation. We see here that God is good not only because he possesses infinite goods, "but that He is good, infinitely good, in the complete *communication* of His goods",[56] the "communication of His infinity".[57] When we glimpse this perfect "generosity" of the Father to the Son, this immanent, boundless donation within the mystery of God himself, the other, created mystery of God's gift to the creature in the communication of the divine nature seems no less wondrous and gratuitous, but certainly less inexplicable and baffling. Without the revelation of eternal Paternity and Filiation within God, the notion of adoptive filiation would be entirely unaccountable and, in Scheeben's view, wholly lacking in any intelligible motive on God's part. The incarnate Son reveals the mystery of divine Paternity and Filiation not primarily in order to subject our humble minds to a divine truth beyond our comprehension, but "to let us know that we too are His children who are to share in His fatherly love, and are called, like the Son, to see the Father face to face".[58] It is precisely

[50] Scheeben, *Nature and Grace*, 147.

[51] Ibid.

[52] Scheeben, *Mysteries*, 142.

[53] Ibid., 125.

[54] Ibid., 128.

[55] Bonaventure, *Itinerarium mentis ad Deum* 5.

[56] Scheeben, *Mysteries*, 128 (emphasis added).

[57] Ibid., n. 3.

[58] Scheeben, *Nature and Grace*, 147.

this revelation of his immanent generative power (rather than his infinite creative power) that "enables us to apprehend that the generation of adoptive children is possible".[59] In the substantial communication of the divine nature from the Father to the other two Divine Persons, we see "the basis for the possibility",[60] the very "conceivability",[61] for the external communication of the divine nature to rational creatures.

The Internal Divine Processions: "The Two-Branched Root of Christian Deification"

So, if Christians are called "sons" and the Father's adopted children (cf. 1 Jn 3:1; Gal 4:4), it is only by way of allusion to the divine Son himself, "the ideal to which we are to be conformed through adoption by God in grace".[62] Scheeben reminds us of one of the core anti-Arian arguments of Athanasius and the Cappadocian Fathers, who argue for the divinity of the Son from the deification of the creature. In other words, the very notion of adoptive filiation is not a random or disconnected revelation of God, but "presupposes natural Sonship".[63] Without the eternally begotten Son of the Father being somehow "present to our minds", we could not "properly regard ourselves as adoptive children of God" at all.[64] It would mean overlooking the very archetype that provides the revelation of adoptive sonship with its natural and metaphysical basis, and by which we glimpse the intelligibility and possibility of "further" sonships. The

[59] Scheeben, *Mysteries*, 142. Scheeben compares what he calls the "accountability" or "basis" of our lives in the orders of nature and grace in this way: "We discover the basis for the possibility, the exemplar, and the motive of our existence in the sole fact that God is being itself, that He is infinite being. God can give existence to finite beings because He is being itself.... [But] God's power to communicate His nature externally and to beget children of grace is conceived by us not on the ground of His creative power, but as correlative to the infinite generative power by which He communicates His nature substantially and begets a Son equal to Himself" (ibid.).

[60] Ibid., 141.

[61] Ibid., 144.

[62] Ibid., 142.

[63] Ibid.

[64] Ibid.

scriptural revelation of Christians enjoying the status of "children of God" or "sons of the Father" necessarily points to an exemplar: the Father's own Son. This internal generation of the Son "provides us with the key", insists Scheeben, which opens for us an "understanding of our elevation" to adoptive sonship.[65]

But if our temporal adoption and regeneration as sons is rooted in the eternal generation of the Son, so it is necessarily rooted in the procession of the Holy Spirit. This is true, thinks Scheeben, not from the standpoint of *what* is effected (that is, adoptive sonship) but "of the *manner* in which it is effected".[66] If the eternal Son proceeds "by real generation" and "by way of natural necessity", adoptive sons participate in the divine nature only "through sheer love and grace".[67] It is in the giftedness and liberty of our sanctification that Scheeben perceives a vital likeness and symmetry between the eternal procession of the Holy Spirit and the Christian's temporal elevation to divine sonship in grace. In the Holy Spirit proceeding internally "by way of pure ... love and liberality", we see here, writes Scheeben, "the first, all-perfect, and innermost fruit of the self-communicating divine love".[68] It is precisely the "first" of many not because further Holy Spirits are to be spirated, but simply insofar as this eternal procession of the Spirit *per modum amoris* stands as the "seed and root" of all the subsequent communications of divine love, all "other fruits which God puts forth by way of His Love".[69] By the grace poured into a sinner's heart what is created is a new son, a true "son in the image of the eternal Son", but the *manner* of the process finds its eternal pattern and exemplar not especially in the Son's eternal generation but in the procession of the Spirit by way of "sheer love". It is the communication of the divine nature from the Father to the Son by generation which is to be reproduced in us as regenerated children of God, but this "can find its way" to man only in the "further communication of the same divine nature to the Holy Spirit by love".[70] If the procession of the Son is the exemplar which "determines the

[65] Ibid.
[66] Ibid., 143 (emphasis added).
[67] Ibid.
[68] Ibid.
[69] Ibid.
[70] Ibid., 144–45.

nature and conceivability" of the filial relationship we are to enter with God, the procession of the Holy Spirit is chiefly "the motive and standard which determines the *way* that relationship is realised".[71] By way of divine love, man is regenerated as a true son of God.

Deification and the Hypostatic Union

So the revelation of the Blessed Trinity is the vital source of light in our understanding of the communication of the divine nature to creatures; any external communication of this nature finds its basis in the hidden, internal divine processions of the Godhead. But this Life would not only be entirely unknowable, but also entirely unattainable, were it not for the coming into our world of the Person of the Son. Indeed, the extension of the trinitarian communications to beings outside of God is made possible by the Son's assumption of a human nature into the unity of his Divine Person. In this "absolutely unique, supereminent union" of flesh and divinity, "the bearer and possessor of the divine nature becomes likewise the bearer and possessor of a human nature."[72] Two infinitely separated orders of being, the divine and the human, are here united "in one personal, hypostatic whole, without at the same time merging or fusing them into one nature".[73]

Importantly for our topic, the consequence for this human nature assumed "in the highest conceivable union with the divinity"[74] is not its dissolution into God, but its incalculable enrichment, its supreme "deification". Such a human nature must, "in a measure equalled by no other", participate in the nature of God. Scheeben enjoys describing the extent to which the assumed flesh is pervaded by the divine life with which it is personally united. As a finite human nature it can do no more than participate in the divinity, yet, still, this most privileged flesh is not only to be elevated above its natural condition by its union with it, but "must be pervaded, shot through, transfigured by it, vitalized by it, must be made conformable and

[71] Ibid., 144 (emphasis added).
[72] Ibid., 319.
[73] Ibid., 318.
[74] Ibid., 323.

like to it, must be fashioned in its image".[75] Though finite, visible, and palpable flesh, "the animating, spiritualizing, divinizing power of God dwells within it",[76] "hous[ing] within it the divine energy of life" (cf. Col 2:9).[77] Indeed, its perfect proximity to the uncreated source of holiness must result in its being supremely conformed to God, supremely deified. This "humanity which belongs to God", this "divine humanity", this "human nature of God's Son",[78] is a humanity "*worthy* of Him",[79] containing within it all the holiness that it is possible for a finite, created nature to possess, indeed "of all creatures combined";[80] it must be, insists Scheeben, "deified to the full capacity of its own condition".[81]

Human Nature: A Capacity for Deification

Before we come to consider how this relates to our own deification, it is worth observing what this reveals about the capacities of human nature in general, in relation to the active agency of God.[82] First of all, if it were not for the Incarnation, we might have suspected that humanity and divinity were discordant, or at least metaphysically incompatible, and hence ununitable, orders of being. But beholding the humanity of Christ "in the highest conceivable union with the divinity"[83] we are able, says Scheeben, to "discern in human nature a potency for union with God".[84] What we find at the Incarnation—namely, a union of a created human nature with God in person, and the resultant supernatural enhancement and ennobling of this nature—tells us that, by the divine power, human nature is both capable of being united to God and, consequently, capable of receiving,

[75] Ibid.

[76] Ibid., 513.

[77] Ibid., 514.

[78] Ibid.

[79] Ibid., 327 (emphasis added).

[80] Ibid., 324.

[81] Ibid., 323.

[82] Theologians refer to this as "obediential potency"—that is, a being's capacity to undergo a supernatural perfection (or miraculous change) that exceeds its natural capacities. It signals the being of an existing creature as obedient, subject, and even positively ordered to God's power to act in it. See *STh* III, q. 11, a. 1.

[83] Scheeben, *Mysteries*, 323.

[84] Ibid., 320. Here Scheeben follows Saint Thomas (*STh* III, q. 4, a. 1).

as Scheeben puts it, a higher supernatural "perfectibility". We learn, in other words, that becoming godlike is possible for mere flesh. Such an elevation is something we could not "in the remotest degree uncover or surmise" without God revealing it to us in Christ.[85]

Now such a disclosure about the possibilities for humble flesh is, once again, of supreme importance for the Christian life. The grace and glory of the sacred humanity of Christ tell us what glorious consequences follow upon human proximity to God, and the elevating—rather than supplanting—effects the supernatural order has upon human nature. But secondly, it also reveals what the divine Son wants to procure in us. For if this "absolutely unique, supereminent union" of human and divine natures in Christ effects not the abolition but the supreme ennobling and supernatural enrichment of his human nature, it is only for our good. "He did not receive sanctification for Himself."[86] The great condescension of the Son into our world and into our flesh is ordered to our own, relative elevation, and this is something the Son effects by means of this same, graced humanity.

The Sacred Humanity of the Son: The Deified Instrument of Deification

Just as we can begin to make sense of our adoptive sonship by means of the natural Sonship of Christ, so we can begin to understand

[85] Scheeben, *Mysteries*, 320. Furthermore, without such a deification of our human nature in mind, it is very difficult to make any sense of the supreme elevation of the human nature we find in Christ. Nothing else, it seems, stands in any intelligible proportion to it. As Scheeben writes, "Only the absolutely supernatural elevation of human nature to participation in the divine nature stands in proportion to the elevation of Christ's humanity to hypostatic union with the divine Word, as to its exemplary and efficient cause" (ibid., 502).

[86] Ibid., 381, n. 33. "Whatever Christ has, that becomes our portion, too. For He did not receive sanctification for Himself, seeing that He is the Sanctifier, but that He might acquire it for human nature; and so He becomes the channel and principle of the goods which have flowed into us. This is why He says: 'I am the Way,' that is, the way by which divine grace has come down to us, exalting and sanctifying and glorifying us, and thus deifying human nature" (Scheeben is quoting from Cyril of Alexandria, *Thesaurus de Sancta et Consubstantiali Trinitate* 20). As Cyril writes elsewhere, "Is it not clear to all that He lowered Himself to a menial condition not to gain anything for Himself by so doing, but to give us Himself, so that we, raised to His own inexhaustible wealth by our resemblance to Him, might be rich by His poverty, and be made gods and sons of God by faith?" (*In Ioan.*, lib. 1, c. 9, no. 24).

something of the supernatural elevation of our natures by considering the elevation of the assumed humanity of the Son.[87] Scheeben sees three ways in which the Son's human nature is elevated above its natural condition, a "threefold deification and sanctification",[88] that relate in important ways to our own. First of all, there is the hypostatic union itself, "whereby the humanity is deified as a nature belonging to God".[89] This is, of course, a wholly unique and incommunicable privilege, but from it emerges the second elevation, in which we are called to share: "springing from this [hypostatic] union and rooted in it come the transfiguration of the humanity and its assimilation to God by grace and glory, wherein it participates in the nature of the divinity".[90] Such participation, as well as our assimilation by grace and (eventual) glory, are privileges that our incarnate Lord intends us to have in common with him, with "due allowance being made for the difference between the two cases".[91] As Scheeben writes, "As the sacred humanity is itself transfigured, glorified, and in the highest measure made to participate in the divine nature by the power of the divinity, it conveys this same power to all men who are in union with it."[92] But what, precisely, allows for such privileges to be communicated, and for this union to be effected? The answer lies in the third great consequence of the hypostatic union, where the assumed humanity "is called to share in the divine power and activity of the person".[93] It thereby becomes, as

[87] The blessings of Christ's sacred humanity, such as his beatific vision, are perfections "to which creatures are raised only gradually and imperfectly.... From the very beginning Christ stood at the end of the road, at the summit of the mountain, which we must strive to gain by degrees, and to which we have to be raised by the grace of God. Christ is a *comprehensor*, as the theologians say. He is not only holy, but also in possession of divine glory and happiness; He is transfigured and beatified" (Scheeben, *Mysteries*, 326).

[88] Scheeben, *Mysteries*, 331.

[89] Ibid.

[90] Ibid.

[91] Ibid., 377. As he says elsewhere, "Since his dignity [as God] is the highest possible, and since on the other hand His humanity also must possess an endowment in keeping with this supreme dignity, this endowment must differ in compass and wealth from the endowment of all mere creatures as heaven differs from earth. And since, further, the humanity of Christ draws its wealth immediately from the divine source abiding in it, that wealth must be so abundant that it surpasses beyond comparison the supernatural riches of all creatures combined, as a mighty torrent surpasses the tiny rivulet that drains off from it" (ibid., 324).

[92] Ibid., 458.

[93] Ibid., 330.

Scheeben writes, following the Greek Fathers and Saint Thomas, a kind of instrument of the divinity, "the *instrumentum coniunctum* [conjoined instrument] of this divine person",[94] the human channel through which the deifying power of God enters us. As Scheeben writes, uniting both the personal and causal privileges enjoyed by the humanity of Christ, "on account of its hypostatic union with the Son of God, the animating, spiritualizing, divinizing power of the Godhead dwells within it; and so, as the organ of the divinity, it also animates, spiritualizes, and divinizes us."[95]

Scheeben assembles many of the great patristic metaphors that illustrate these privileges of the assumed humanity of the Son. The ancient figure of his flesh as a "glowing coal", aflame with divine energy, is the commonest, and Scheeben interprets it for us: "His divinity is the fire that is to pervade, illuminate, and transform the whole human race; but His humanity is the glowing coal in which the fire dwells and from which it is diffused over the whole human race."[96] Indeed, the deifying power of the divinity permeates the assumed flesh like fire pervading a live coal and, like a burning coal communicating its flame to other coals, those who come into contact with the flesh of the Word are also to be enlivened and enflamed by its purifying, revitalising energy. Of course, "the flesh is of no avail" (Jn 6:63)[97] but, in the case of Christ, like humble coal enflamed with fire, lowly flesh has been raised to an unimaginable dignity: "The coal," Scheeben explains, "does nothing of itself to kindle fire in other substances; but since it bears fire within itself, it brings fire to all objects coming into contact with it."[98] So it is with the sacred humanity of Christ.

[94] Ibid.

[95] Ibid., 513. Cf. Cyril of Alexandria, *In Ioan.*, lib. 4, c. 3.

[96] Scheeben, *Mysteries*, 459.

[97] Here is Scheeben, speaking in the place of Christ, interpreting Christ's words in John 6:63: "That is, My flesh, as mere flesh like any other, can be of no help to you whatever; it imparts life not by being torn to pieces and devoured, but by the Spirit, the divine energy residing in it. It gives life not as a dead and bleeding corpse, but as living flesh, permeated by the Spirit of God. What I said of the flesh is to be understood with reference to this life-giving energy present in the flesh. Therefore whoever believes that My flesh is not an earthly but a heavenly bread, into which a divine strength has come down from heaven, and which because of this same divine strength belongs to heaven and will ascend thither, cannot see anything objectionable in My words" (Scheeben, *Mysteries*, 517).

[98] Ibid., 459.

Christ and the Sacraments: A Deifying Contact

If the Incarnation brings about, as Saint Paul and the Fathers teach, the *admirabile commercium*, the "wonderful exchange" of divine and human properties, the deifying blessings of such an exchange are realised for each person by means of the "contact" to which Scheeben has just referred. In the measure apportioned to mere creatures, we are to say with the Fathers, "What man is, Christ wished to be, that man in turn *might* be what Christ is."[99] The patristic author adds "might" here because our deification and adoptive sonship is not a process that automatically follows upon the Incarnation. If the Son became "what we are" at his Incarnation, we can only become "what Christ is" by means of theological faith and a particular kind of contact with him. The contact to which Scheeben refers ought to be analogous to the healing and sanctifying contact exerted by Christ throughout his earthly ministry, as Scheeben's great mentors, Cyril and Thomas, frequently teach.[100] "Is there, then, such a real, physical contact of Christ's humanity with us?"[101] Scheeben asks.

It is in answer to this question that Scheeben turns his attention to the sacraments, for "what else is sacramental Communion but such a real contact?"[102] In continuity with the Fathers, Scheeben's favoured image to illustrate this deifying union with Christ is that of marriage—a loving, fructifying, and indissoluble coming together

[99] Ibid. This is a quote from Saint Cyprian (*De idolorum vanitate*, c. 11; emphasis added).

[100] For Cyril, see *In Ioan.*, lib. 3, c. 5. In his commentary on the Gospel of John, Saint Thomas also uses the earthly ministry of Christ to illuminate truths of the sacramental order. "He then speaks of his body when he says, 'And the bread which I will give is my flesh.' For he had said that he was the living bread; and so that we do not think that he is such so far as he is the Word or in his soul alone, he shows that even his flesh is life-giving, for it is an instrument of his divinity. Thus, since an instrument acts by virtue of the agent, then just as the divinity of Christ is lifegiving, so too his flesh gives life (as Damascene says) because of the Word to which it is united. *Thus Christ healed the sick by his touch.* So what he said above, I am the living bread, pertained to the power of the Word; but what he is saying here pertains to the sharing in his body, that is, to the sacrament of the Eucharist" (*In Jo.*, ch. 6, lect. 6, 959). See also *STh* III, q. 84, a. 10, obj. 3 and ad. 3, where Thomas draws a parallel between Christ's healing ministry on earth and the sacrament of penance. See also Thomas Weinandy, "The Human Acts of Christ and the Acts That Are the Sacraments", in *Ressourcement Thomism: Sacred Doctrine, the Sacraments, and the Moral Life* (Washington, D.C.: Catholic University of America Press, 2010), 150–68.

[101] Scheeben, *Mysteries*, 462.

[102] Ibid., 463.

of Christ and the Christian, and such a "union is not established between Christ and us except by baptism and the Eucharist."[103] As we have touched upon, baptism effects man's regeneration as adopted sons, sons in the Son. By it "we are received into the mystical body of Christ.... Through it we acquire for the first time a share in Christ's supernatural life. In it we are born as children of God."[104] Man's supernatural elevation, his participation in the divine nature, undoubtedly begins here, but Scheeben insists that what is communicated at baptism is received in anticipation of something greater, for "this membership looks forward to a closer, substantial fellowship in His body that is to be effected later."[105] Thus, it is not the effects of baptism but rather of the Eucharist that Scheeben prefers to associate most explicitly with man's deification. Scheeben conveys the progression from one to the other in this way:

> Man is to attach himself to his divine bridegroom by faith; and the bridegroom seals His union with man in baptism, as with a wedding ring. But both faith and baptism are mere preliminaries for the coming together of man and the God-man in one flesh by a real Communion of flesh and blood in the Eucharist, and hence for the perfect fructifying of man with the energizing grace of his head.[106]

Here, and only here before the face-to-face perfections of heavenly beatitude, does the Christian enjoy what Scheeben calls "a real contact with the source" of his deification.[107] The conversion of the substances of bread and wine into the substances of Christ's Body and Blood[108] means that divine grace is not imparted merely "as a gratuitous influx from without",[109] but that a real union of our substance with the very substance of the risen and glorious God-Man is

[103] Ibid., 374.

[104] Ibid., 572.

[105] Ibid., 542.

[106] Ibid., 543.

[107] Ibid., 385.

[108] Scheeben sees the mystery of Transubstantiation as a sign of the communicant's elevation through Holy Communion: "It is only the sublime and mysterious transformation of our nature ... which is proportionate to the conversion of bread into the body of Christ.... The same Holy Spirit who upon the altar changes earthly bread into heavenly bread changes us from earthly men to heavenly, deified men" (ibid., 502).

[109] Ibid.

brought about, effecting "a bond that is essentially intrinsic".[110] Such a direct level of contact, such "a real, physical, substantial union",[111] with Christ is ordered, purely and simply, to the deification of the recipient. Of all the dimensions of the Eucharistic mystery, nothing else seems more obvious to Scheeben than this.[112] If we abandon "the idea of man's elevation to a true participation in the divine nature," he says, the Eucharist soon appears to us as an "isolated, insufficiently motivated, and inexplicable work of God".[113]

The Eucharist: A Deifying Assimilation

The notion of the communicant's deification through the Eucharist becomes obvious once the connection between this and his Eucharistic transformation is understood. "Nothing else," Scheeben quotes Saint Leo as saying, "is aimed at in our partaking of the body and blood of Christ, than that we change into what we consume."[114] Following the Fathers and Saint Thomas, the decisive feature of normal, bodily eating that Scheeben seeks to apply, in an analogous sense, to the supernatural or "sacramental" eating of the Eucharist is this very notion of *change* (or as Augustine and Thomas put it, *conversio* or *mutatio*) through the interaction of food with the one nourished. If, on the biological level, a certain incorporation can be observed,

[110] Ibid., 485. "In the Eucharist He brings us into closest contact with the divine source of that life, most generously guarantees our stability and perseverance therein, [and] firmly binds us to God in living union" (ibid., 489).

[111] Ibid., 483.

[112] As he writes, "For how could we account for this ineffable miracle of divine love in the Eucharist, if it were not God's intention to treat us merely as His servants, and if it were not His will to raise us above our nature and take us to His fatherly bosom? Whence comes this heavenly, divine nourishment, and to what end is it directed, if we are not born to a supernatural, divine life? Why this stupendous, substantial union of the new Adam with man, if He wishes to do no more than offer satisfaction for our sins, or merit God's assistance for us, and does not intend, as supernatural progenitor of the race, to recharge our nature with divine energy, and to be for it the seed of a life that is not only humanly good and just, but divinely holy and blessed? Why, I repeat, this substantial union of God with us, unless it is to be a communication and an image of that inexpressible union which in the Trinity binds the Father to the Son in the Holy Spirit? Why all this, if Christ does not purpose to pour out upon us, along with His substance, His own divine life, just as the Father, in communicating His substance to the Son, floods Him with His own life?" (ibid., 479–80).

[113] Ibid., 480.

[114] Pope Leo the Great, *Sermo* 63 (PL 54, 357).

where the food "is changed into us, nourish[ing] only our body",[115] the very opposite takes place through the sacramental eating of the Body of Christ. Here we have a reversal of the typical active and passive principles peculiar to normal eating. In this unique instance, the assimilation is not of food into the body of the consumer, but of the consumer into the supernatural food of Christ himself. Though Holy Communion effects, says Scheeben, "the union of one living body with another living body",[116] it is—in relation to the powers exerted—an entirely uneven union, for the powers which "go forth" (see Lk 8:46) from the living Body of the God-Man are infinitely more powerful than the assimilating powers of the communicant. The glorious Body is not incorporated into the sinner but rather exerts its assimilating, incorporating powers upon him, "so that our bodies themselves are, as it were, changed into the body of Christ".[117] This hidden Body of Christ, "animated and transfigured by the divinity",[118] and now an "immutable, imperishable, insoluable substance",[119] acts "not by being absorbed into us, but by changing us into itself".[120] In other words, Christ's glorious and divinising flesh suffers no destruction, loss, absorption, nor material integration, but exerts its own incorporating and assimilating powers upon the recipient, changing him into himself, deifying him. "The change is entirely on our side, not on his."[121] Thus, in the worthy reception of the Son's very own flesh, the Christian is to be assimilated and conformed to him by this closest of preheavenly communions. By such a coming together, "we must be deified."[122]

It follows, then, that the risen Body of Christ sacramentally entering the fallen body of the Christian comes to make man *wholly* deified, for it is the cause and pledge both of his spiritual and bodily glory. Here, the whole Christ exerts his deifying power upon the whole man. Since, as Scheeben states, "we must become one with this body so as to share in the energy residing and functioning in

[115] Scheeben, *Mysteries*, 514.
[116] Ibid., 483.
[117] Ibid., 501.
[118] Ibid., 515.
[119] Ibid., 514.
[120] Ibid.
[121] Marie-Joseph Nicholas, O.P., *The Eucharist*, trans. Reginald F. Trevett (London: Burns and Oates, 1960), 53.
[122] Scheeben, *Mysteries*, 487.

it",[123] such a sharing will ensure, by a certain logical necessity,[124] not only the Christian's spiritual deification, but also his bodily glory, making "our body conformable to the body of His glory".[125] That such a transformation is, at this present time, "mainly interior and hidden" is testimony to the depth of activity of Christ's glorious Body in the communicant. But Christ's deifying objective here touches the whole man: he "must pervade and encompass the entire being of each person to whom He unites Himself in the Host".[126] As we have observed, the Word's own flesh is not food of the natural order, but supernatural food that "descends into the depths of the soul",[127] sanctifying man from his root upward, bringing about an external, bodily glory—a comprehensive deification—at the end of time.

Conclusion

We began this exposition with Scheeben's understanding of the trinitarian origins of man's deification, and his belief that the communication of the divine life to mankind is "to be regarded as an extension and continuation of that communication of life which is transmitted from the Father to the Son in God".[128] We have concluded with the moment when the Son "brings us into closest contact with the divine source" of that same life,[129] when the immediate, "real cause of grace [enters] into contact with the recipient",[130] conforming us to himself. Scheeben thinks that such an occurrence is "brought about most perfectly" not from without, but "if we come into a union of continuity with God's Son as His body"[131]—that is, by means of the very sacrament of his Body. Immediately the mystery of deification

[123] Ibid., 513.

[124] According to Saint Thomas, if the Christian places no obstacle, the resurrection of the body will follow infallibly from the Christian's union with Christ (see *STh* suppl. 76, 1 ad. 1). Similarly, Cyril insists that "it is impossible that [Christ] should not endow those with Life those in whom he comes to dwell" (*In Jo.* 6:54).

[125] Scheeben, *Mysteries*, 504.

[126] Ibid., 512.

[127] Ibid., 514.

[128] Ibid., 392.

[129] Ibid., 489.

[130] Ibid., 461–62.

[131] Ibid., 392.

is seen in its connection with the principal mysteries of the faith, for "the divine life passes from the Father into the Son, in order to be transferred to us in the Son and through the Son."[132] If we began with the Trinity and ended our exposition with the "the supernatural grace in the creature", in between them Scheeben places the Incarnation which, both chronologically and ontologically, "takes its place in the middle", between these two mysteries, "in order to join them together and to fit them to each other".[133] Scheeben's theology of deification is, thus, deeply Christocentric; the Son becomes man not merely to offer satisfaction for sin, nor merely to restore and heal, but to effect "an absolutely supernatural elevation of mankind".[134] In the enfleshed Son is manifested and realised God's will to deify us, for in becoming man he became "the organ and center of an inexpressible, inconceivably intimate union of mankind with God".[135] The consequences that follow upon this would "strike us as rash and blasphemous"[136] had not God himself revealed them to us. For the supernatural rebirth of sinners as brothers of the Son, sons of the Father, and children of God involves, Scheeben perceives, an astounding consequence: because of God's great love for us, "the twofold supernatural glorification which God the Father wills to receive from His natural Son and His adopted children now merges into a single harmonious, divine hymn."[137]

Readings for Further Study

Scheeben, Matthias. *Glories of Divine Grace*. Rockford, Ill.: Tan Books, 2001.

_____. *The Mysteries of Christianity*. Translated by Cyril Vollert, S.J. New York: Crossroad Publishing, [1948] 2008.

_____. *Nature and Grace*. Translated by Cyril Vollert, S.J. Saint Louis: Herder, 1954.

[132] Ibid.

[133] Ibid., 398.

[134] Ibid., 399.

[135] Ibid.

[136] Scheeben, *Nature and Grace*, 131.

[137] Scheeben, *Mysteries*, 398.

Chapter Twelve

BETWEEN THE VATICAN COUNCILS: FROM VATICAN I TO VATICAN II

Adam G. Cooper

The First Vatican Council (1869–1870) is widely remembered for promulgating the decree on papal primacy and infallibility, not for contributing in any way to the doctrine of deification. Recounting the tradition of the doctrine of deification for the period between the two Vatican Councils presumes familiarity with the decades before Vatican I and with two major renewals, the first represented by the Tübingen School of theology, pioneered by Johann Sebastian Drey (1777–1853) and Johann Adam Möhler (1796–1838), and the second represented by the Cologne patristic and dogmatic theologian Matthias Scheeben (1835–1888).

Seeking to reunite theology and culture, doctrine and life, the Catholic Tübingen theologians revitalised the ancient sense of the Church as an organic extension of the Incarnation and therefore as the living, historical community in which man is granted a vital share in the life of God.[1] Scheeben, on the other hand, hailed by Hans Urs von Balthasar as "the greatest German theologian to date",[2] emerged as an early protagonist of what would later become known as *ressourcement*: a return to the primary wellsprings of theological reflection, combined with the affective and speculative appropriation of the fruits of that reflection in the light of

[1] See Donald J. Dietrich and Michael J. Himes, *The Legacy of the Tübingen School: The Relevance of Nineteenth Century Theology for the Twenty-first Century* (New York: Crossroad, 1997); Michael J. Himes, *Ongoing Incarnation: Johann Adam Möhler and the Beginnings of Modern Ecclesiology* (New York: Crossroad, 1997).

[2] Hans Urs von Balthasar, *The Glory of the Lord: A Theological Aesthetics*, vol. 1, *Seeing the Form*, trans. Erasmo Leiva-Merikakis (San Francisco: Ignatius Press, 1982), 104.

contemporary thought and life.[3] Scheeben's aesthetic expositions on traditional Scholastic categories were integrated with a lively pneumatology, a profound pastoral bent, and an unshakable conviction that grace brings about not just a new situation but a "new being".[4] The effects of his recovery of the doctrine of deification were far reaching, though formal ecclesial substantiation for developing theology in this direction would only come after his death during the pontificate of Leo XIII (d. 1903). Pope Leo of course is the author of the famous encyclical *Aeterni patris* (1879), on the restoration of the philosophy of Saint Thomas. Yet, numerous figures, including the influential Salamancan Dominican Juan Gonzalez Arintero (1860–1928), would invoke this pope's promotion of renewed devotion to the Holy Spirit and surrender to "uncreated Love" enshrined in such encyclicals as *Divinum illud munus* (1897), as authorisation for an all-out recovery of deification as the lost but crucial plot of the Christian gospel and the key to human fulfillment.

Juan Gonzalez Arintero

Juan Gonzalez Arintero joined the Dominican novitiate in 1875 and, after studying at the University of Salamanca, lectured all over Europe in the natural sciences until a dramatic turn to spiritual theology in 1903.[5] In his definitive classic *The Mystical Evolution in the Development and Vitality of the Church* (1908), many of the themes traditionally associated with the doctrine of deification are developed with explicit and vigorous urgency.[6] Arintero underscores the necessity of the doctrine for spiritual flourishing, repeatedly lamenting the loss of its central profile in Christian consciousness. "This deification, so well known to the Fathers but unfortunately forgotten today, is the primary purpose of the Christian life."[7] "So common were these

[3] See Aidan Nichols, "Homage to Scheeben", in *Scribe of the Kingdom: Essays on Theology and Culture* (London: Sheed and Ward, 1994), 205–13.

[4] Yves Congar, *A History of Theology*, trans. H. Guthrie (New York: Doubleday, 1968), 193.

[5] See "Biographical Note", in John G. Arintero, *The Mystical Evolution in the Development and Vitality of the Church*, vol. 1, trans. J. Aumann (Saint Louis: B. Herder, 1950), xi–xiii.

[6] John G. Arintero, *The Mystical Evolution in the Development and Vitality of the Church*, 2 vols., trans. Jordan Aumann (Saint Louis: B. Herder, 1949–1951).

[7] Ibid., 1:23; cf. 29, 38.

ideas concerning deification that not even the heretics of the first centuries dared to deny them."[8] Yet, despite "the universal forgetfulness" and "the shameful deviations" from this traditional teaching, it can still be heard from numerous "dominant and authoritative voices". It is here that Arintero refers explicitly to Leo XIII and his advocacy of devotion to the Paraclete: "This augurs a happy rebirth of these fundamental doctrines which are the very soul and substance of the Christian life."[9]

What are the features of Arintero's exposition of the doctrine? Quoting Dionysius the Areopagite, he defines deification as "the most perfect possible assimilation, union, and transformation in God".[10] This union constitutes the very goal and purpose of the Incarnation. "For this was God made man: to make men gods and to take His delight in them."[11] Arintero denies any association between this teaching and any "absurd Gnostic emanation" or "repugnant pantheistic fusion". "God remains ever the same—God is immutable—but man, without ceasing to be man, is deified."[12]

Our deification involves us in a paradox. On the one hand, "we need the animation of a new vital principle that far transcends our own." In other words, we need a new life from outside of us. On the other hand, this principle must "give us a new sort of being, a second nature with its own proper faculties or potencies, so that we shall be able to live and work divinely and produce fruits of eternal life".[13] In other words, this new life needs to be intrinsically our own, fitted to our creaturely and psycho-physical nature, and not merely imposed from above. Sanctifying grace, the seed and sap of divine life as communicated and adapted to the created order, fulfills both these conditions:

> God respects us and does not destroy the nature formed by Him to be a subject of grace.... When [God's own life] is reproduced in us to the greatest possible extent and in harmony with our own life, it does not

[8] Ibid., 29.

[9] Ibid., 38.

[10] Ibid., 355 and 65. Cf. Dionysius the Areopagite, *Ecclesiastical Hierarchy* 1.3.

[11] Arintero, *Mystical Evolution*, 1:350. Cf. Athanasius, *On the Incarnation* 54.

[12] Arintero, *Mystical Evolution*, 1:57.

[13] Ibid., 71.

> make us cease to be men; rather it makes us perfect men at the same time that it deifies us.[14]

Constantly we find Arintero emphasising this intrinsic character of our deifying transformation, the fact that it consists not simply in an extrinsic relation with God or his grace, nor only in a moral or affective inclination, but in an ontological transformation of the individual person. "Sanctifying grace truly ... transforms us to our very depths and makes us like unto God as His sons in truth, and not in name only or merely in appearance. It is the true divine life."[15] This grace "is received into the very substance of the soul and makes us a new creature and so transforms and divinizes us. It gives a manner of life which is truly divine; whence flow certain powers and energies likewise divine."[16] In order to be deified, "the conformity of wills is not enough; there must be a conformity of nature."[17] God must become the very life of our souls, as the soul is the life of our bodies. "To dwell in the soul, to vivify and refashion it, God must penetrate it substantially, and this is proper and exclusive to God."[18] This explains why Arintero finds human adoption a poor analogy for divine adoption. "Earthly adoption is nothing more than a moral union. It confers new rights, but it does not change the nature of the adopted.... Divine adoption, on the other hand, not only implies the name, but also the reality of filiation."[19]

Because it effects an ontological change, deification enables the individual person to perform a range of new and divine acts. Human beings become capable of knowing and loving God as God knows and loves himself. Arintero's description of the trinitarian "shape" of this deified love is especially striking:

> The functions and essential or characteristic operations of this [deified] life are a divine love and knowledge caused in us by the Spirit.... As directed to the Father, this love should be a filial love; as

[14] Ibid., 60.
[15] Ibid., 67.
[16] Ibid., 24.
[17] Ibid., 33.
[18] Ibid., 30.
[19] Ibid., 348.

> directed to the Son, it should be fraternal, marital, and even organic, vital, for He is the first-born, the Spouse of our souls, and the Head of the mystical body of the Church. Finally, as directed to the Holy Ghost, that love must be a love of affectionate friendship and, so to speak, an experimental and vital love, full of sentiment and life and intimate affections.[20]

This passage reveals the way Arintero believes that the deified soul properly bears the marks of the trinitarian processions. Deification is a "trinification" inasmuch as it is "a resemblance of and participation in the inner life of God, one and three".[21] It also reveals his sense that deification is as much experienced or "suffered" as it is actively achieved. "Experimental" knowledge is not the fruit of discursive reason, but a "knowing" that arises from the intimate experience of another through love. "The knowledge which accompanies this love must not be an abstract knowledge but one that is concrete and ever more experimental, because it treats of an admirable and incomprehensible fact that can be realized only by living and experiencing it."[22]

Karl Adam

While Arintero was championing deification amongst neo-Thomists in Rome and Spain, Karl Adam (1876–1966) was doing so in Germany in the spirit and eventually also the surrounds of the great Tübingen School. Trained in Regensburg and Munich with doctoral theses on Tertullian and Augustine, Adam became one of the most widely read theologians in the twentieth century.[23] In his justly famous book *The Spirit of Catholicism* (1924), which manifests deep affinity with the mystical ecclesiology that eventually flowered at Vatican II,[24] we discover a strongly ecclesiocentric and sacramental exposition of deification, which he expounds in terms of participation in the

[20] Ibid., 353–54.

[21] Ibid., 44.

[22] Ibid., 354.

[23] See Robert Anthony Krieg, *Karl Adam: Catholicism in German Culture* (Notre Dame, Ind.: University of Notre Dame Press, 1992).

[24] Karl Adam, *The Spirit of Catholicism*, trans. J. McCann, from the 4th German ed. (London: Sheed and Ward, 1929). Cf. Krieg, *Karl Adam*, 51–56.

Church which, as the Body of Christ, has been established by Christ as the living and dynamic *locus deificandi* in history. Like Arintero and Scheeben, Adam argued that the Church's message of salvation does not simply concern the redemption of humanity from a state of sin and its restitution to a pristine natural condition. "The Church's doctrine of justification is based upon the presupposition that man is not only called to a natural end,... but also beyond that, to a supernatural elevation of his being which entirely surpasses all created aptitudes and powers, to sonship with God, to participation in the divine life itself."[25] This glorious end constitutes "the central fact" of the gospel. The likeness to which we are being conformed "consists, according to the Second Epistle of St. Peter, in an enrichment by grace, in a fulfilling and permeation of our being by divine and holy forces.... Therefore man's end lies, not in mere humanity, but in a new sort of superhumanity, in an elevation and enhancement of his being, which essentially surpasses all created powers and raises him into an absolutely new sphere of existence and life, into the fullness of the life of God."[26]

For Adam, deification and incarnation are almost reversible terms. He speaks of "this incarnation, this raising of man to the fullness of the divine life".[27] Grace is "a vital force" which "does not come from outside like some alien charm" but, rather, presupposes our humanity and calls for accompanying human activities and psychological points of contact.[28] Yet, it is thoroughly divine, "a sort of overflow of the eternal and infinite life within the soul". "It is not of me, yet it is wholly mine." The expression "infusion of charity" means "that the new love flows into me out of a primal source which is not my own self. But this primal source is not far from me, but within me, for it is the basis of my being." It is on this transcendent, intrinsically communicated divine power that the entire Christian life depends. "If a man denies it theological substance, then his theology is an unsatisfactory subjectivism."[29] Adam's modes of expression were not as precise as those of Arintero or Scheeben, but he has certainly become

[25] Adam, *Spirit of Catholicism*, 177.
[26] Ibid., 177–78.
[27] Ibid., 178.
[28] Ibid., 179–81.
[29] Ibid., 181.

the better known theologian outside his own circle and remains one of the key inspirations behind many Protestant conversions to the Catholic Church.

Réginald Garrigou-Lagrange

Meanwhile, a very different protagonist was coming to the fore in the heart of the Church's curial environs. Arintero's turn to spiritual theology led him to teach for some years at the Angelicum in Rome. It was here in 1909 that he developed a collegial friendship with the Dominican neo-Thomist Réginald Garrigou-Lagrange (1877–1964). Garrigou-Lagrange is best known for his role in the offensive against the so-called *nouvelle théologie* movement culminating in Pius XII's encyclical *Humani generis* (1950).[30] His suspicion of the younger generation's philosophy and theology as a front for modernist relativism has been well documented.[31] M.-D. Chenu famously criticized Garrigou-Lagrange's style of theology as a Thomism that had lost its Augustinian sap and Dionysian mysticism and become a virtual positivism.[32] R. H. Bulzacchelli has posed an even sharper division between Garrigou-Lagrange's overall enterprise and the direction of the Magisterium during the pontificates of John Paul II and Benedict XVI.[33]

But alongside these problems there are some mitigating factors. Garrigou-Lagrange was no stranger to the belief that Christians need a living experience of the divine realities which they profess. His encounter with Arintero's doctrine of deification left a deep

[30] For a detailed account, see Jürgen Mettepenningen, *Nouvelle Théologie: Inheritor of Modernism, Precursor of Vatican II* (London: T&T Clark, 2010).

[31] See Fergus Kerr, "A Different World: Neoscholasticism and Its Discontents", *International Journal of Systematic Theology* 8, no. 2 (2006): 128–48; Aidan Nichols, "Thomism and the Nouvelle Théologie", *The Thomist* 64, no. 1 (2000): 1–19.

[32] M.-D. Chenu, *Une école de théologie: Le Saulchoir* (1937), summarised by Fergus Kerr in "Chenu's Little Book", *New Blackfriars* 66, no. 777 (1985): 108–12.

[33] R. H. Bulzacchelli, "Dives in Misericordia: The Pivotal Significance of a Forgotten Encyclical", in N. M. Billias et al. (eds.), *Karol Wojtyla's Philosophical Legacy* (Washington, D.C.: Council for Research in Values and Philosophy, 2008), 125–36. A balanced introduction to Garrigou-Lagrange's theology can be found in Aidan Nichols, *Reason with Piety: Garrigou-Lagrange in the Service of Catholic Thought* (Naples, Fla.: Sapientia Press, 2008).

impression on him, and the two kept up a lively correspondence.[34] According to Arintero's translator, Jordan Aumann:

> In the short time that he taught at the Angelicum in Rome, Arintero inspired Reginald Garrigou-Lagrange to take up his pen and write for the same cause. Garrigou-Lagrange became known throughout the world as his works in spiritual theology were translated into various languages. Nevertheless, to Arintero belongs the credit for being the champion of the return to traditional teaching in spiritual theology and in this field he must likewise be considered the master of Garrigou-Lagrange.[35]

In Garrigou-Lagrange's spiritual works a number of now-familiar themes emerge. Christ's mission was not simply to redeem humanity from sin, but to elevate it to participate in the life of the triune God. The soul achieves union with God by docility to the Holy Spirit, by prayer, and by bearing sufferings with patience, gratitude, and love. Union with God is an unfolding process that begins already in this life and is not just a goal. The individual person relies utterly upon the prevenient grace of God, whose merciful power underlies all of one's undertakings and assimilates one to himself. Garrigou-Lagrange draws a distinction between God's general "presence of immensity" in things, as cause in effect, and his special presence in the just, which comes about not only in the form of created grace, but by the actual indwelling of the three Divine Persons themselves.[36] Commenting on Jesus' words, "If anyone loves me ... my Father will love him and we will come to him and make our home in him" (Jn 14:23), the Dominican fixes upon the personal and communional nature of this mysterious indwelling: *we* will come. To what does this "we" refer ? "Created effects? Supernatural gifts? No. Those

[34] See Richard Peddicord, *The Sacred Monster of Thomism: An Introduction to the Life and Legacy of Reginald Garrigou-Lagrange, O.P.* (South Bend, Ind.: St. Augustine's Press, 2005), 14. Garrigou-Lagrange's unpublished letters that were written to Arintero 1911–1927 are preserved by the Archivo del P. Arintero in Salamanca (see Inner Explorations, accessed December 8, 2015, http://www.innerexplorations.com/chmystext/reginald.htm).

[35] Jordan Aumann, *Christian Spirituality in the Catholic Tradition* (San Francisco: Ignatius, 1985), 274.

[36] Réginald Garrigou-Lagrange, *The Love of God and the Cross of Jesus*, vol. 1, trans. Jeanne Marie (Saint Louis: Herder, 1947), 136–38.

who love and those who come are the same, the Divine Persons, Father, Son and inseparable Spirit promised us by our Lord and sent visibly to His Church on Pentecost."[37] Garrigou-Lagrange insisted upon the tri-personal character of the divine indwelling in the elect and the experiential character of our resultant knowing and loving. "In those who possess grace the three divine Persons are present as an object known in the knower, as an object loved in the lover; no distance divides Them from Their host who really possesses Them and enjoys a quasi-experience of Their presence."[38]

It is for this reason that Garrigou-Lagrange takes issue with any reduction of the union between God and man to a matter of spiritual friendship. The problem with this, he contends, is that it still does not imply a *substantial* presence. "After all, separated friends are bound together with ties of affection, yet distance lies between them just the same; for friendship as such makes us desire the real presence of the one we love, but it cannot bring him to us."[39] Love may tend toward union with the beloved, but only *actual presence* effects it. By sanctifying grace, God becomes present in a new way, so that there arises an "experimental" knowledge and affective delight. "In this life we do not see God, but believe in Him and, in the obscurity of faith, we can have a quasi-experimental knowledge of Him such as the Scriptures frequently describe, and sometimes, by a gift of His good pleasure, we may experience Him in us through the gift of wisdom."[40]

We have now a number of times come across the term "experimental" or "quasi-experimental" knowledge. While the idea of an experimental or experiential knowledge of God was commonplace in medieval sources, the qualification "quasi" seems to be a unique contribution by Aquinas.[41] Quasi-experimental knowledge is not knowledge that one comes to by reasoning. It is rather the knowledge that rises from "a certain connaturality or conformity to divine things".[42]

A determinative text for Garrigou-Lagrange on this point is 1 John 4:16: "God is love: and he who abides in love abides in God, and

[37] Ibid., 138.

[38] Ibid., 142.

[39] Ibid., 143.

[40] Ibid., 144–46.

[41] See J.-P. Torrell, *Saint Thomas Aquinas*, vol. 2, *Spiritual Master*, trans. R. Royal (Washington, D.C.: Catholic University of America Press, 2003), 90–100.

[42] Garrigou-Lagrange, *Love of God*, 154, with reference to *STh* II–II, q. 45, a. 2.

God in him." The subjective experience of love, it seems, more than objective knowledge, is the glue or uniting force in this union of mutual indwelling. True, one cannot love what one does not somehow know, yet the indwelling of God begins "generally without any consciousness of it on our part."[43] "At the moment of justification, without any consciousness of our own, our spiritual life begins with God's indwelling."[44] The grace given by and with the Holy Spirit constitutes a proximate power or principle that needs to be actualized, such that one can say that the intimate contact implied in knowing and loving God comes about *per operationem creaturae*. In Thomas' words, "The rational creature by its own operation of knowledge and love attains to God Himself."[45] The Divine Persons present themselves, give themselves, to be known and possessed in just this way.

Garrigou-Lagrange asks why this knowledge should be deemed *quasi*-experimental and not simply experimental.[46] What Thomas seems to indicate by the term "experimental" or "quasi-experimental knowledge" is the unity of the intellectual and affective dimensions of the individual person in his fellowship with God. Torrell comments: "Basically, the word *experience*, borrowing from the vocabulary of the senses, suggests something of direct contact with reality transposed into the realm of divine things."[47] We are here close to the Dionysian and patristic doctrine of knowledge not by learning but by "suffering divine things".[48] In fact Thomas quotes this very phrase to make the point that by means of affective or experimental knowledge one tastes and proves the goodness of God in one's own living experience.[49]

[43] Garrigou-Lagrange, *Love of God*, 136.

[44] Ibid., 153.

[45] *STh* I, q. 43, a. 3.

[46] Garrigou-Lagrange, *Love of God*, 156–57.

[47] J.-P. Torrell, *Saint Thomas Aquinas*, 2: 95–96. For a closer analysis of texts, see J. F. Dedek, "*Quasi Experimentalis Cognitio*: A Historical Approach to the Meaning of St. Thomas", *Theological Studies* 22 (1961): 357–90; A. Patfoort, "Missions divines et expérience des Personnes divines selon S. Thomas", *Angelicum* 63 (1986): 545–59.

[48] Dionysius the Areopagite, *Divine Names* 2.9.

[49] *STh* II–II, q. 97, a. 2: "There are two ways of knowing the goodness or will of God. One is speculative, and from that point of view, we are allowed neither to doubt the divine goodness nor to put it to the test.... The other is an affective or experimental knowing of the divine goodness or will, when one personally experiences the taste of the divine sweetness and the delight of his will, after the fashion of Hierotheos, whom Dionysius says 'learned divine things through experiencing them.' It is from this point of view that we are told to 'prove' the divine will and 'taste' his sweetness."

For Garrigou-Lagrange this fact confirms his conviction that "infused contemplation of the mysteries of faith belongs to the normal progress of sanctity". The indwelling of the holy Trinity "is explicable only so far as God can be known and loved as the object of quasi-experimental knowledge"—that is, a knowledge that transcends discursive analysis and that involves the affective and connatural assimilation of the soul to God.[50] Through his exposition of the work of seventeenth-century Thomist Louis de Chardon (d. 1651), Garrigou-Lagrange confronts overly rational approaches with a more affective, performative mysticism of love. In his spiritual masterpiece *La Croix de Jésus* (1647) Chardon had posited the Divine Persons not only as objects known and loved but as the principles of supernatural operation in the soul.[51] "They are no longer present to us simply as objects powerfully attracting our operations but as actualizing, effecting, applying, and directing our operations."[52] Chardon also drew a close parallel between the "internal/eternal" and "external/temporal" processions in the Godhead: "The temporal mission of a divine Person is only an extension of the eternal procession in God.... Thus the Word, begotten by the Father from all eternity, and with Him the Holy Ghost, are invisibly sent to the just at the moment of conversion."[53] Having quoted these passages, Garrigou-Lagrange goes on to reflect approvingly on an emphasis in Chardon's spiritual theology upon the passivity of the soul in respect to the deiform life:

> Charity may at times act with such efficacious strength that it reduces souls to a passive state in regard to divine things; they are no longer conscious of their cooperation and concurrence in supernatural and Godlike acts. They do not so much live the life of God as the life of God lives in them; they are more loved than loving; and even when they love, they receive rather than give.[54]

On this passivity or, as we might prefer to call it, active receptivity, Garrigou-Lagrange comments: "In the passive state which Chardon refers to here, God accomplishes in us and for us a much more perfect

[50] Garrigou-Lagrange, *Love of God*, 159.

[51] Ibid., 161. The English translation of Chardon's work is *The Cross of Jesus*, trans. R. T. Murphy (St. Louis: Herder, 1957).

[52] Garrigou-Lagrange, *Love of God*, 162.

[53] Ibid., 162.

[54] Ibid., 163.

and complete giving of ourselves than we could ever achieve by our own efforts with ordinary actual grace."[55] By indwelling the soul God "penetrates all and destroys nothing, making us participants of His divine society and sharers, by imitation, in His own natural life that we may be caught and embraced by the fullness of Divinity."[56] Here, he summarises, "in a really vital way, [Chardon] brings us back to the very source of theology, the truths of Scripture and tradition."[57] This is why, in the final deified state, human action eventually seems to play no part, or is at least indistinguishable from the action of God. In this state of sublime pathos, says Saint John of the Cross, "the soul can perform no acts, but it is the Holy Spirit that moves it to perform them."[58]

We do not have space here to develop the christological corollary of this doctrine, other than to mention briefly the unique way Garrigou-Lagrange expounds a structural analogy between deification and the hypostatic union. In the Incarnation, God, who is essentially diffusive goodness, communicated himself so fully and intimately that the human "personality" of Christ was effaced, without his human nature in any way being diminished. In a similar way, human beings are deified, or receive God's intimate self-communication, to the degree that they efface themselves or "depersonalise" their own ego. Just as the deprivation of the dimension of personal existence renders Christ's humanity more absolutely open to the deifying influence of the divine Logos, so too does the Christian realise deification in a dramatic and ecstatic self-mortification. This means that cruciform humility, not egoistic virtuosity, is the characteristic mark of deification in this life.[59]

Émile Mersch

Despite his enthusiastic exposition of these aspects of the great spiritual tradition, Garrigou-Lagrange had difficulty in allowing them

[55] Ibid.

[56] Ibid., 163–64.

[57] Ibid., 165.

[58] Garrigou-Lagrange, *The Three Conversions in the Spiritual Life* (1933; Rockford, Ill.: Tan Books, 2002), 99, quoting John of the Cross, *The Living Flame of Love* 1.4, English translation in *The Collected Works of St. John of the Cross*, trans. K. Kavanaugh and O. Rodriguez (Washington, D.C.: Institute of Carmelite Studies, 1991), 642.

[59] See Réginald Garrigou-Lagrange, *Our Savior and His Love for Us*, trans. A. Bouchard (Saint Louis: Herder, 1951).

to broaden, correct, and reconfigure his metaphysics. Already in the 1920s, perhaps due in part to the widening dissatisfaction with Aristotelian metaphysical categories to account adequately for the mystery of human deification in Christ, and due also to a conscious interest in conforming theology more closely to the language of Scripture and concrete personal experience, there develops in Catholic tradition a more fluid and symbolic terminology to describe the dynamics involved in conversion, faith, love for God, and the passage to final beatitude. In the judgment of Émile Mersch, author of the highly influential study *The Theology of the Mystical Body* composed mainly in the 1930s, "Aristotle's categories are too narrow for this mystery of the Most High that comes to elevate and enlarge infinitely the natural universe."[60] On the basis of renewed reflection on precisely what happens in the human being in deification, and inspired by more personalist currents in philosophy, theologians began to explore new ways of articulating the causal dynamics at work in the creature's transformation and participation in God. One particular example crucial to our topic was the development of the notion of "quasi-formal" causality. According to classic Thomistic metaphysics, formal causality consists in "the communication of the entire act or perfection of the form, formally as such, to its perfectible term, when it is united intrinsically and immediately, formally as such, to that term".[61] Mersch adapted and modified this concept first of all to account for the perfection of the assumed human nature in Christ. In the Incarnation we discover an utterly new kind of divine causality, distinct from the "efficient" causality involved in creation.

> By creation God establishes beings in themselves, outside the Godhead. By the Incarnation considered *in facto esse*, God establishes a being in the Godhead and above the being's own nature, by suppressing all distance and by becoming strictly immanent in that being. Creation, in the thing created, consists in having the cause of being outside the being; the Incarnation, considered in the assumed nature, consists in having the cause of being in the being itself, as its sole personality. Hence this is a new kind of action.[62]

[60] Émile Mersch, *The Theology of the Mystical Body*, trans. Cyril Vollert (Saint Louis: Herder, 1952), 473.

[61] Kevin F. O'Shea, "Pure Uncreated Unity", *Irish Theological Quarterly* 30, no. 4 (1963): 350.

[62] Mersch, *Theology of the Mystical Body*, 471.

According to Mersch, the hypostatic union perfects the assumed human nature of Christ not by way of efficient causality but by way of "quasi-formal" causality.[63] If we are not to reduce the union of natures in Christ to a "local juxtaposition", "mechanical juncture", or "juridical fiction", we have to admit the causal operation of something that is both human and divine, "because it makes the humanity the humanity of God".[64] That "something", says Mersch, is grace, "by which the gift that God gives in a divine way exists in a man in a human way; it is that which makes man formally what the coming of God makes him effectively."[65]

Having explored the christological mystery in this way, Mersch went on to suggest an analogous relation between this causal dynamism in the Incarnation and that which takes place in deification. The operation of divine grace in Christ is not far removed from its operation in the Christian, for the divinization of Christ "is radically the divinization of all humanity".[66] Of course some distinction must be observed: Christ's humanity "must be truly, intrinsically, and objectively the humanity of God". Its divinisation is achieved not by efficient or instrumental means, but quasi-formally. By contrast, "as far as its mode of existing is concerned", grace "can be nothing else than an accident in man". Yet, it is a truly supernatural and divine accident,

> because it is an "entity of union" modeled on the hypostatic union.... Therefore divinization, and consequently grace, is something essentially ontological. It does not merely confer this or that new perfection, but makes the recipient exist in a different way, by actuating the remotest capacities of finite being.[67]

Maurice de la Taille and Karl Rahner

Two other well-known theologians in the 1920s and 1930s adopted the language of quasi-formal causality to express what takes place in

[63] Ibid., 208.
[64] Ibid., 602.
[65] Ibid., 610.
[66] Ibid., 618.
[67] Ibid.

deification—namely, Maurice de la Taille and Karl Rahner.[68] Like Mersch, both thinkers were trying to account for the distinctly *immanent* character of the divine indwelling in the Christian and the operation of grace. Once again the notion of efficient causality was found to be inadequate: by it one produces a being without oneself being a part of it. In the case of Christian transformation, the notion of efficient causality does not call for or imply any connatural community between God and man; it does not require any kind of intimate, ontological self-communication. Yet, on its own, the notion of formal causality, properly speaking, implies too much: God cannot have any immediate, formally causal relation with a creature, since that would be to enter into composite, essential relation with it, to become its very form and act. There would arise not an ontological *union*, but, impossibly, an ontological *fusion*. By means of his controversial formula "the created actuation by the uncreated Act", de la Taille coordinated three key realities—the Incarnation, sanctifying grace, and the beatific vision—into a single harmonious economy. Each embodies a distinct yet intrinsically related instance of God's real self-donation, his utter self-communication in such a way that there necessarily follows some concomitant enriching and substantially perfecting actuation in the creature.

[68] Maurice de la Taille, "Actuation créée par Acte incréé", *Recherches de science réligieuse* 18 (1928): 753–68. English translation in Maurice de la Taille, *The Hypostatic Union and Created Actuation by Uncreated Act*, trans. C. Vollert (West Baden Springs, Ind.: West Baden College, 1952), 29–41. Karl Rahner, "Zur Begrifflichkeit der ungeschaffenen Gnade", *Zeitschrift für katholische Theologie* 63 (1939): 137–71, reprinted in Karl Rahner, *Schriften zur Theologie* 1 (1954): 347–75. English translation: "Some Implications of the Scholastic Concept of Uncreated Grace", in *Theological Investigations*, trans. Cornelius Ernst (London: Darton, Longman, and Todd, 1961), 1:319–46. Rahner refers to de la Taille's work, published some ten years earlier, in support of the probability of his thesis (*Theological Investigations*, 340, n. 2). These works gave rise to a series of articles debating the question in some detail. In support of the notion of quasi-formal causality, see P. de Letter, "Created Actuation by the Uncreated Act: Difficulties and Answers", *Theological Studies* 18, no. 1 (1957): 60–92; "Divine Quasi-Formal Causality", *Irish Theological Quarterly* 27, no. 3 (1960): 221–28; "'Pure' or 'Quasi'-Formal Causality?", *Irish Theological Quarterly* 30, no. 1 (1963): 36–47; "The Theology of God's Self-Gift", *Theological Studies* 24 (1963): 402–22. More critical are the following: Kevin F. O'Shea, "Pure Formal Actuation", *Irish Theological Quarterly* 28, no. 1 (1961): 1–15; "Pure Uncreated Unity", *Irish Theological Quarterly* 30, no. 4 (1963): 347–53; "Divinization: A Study in Theological Analogy", *The Thomist* 29, no. 1 (1965): 1–45; B. Kelly, "Divine Quasi-Formal Causality", *Irish Theological Quarterly* 28, no. 1 (1961): 16–28. For a general summary of the issues from a contemporary systematic theological perspective, see Ralph del Colle, *Christ and the Spirit: Spirit-Christology in Trinitarian Perspective* (New York: Oxford University Press, 1994), 64–90.

While de la Taille never used the term "quasi-formal" itself, Karl Rahner (1904–1984) explicitly adopted it to designate the individual person's infusion with "uncreated grace" or the self-communication of God. This way of understanding deification stands right at the heart of Rahner's entire theological project. His representative article in the multivolume *Lexikon für Theologie und Kirche* on the classic Scholastic category of "sanctifying grace" amounts essentially to an attempted recovery, under that term, of the biblical and patristic understanding of uncreated grace as *Vergöttlichung* (deification), *die Selbstmitteilung Gottes* (the self-communication of God), or *die vergöttlichenden Teilnahme an der göttliche Natur* (deifying participation in the divine nature).[69] Far from this process of human *theopoiesis* being a peripheral element in Rahner's theological world view, it forms "the center of gravity" around which revolves his "understanding of creation, anthropology, Christology, ecclesiology, liturgy, and eschatology".[70]

According to Rahner, the schools tended to posit uncreated grace as a consequence of created grace, so that modifications in the soul by virtue of created grace are made the basis for the union constituted by the divine indwelling. In the Scriptures and the Greek Fathers, by contrast, the created gifts are seen to be the consequence of God's "substantial" self-communication. The Holy Spirit is himself the inchoate seed and homogeneous commencement of the beatific life.[71] If this is true, Rahner argues, then it is not inappropriate to apply to the life of earthly Christian pilgrimage "the concepts of formal ontology relating to the possession of God in the *visio beatifica*".[72] In this connection Rahner invokes the approval of the encyclical *Mystici Corporis* of Pope Pius XII (1943), which determined that the

[69] Karl Rahner, "Heiligmachende Gnade", in J. Höfer and K. Rahner, eds., *Lexikon für Theologie und Kirche*, vol. 5 (Freiburg: Herder Verlag, 1960), 138–42. Although the article is brief, it should be noted how heavily weighted the bibliography is with numerous works from the 1920s that explicitly treat the topic of deification.

[70] Francis J. Caponi, "Karl Rahner: Divinization in Roman Catholicism", in *Partakers of the Divine Nature: The History and Development of Deification in the Christian Traditions*, ed. M.J. Christensen and J.A. Wittung (Grand Rapids, Mich.: Baker, 2007), 259.

[71] For differing views on the validity of this claim and its relation to patristic and Eastern Orthodox theology, see A.N. Williams, *The Ground of Union: Deification in Aquinas and Palamas* (New York: Oxford University Press, 1999); Bruce D. Marshall, "*Ex Oriente Lux?* Aquinas and Eastern Orthodox Theology", *Modern Theology* 20, no. 1 (2004): 23–50.

[72] Rahner, "Some Implications of the Scholastic Concept of Uncreated Grace", 1:334.

essence of grace in this life, being as it is the *inchoatio gloriae*, is properly known as it is by reference to the beatific vision.[73] Importantly, this must include reference to the act of knowing that comes about in the beatified person according to which God's own essence takes the place of the impressed species. This would mean that, insofar as in the act of knowledge knower and known are identified, the beatified human may be said to be, or to have in himself, the form or essence of God.

Accordingly, this dynamic state of supernatural union with God, says Rahner, should be considered not under the category of efficient causality, but under the category of formal causality—that is, a taking up *into* the ground or *forma* ("ein In-den-Grund[forma]-*Hinein*nehmen").[74] What distinguishes this graced state of glory from the case of the hypostatic union was initially indicated by Rahner by the prefix "quasi", so that one may speak of God exercising a quasi-formal causality. "All this 'quasi' implies is that this 'forma,' in spite of its formal causality, which must be taken seriously, abides in its absolute transcendence (inviolateness, 'freedom')."[75] The metaphysical assumptions present in this claim are astounding: in the beatitude that constitutes final deification, God stands in relation to the believer not simply as Creator to a creature distinct from him, but as God to his own self, as it were—that is, as a sort of formal cause. If the perfectly graced life is truly supernatural, and if by "supernatural" we mean something "absolutely mysterious", then, concludes Rahner, "God himself must belong to what constitutes it, i.e., God in so far as he is not merely the ever transcendent Creator, the efficient cause of something finite which is distinct from him, but in so far as he communicates himself to the finite entity in quasi-formal causality."[76]

After Vatican II Rahner consolidated his commitment to the primacy of uncreated grace, dropping the "quasi" to speak simply of formal causality. He reiterated the claim that "God does not confer on man merely created gifts as a token of his love. God communicates *himself* by what is no longer simply efficient causality. He makes

[73] Ibid., 340.

[74] Ibid., 329 (emphasis in original).

[75] Ibid., 330.

[76] Ibid., 333–34, n. 3.

man share in the very nature of God."[77] But even "share" was too weak a word. Rahner's most mature expression concerning grace, causality, and deification is finally that God "in his own most proper reality makes himself the innermost constitutive element of man".[78]

Henri de Lubac

Rahner's influence in theology prior to and after Vatican II would be difficult to exaggerate. However among the new generation of theologians in the twentieth century it would be another Jesuit, Henri de Lubac (1896–1991), whose more Christo- and ecclesiocentric theology of deification would come to be more expressly substantiated by magisterial teaching.[79] De Lubac was also distinguished by having been appointed a cardinal (in 1983), an honour that can be taken as vindication of his fundamental theology.

How is it possible to classify his theological output? "Whoever stands before the forty or so volumes of Henri de Lubac's writings ... feels as though he is at the entrance to a primeval forest."[80] He was completely conversant with the entire tradition of Christian thought, having additional recourse in his research to the ever-increasing number of specialist studies devoted to the theology of the Fathers and especially to deification. Among these mention may be made in particular of J. Gross' book *The Divinization of the Christian according to the Greek Fathers* (1938), along with articles by O. Faller (1925), M.-J. Congar (1935), H. Rondet (1949), É. des Places (1957), as well as those by the Russian Orthodox theologian M. Lot-Borodine

[77] Karl Rahner, "Grace II: Theological", in Karl Rahner, ed., *Encyclopedia of Theology: A Concise Sacramentum Mundi* (London: Burns and Oates, 1975), 588 (emphasis in original).

[78] Karl Rahner, *Foundations of Christian Faith: An Introduction to the Idea of Christianity*, trans. W. Dych (London: Darton, Longman, and Todd, 1978), 116. For a brief overview of Rahner's teaching on grace, see Stephen J. Duffy, "Experience of Grace", in D. Marmion and M. E. Hines, eds., *The Cambridge Companion to Karl Rahner* (Cambridge: Cambridge University Press, 2005), 43–62.

[79] For a brief but reliable introduction to his life and work, see Rudolph Vodeholzer, *Meet Henri de Lubac: His Life and Work* (San Francisco: Ignatius, 2008). Also A. Komonchak, "Theology and Culture at Mid-Century: The Example of Henri de Lubac", *Theological Studies* 51 (1990): 579–602.

[80] Hans Urs von Balthasar, *The Theology of Henri de Lubac* (San Francisco: Ignatius, 1991), 23.

(1932).[81] Philosophically de Lubac was indebted to the revitalised Thomism of Pierre Rousselot (1878–1915) and the action theory of Maurice Blondel (1861–1949).[82] Above all he benefitted from the collaboration of expert friends such as Hans Urs von Balthasar and Jean Daniélou. It was with Daniélou and Claude Mondésert that de Lubac founded the famous series *Sources chrétiennes* (1942), a publishing event which, through its printing of now over five hundred edited and translated volumes of patristic texts, arguably has done more to open access to the patristic doctrine of deification than any other.

Already during and especially after Vatican II, de Lubac discerned a disconcerting falling away on the part of many leading bishops and theologians from the fundamentals of the faith and a troubling penchant for revisionist interpretations ultimately subversive of the revealed objectivity of creation and incarnation, redemption and resurrection. As an antidote to this shortsighted emptying of the Christian faith of all substance, he counselled a return to the timeless fecundity of the Fathers.[83] His understanding of deification functions as a corollary of this concern to restore to humanity—and to the Church—what is essential for their being, self-understanding, and destiny.

The idea of deification originates not in an ideology, but in a wonderful fact. "Our 'deification' is an incredible marvel, and we

[81] Gross' work, written in French, has been translated into English by Paul A. Onica in *Divinization of the Christian according to the Greek Fathers* (Anaheim, Calif.: A&C Press, 2002); O. Faller, "Griechische Vergottung und christliche Vergöttlichung", *Gregorianum* 6 (1925): 405–35; M.-J. Congar (=Yves), "La Déification dans la tradition spirituelle de l'Orient", *Vie spirituelle* 43 (1935): 91–107; H. Rondet, "La divinisation du chrétien", *Nouvelle Revue Théologique* 71 (1949): 449–76, 561–88; the article by Édouard des Places is in fact a long multi-authored study on "Divinisation", published in the *Dictionnaire de Spiritualité*, vol. 3 (Paris, 1957), cols. 1370–1459. M. Lot-Borodine's articles, first published between 1932 and 1933 in *Revue d'histoire des religions*, were reprinted in the single volume *La Déification de l'homme selon la doctrine des Pères grecs* (Paris: Cerf, 1970), with a preface by Jean Cardinal Daniélou.

[82] Rousselot's *The Eyes of Faith* (1910) has been "widely acknowledged as a major turning point in the development of modern Catholic theology". See John M. McDermott, "Introduction" to Pierre Rousselot, *The Eyes of Faith*, trans. Joseph Donceel (New York: Fordham, 1990), 1. Similarly influential, Blondel's *Action (1893)*, trans. Oliva Blanchette (Notre Dame, Ind.: University of Notre Dame Press, 1950), examines the transcendent grounds and conditions of all human activity.

[83] Henri de Lubac, *At the Service of the Church*, trans. Anne Elizabeth Englund (Communio Books; San Francisco: Ignatius Press, 1993), 319.

can believe it only because of that even greater marvel in which it originated—the Son of God becoming a son of man."[84] Truth for de Lubac is invariably marked by paradox, and the Incarnation is "the paradox of paradoxes".[85] Human beings are similarly paradoxical. Being a unity of body and soul, they are bound to the material and historical structures of this world. But they are also created spirits, bearing in themselves the stamp of their divine origin. They can only fully become themselves by infinitely transcending themselves. Created spirits are unlike the natures of other created beings. "There is something in man, a certain capacity for the infinite, which makes it impossible to consider him one of those beings whose whole nature and destiny are inscribed within the cosmos.... Congenitally, the end of the spiritual creature is something that surpasses the powers of his nature."[86] Human action translates a divinely initiated movement present deep within as image called and destined to attain deifying likeness to God.[87]

These were the themes which de Lubac expressed a little more stridently in his famous *Surnaturel* (1946), a work which precipitated a theological revolution.[88] In it de Lubac demolished extrinsicist theories that, in order to protect the gratuity of grace, had posited a natural, this-worldly end for mankind proportionate to man's natural desires. De Lubac by contrast pressed the case for a supernatural finality paradoxically inscribed within the very being of the human creature. Many

[84] Henri de Lubac, *The Mystery of the Supernatural*, trans. R. Sheed (1965; New York: Crossroad, 1998), 21.

[85] See Henri de Lubac, *Paradoxes of Faith*, trans. Sadie Kreilkamp (San Francisco: Ignatius Press, 1987).

[86] De Lubac, *Mystery of the Supernatural*, 110–11.

[87] See Eric de Moulins-Beaufort, "The Spiritual Man in the Thought of Henri de Lubac", *Communio* 25 (1998): 287–302.

[88] The literature discussing de Lubac's *Surnaturel* is vast. One may consult with especial profit the essays in Serge-Thomas Bonino, ed., *Surnaturel: A Controversy at the Heart of Twentieth-Century Thomistic Thought* (Ave Maria, Fla.: Sapientia Press, 2009). See also Nicholas J. Healy, "Henri de Lubac on Nature and Grace: A Note on Some Recent Contributions to the Debate", *Communio* 35, no. 4 (2008): 535–64. For an account of the events between de Lubac's publication of *Surnaturel* and his temporary suspension from teaching in 1950, see Jürgen Mettepenningen, *Nouvelle Théologie: Inheritor of Modernism, Precursor of Vatican II* (London: T&T Clark, 2010). On the patristic *ressourcement* in *nouvelle théologie* circles in general, see Brian Daley, "The *Nouvelle Théologie* and the Patristic Revival: Sources, Symbols and the Science of Theology", *International Journal of Systematic Theology* 7, no. 4 (2005): 362–82.

have found in this a synthesis of the Latin idea of grace perfecting nature and the Greek patristic doctrine of deification. But some have gone further, finding in the vision of beatitude described by *Surnaturel* an elimination of the concept of nature altogether. Through our total transfiguration by the divine light, interprets John Milbank, "we *become* the reception of this light and there is no longer any additional 'natural' recipient of this reception."[89] "This," Milbank suggests, "is perhaps the subtle heart of de Lubac's theology."[90]

Yet, de Lubac never lost sight of what philosopher Maurice Blondel called the "abyss" or "radical heterogeneity" that obtains between God and man, such that what is required for the passage to divine life is not simply a spontaneous *epistrophe* but a thoroughgoing mortification, death, and rebirth. Although creation and deification are structurally parallel, although they are given together in the very summoning of my being into existence, they are nevertheless strictly incommensurable.[91] De Lubac happily jettisoned the neo-Scholastic theory of "pure nature" and man's "two ends" (*fines duo*), but he nonetheless retains the adjective "twofold" (*duplex*) as an indispensable means of expressing an irreducible categorical distinction:

> I must carefully distinguish and always maintain a twofold gratuity, a twofold divine gift, and therefore, if one may say so, a twofold divine freedom. There are here, as it were, two successive planes, like two landings without any communication from the bottom one to the one above. A twofold ontological passage, doubly impassable to the creature without the twofold initiative that arouses and calls him.... Between the existent nature and the supernatural to which God destines it, the distance is as great, the abyss is as profound, the heterogeneity is as radical as between being and nonbeing.[92]

Referring again to humanity's need for repentance—that is, a radical ontological requalification—de Lubac quotes the biblical idea of a

[89] John Milbank, *The Suspended Middle: Henri de Lubac and the Debate concerning the Supernatural* (Grand Rapids, Mich.: Eerdmans, 2005), 46–47 (emphasis in original).

[90] Ibid., 47.

[91] Regarding Blondel on this point, see the "Introduction" to Maurice Blondel, *The Letters on Apologetics and History and Dogma*, ed. and trans. A. Dru and I. Trethowan (Grand Rapids, Mich.: Eerdmans, 1964), 74–77; also Oliva Blanchette, *Maurice Blondel: A Philosophical Life* (Grand Rapids, Mich.: Eerdmans, 2010), 657–723.

[92] De Lubac, "Mystery of the Supernatural" (1949), in *Theology in History*, trans. Anne Englund Nash (San Francisco: Ignatius Press, 1996), 302.

new creation, one which is "without common measure with the first creation.... This gift constitutes for nature a real *sublimation*, a real *exaltation* above itself, in brief, a real *deification*."[93]

In this journey to our goal, Church and Scripture are crucial. The Church is the realm of liturgical and sacramental incorporation into the one deified humanity of Christ. Between the Church and the final union of humanity with God, there is not an extrinsic relationship. Rather, they are "two states of the same body".[94] Nor is Scripture some external help along the way. By attending to the inner meaning of Scripture, by not stopping at the external letter but, in faith, internalising its performative, "action-producing words"[95] and penetrating to their mystical heart, the Spirit-enlightened soul encounters Christ the Logos himself and undergoes a dramatic pedagogical journey by which it is interiorly assimilated to God.[96]

Earlier in his 1938 *Catholicism*, de Lubac had already pursued these themes in a brief and accessible form. The whole mystery of Christ is a mystery not only of resurrection, but also of death. "Pasch means passing over. It is a transmutation of the whole being, a complete separation from oneself which no one can hope to evade. It is a denial of all natural values in their natural existence and a renunciation even of all that had previously raised the individual above himself."[97] The terrible shadow of the Cross must encompass everything human, dimming all natural light. Only through the painful way of negation can what is human attain its proper glory. Participation in the agony of the Son's kenosis and sacrifice is the efficacious means to union with the Father.

> There is no smooth transition from a natural love to a supernatural love. To find himself man must lose himself.... *Exodus* and *ecstasy* are governed by the same law. If no one may escape from humanity,

[93] Ibid., 303 (emphasis in original).

[94] Henri de Lubac, *Catholicism*, trans. L. C. Sheppard (London: Burns and Oates, 1950), 27.

[95] Henri de Lubac, *Medieval Exegesis*, vol. 2, trans. E. M. Macierowski (Grand Rapids, Mich.: Eerdmans, 2000), 140, quoting Paul Claudel.

[96] See Henri de Lubac, *History and Spirit: The Understanding of Scripture according to Origen*, trans. Anne Englund Nash (1950; San Francisco: Ignatius, 2007); Henri de Lubac, *Medieval Exegesis*, 3 vols., trans. M. Sebanc et al. (1959–1964; Grand Rapids, Mich.: Eerdmans, 1998–2009).

[97] De Lubac, *Catholicism*, 209.

> humanity whole and entire must die to itself in each of its members so as to live transfigured in God.[98]

Later, in a lecture given to fellow priests at the *Semaine sociale* in Paris in 1947, de Lubac repeated numerous expressions word for word from this last page of *Catholicism*, adding, however, one or two vital comments that reveal his essential congruity with authentic Thomism. Emphasising the need for supernatural agency in the full actualisation of human nature, he writes: "Whatever therefore might be the natural progress gained, even in moral values, whatever might be the new idea elaborated, something else must intervene in order to confer on all this its definitive value: a transfiguration, incommensurate with all natural transformations."[99] This transformation does not spell the destruction of nature. "The bonds are real and close between nature and the supernatural, since it is the first that weaves, so to speak, the body of the second."[100] Even so,

> it is not a question of passing over into a new degree in the same order. The *supernatural* is not a higher, more beautiful, richer or more fruitful nature. It is not, as is sometimes said today through a poor neologism, an overnature. It is the irruption of a totally different principle. A sudden opening of a kind of fourth dimension, without proportion of any kind with all the steps provided in natural dimensions.[101]

Does this mean man should make no effort to prepare the way for this irruption? Is there no more proximate goal for human nature, nothing one can "do" to anticipate or advance the advent of ultimate happiness? De Lubac does not let us off the hook so easily. Some inner restlessness, some creaturely compulsion or calling, drives us forward, even if, in the end, we can only wait with open hands:

> Let man, therefore, confident of divine assistance, take responsibility once again for the work of the six days. Let him prolong it throughout the seventh day. Let him be bold, victorious, inventive.... But

[98] Ibid., 209–10.
[99] "La Recherche d'un homme nouveau", in de Lubac, *At the Service of the Church*, 243.
[100] Ibid., 244.
[101] Ibid., 243–44.

the eighth day, on which alone everything is brought to completion and renewed, is the day of the Lord: man can only receive it. Let him pursue, as long as the world lasts, the activities of Prometheus: let him light in every century a new fire, the material basis for new human strides, new problems and new anguish. But at the same time, let him beg for the descent of the unique Fire without whose burning nothing could be purified, consumed, saved, eternalized: *Emitte Spiritum tuum et creabuntur, et renovabis faciem terrae.*[102]

Conclusion

The aim of this chapter has been to offer a representative sampling of thought on the doctrine of deification in the period between the councils. Given the variety of formulations, which here and there may even indicate fundamental theological divergences, it is providential that the Council Fathers of Vatican II did not leave the question unaddressed. Although they nowhere used the word "deification" as such, the theological anthropology of the council documents clearly expresses the conviction that a purely natural account of the human situation, one which fails to include deification as integral to man's fulfillment, remains incomplete at best. "For faith throws a new light on everything."[103] "When a divine instruction and the hope of life eternal are wanting, man's dignity is most grievously lacerated."[104] "Only in the mystery of the incarnate Word does the mystery of man take on light."[105] Christ alone "fully reveals man to himself and makes his supreme calling clear."[106] Only God "meets the deepest longings of the human heart, which is never fully satisfied by what this world has to offer."[107] These and many similar expressions indicate a subtle return to what might be called an anthropology of the restless heart. In so doing Vatican II reiterated the traditional teaching, indeed, the traditional hope, that the only end worthy of the individual, the only

[102] Ibid., 244.

[103] Vatican Council II, Pastoral Constitution on the Church in the Modern World, *Gaudium et spes*, December 7, 1965, no. 11.

[104] Ibid., no. 21.

[105] Ibid., no. 22.

[106] Ibid.

[107] Ibid., no. 41.

end that really fulfills us, lies in glorious, deifying communion with the Holy Trinity.

Readings for Further Study

Adam, Karl. *The Spirit of Catholicism*. Translated by Justin McCann. New York: Crossroad, 1997.

Caponi, Francis J. "Karl Rahner: Divinization in Roman Catholicism". In *Partakers of the Divine Nature: The History and Development of Deification in the Christian Traditions*, edited by M.J. Christensen and J.A. Wittung, 259–80. Grand Rapids, Mich.: Baker, 2007.

De Lubac, Henri. *Catholicism: Christ and the Common Destiny of Man*. Translated by Lancelot C. Sheppard and Elizabeth Englund. San Francisco, Calif.: Ignatius Press, 1988.

Garrigou-Lagrange, Réginald. *The Love of God and the Cross of Jesus*. 2 vols. Translated by Jeanne Marie. Saint Louis: Herder, 1947.

Gonzalez Arintero, John. *The Mystical Evolution in the Development and Vitality of the Church*. 2 vols. Translated by Jordan Aumann. Saint Louis: Herder, 1949–1951.

Mersch, Émile. *The Theology of the Mystical Body*. Translated by C. Vollert. Saint Louis: Herder, 1952.

Chapter Thirteen

VATICAN II, JOHN PAUL II, AND POSTCONCILIAR THEOLOGY

Tracey Rowland

The notion that man has been made in the image of God to grow into the image of Christ is an element of Christian belief that has profoundly shaped the areas of theological anthropology and moral theology in the postconciliar era. It is a recurring theme in the magisterial teaching of past pontificates: Paul VI, John Paul II, and Benedict XVI, and it is central to the renewal of moral theology where the emphasis is now placed on man's participation in the life of the Holy Trinity and on what is called "nuptial mystery" theology.

Ressourcement, Vatican II, and John Paul II

It is generally acknowledged that as a concept deification or theosis has been much stronger in the Greek than in the Latin Church Fathers, and that while the Latin branch of the Church never rejected the idea, it was somewhat eclipsed in the period between the fourteenth and nineteenth centuries.[1] It was the patristic revival in late nineteenth-century Oxford and a parallel development in Rhineland Catholic academies that fostered a renewal of interest in the subject. In Oxford the topic of deification came to the attention

[1] Anna Williams argues that the *Summa theologiae* of Saint Thomas Aquinas contains a highly developed doctrine of deification and thus that the eclipse takes place after Aquinas (1225–1274). See Anna Williams, "Deification in the *Summa Theologiae*: A Structural Interpretation of the Prima Pars", *The Thomist* 61, no. 2 (April 1997): 220. See also Daniel A. Keating, *Deification and Grace* (Naples, Fla.: Sapientia Press, 2007), and "Justification, Sanctification and Divinization in Thomas Aquinas", in *Aquinas on Doctrine: A Critical Introduction*, ed. Thomas Weinandy et al. (London: Continuum, 2004), 139–58.

of John Henry Newman in his studies of Saint Athanasius, while in Cologne, Matthias Joseph Scheeben linked the notion of deification to a nuptial union between God and the individual person.[2] The patristic revival was continued by the *ressourcement* scholars in the first half of the twentieth century, leading to publications such as Yves Congar's seminal "La deification dans la tradition spirituelle de l'Orient" in 1935; Jean Daniélou's translation of *Grégoire de Nysse: Contemplation sur la Vie de Moïse, ou Traité de la Perfection en Matiére de Vertu* in 1942; and Benoit Pruche's *Basile de Césarée: Traité du Saint-Esprit* in 1947.[3]

In his translation of Saint Gregory of Nyssa's essay on the life of Moses, Daniélou described deification as the soul's recovery of the divine image within it through a movement of purification. According to Daniélou no one has taught the gratuity of grace more emphatically than Gregory of Nyssa, but "at the same time no one has so made it constitutive of the being of man."[4] As a consequence, in a review of Daniélou's translation, John Courtney Murray concluded that "the choice put to human freedom is not between good and evil in the abstract, but between participation in fallen humanity or in humanity risen in Christ."[5] As Saint Ignatius of Antioch expressed the idea: "Just as there are two coinages, one of God and the other of the world, each with its own image, so unbelievers bear the image of this world, and those who have faith with love bear the image of God the Father through Jesus Christ."[6] In his review published in 1948 Murray declared:

[2] John Henry Newman to John Douglas Sandford, May 6, 1877, in *Letters and Diaries*, vol. 18, ed. Charles Dessain (London: Nelson, 1967), 197. See also Austin Cooper, *John Henry Newman: A Developing Spirituality* (Melbourne: St. Paul's Publications, 2012), 90; Matthias Joseph Scheeben, *The Mysteries of Christianity* (Saint Louis: Herder, 1961); Aidan Nichols, *Romance and System: The Theological Synthesis of Matthias Joseph Scheeben* (Denver: Augustine Institute, 2010).

[3] Yves Congar, "La deification dans la tradition spirituelle de l'Orient", *Vie Spirituelle* 43 (1935): 91–107, and Jean Daniélou's translation *Grégoire de Nysse: Contemplation sur la Vie de Moïse, ou Traité de la Perfection en Matiére de Vertu* (Paris: Cerf, 1942); Benoit Pruche's *Basile de Césarée: Traité du Saint-Esprit* (Paris: Cerf, 1947).

[4] Daniélou, *Grégoire de Nysse*, 34.

[5] John Courtney Murray, "Current Theology: *Sources Chrétiennes*", *Theological Studies* 9 (1948): 255.

[6] Saint Ignatius of Antioch, *Letter to the Magnesians* 5.2, in Michael W. Homes, *The Apostolic Fathers in English*, 3rd ed. (Grand Rapids, Mich.: Baker Academic, 2006), 104.

> Perhaps no other single notion is capturing such wide interest in a variety of circles today as that of the "image of God in man". It is being recognised as the necessary inspiration of social reconstruction; and this fact has made it the object of considerable philosophical interest. Theologians too, are turning to it in the contemporary effort to give fuller theological and metaphysical explanation of man's mysterious capacity for the supernatural.... Maréchal has pointed out that the doctrine of the image of God in man, and of man's participation in the divinity, of which it is the pendant, stands at the centre of Gregory of Nyssa's mystical theology.[7]

Murray suggested that this vision of the individual person carried with it a "joyous mystique" since it "vanquished the sad determinism of the Greeks" and makes the "modern 'liberal' sort of thing, seem very pale".[8]

With the renewal of interest in the *imago Dei* came a renewal of interest in the role of the Holy Spirit in the economy of salvation. In his notes on Saint Basil's treatise on the Holy Spirit, Benoit Pruche wrote:

> He [Saint Basil] grasped the sanctifying role of the Spirit in really new perspectives—doubtless the prolongation of insights of Athanasius; yet ideas like those of perfection, sanctification, "deification" implied therein are met with again and unified on a loftier level, where the mysterious operations of the Holy Spirit originate, through a mode of causality reserved to Him, in the bosom of the indivisible and inseparable action of the three divine persons, "unique Principle of all that is."[9]

At the Second Vatican Council these patristic ideas with their scriptural foundations percolated to the surface and were embedded in the document *Dei verbum*:

> In His goodness and wisdom God chose to reveal Himself and to make known to us the hidden purpose of His will (see Eph 1:9) by

[7] Murray, "Current Theology", 260.

[8] Ibid., 261.

[9] Benoit Pruche as translated into English by Walter J. Burghardt, "Current Theology: *Sources Chrétiennes*", *Theological Studies* 9 (1948): 284.

> which through Christ, the Word made flesh, man might in the Holy Spirit have access to the Father and come to share in the divine nature (see Eph 2:18; 2 Pet 1:4).[10]

The logic of *Dei verbum* was followed through in *Gaudium et spes*:

> The truth is that only in the mystery of the incarnate Word does the mystery of man take on light. For Adam, the first man, was a figure of Him Who was to come, namely Christ the Lord. Christ, the final Adam, by the revelation of the mystery of the Father and His love, fully reveals man to man himself and makes his supreme calling clear.[11]

This particular paragraph became something of a "signature tune" for the entire pontificate of Pope Saint John Paul II. It reverberates through his many homilies and encyclicals, but it is found in its strongest manifestation in his trinitarian encyclicals: *Redemptor hominis* (1979), *Dives in misericordia* (1980), and *Dominum et vivificantem* (1986). According to the late pontiff, the fact of having been made in God's image does not mean, *merely*, that man has a rational intellect and a free will, as this is so often stated, *but also*, that he has from the beginning the capacity of having a personal relationship to God. Thus, in *Redemptor hominis* John Paul II stated that the man who wishes to understand himself thoroughly must draw near to Christ and appropriate and assimilate the whole of the reality of the Incarnation and redemption in order to find himself.[12] In *Dives in misericordia*, the encyclical on the individual person's relationship to God the Father, mention was made of the fact that the Father does not merely remain closely linked with the world as the Creator and the ultimate source of existence, but he remains linked to the individual person in a bond still more intimate than that of creation.[13] Each person has the potential to become an "adopted son" and a sharer in the truth and love that is in God and proceeds from God.[14]

[10] Vatican Council II, Dogmatic Constitution on Divine Revelation, *Dei verbum*, November 18, 1965, no. 2.

[11] Vatican Council II, Pastoral Constitution on the Church in the Modern World, *Gaudium et spes*, December 7, 1965, no. 2.

[12] Pope John Paul II, Encyclical Letter *Redemptor hominis*, March 8, 1979, no. 10.

[13] Pope John Paul II, Encyclical Letter *Dives in misericordia*, November 30, 1980, no. 7.

[14] Ibid.

In *Dominum et vivificantem*, the encyclical on the Holy Spirit, John Paul II described the farewell discourse at the Last Supper as the "highest point of the revelation of the Trinity", and he argued that the trinitarian formula used in the sacrament of baptism "brings about sharing in the life of the Triune God, for it gives sanctifying grace as a supernatural gift to man."[15] The foregoing reiterated themes in the encyclical *Ecclesiam suam* of Paul VI to the effect that those who are baptised are incorporated into Christ's Mystical Body and are thereby raised "to a higher status, of being reborn to a supernatural life, there to experience the happiness of being God's adopted sons, the special dignity of being Christ's brothers, the blessedness, the grace and the joy of the indwelling Holy Spirit".[16] According to Paul VI, the sacrament of baptism for a baptised person is a kind of " 'illumination which draws down upon his soul the life-giving radiance of divine truth, opens heaven to him, and sheds upon this mortal life that light which enables him to walk as a child of the light toward the vision of God."[17]

In *Dominum et vivificantem* John Paul II also emphasised that the divine filiation planted in one's soul through sanctifying grace is the work of the Holy Spirit.[18] As a consequence one's life becomes permeated, through participation, by the divine life, and itself acquires a divine, supernatural dimension which includes access to the Father in the Holy Spirit.[19] The logic of these trinitarian encyclicals is that grace "bears within itself both a Christological aspect and a pneumatological one, which becomes evident above all in those who expressly accept Christ".[20]

In *Dominum et vivificantem*, John Paul II linked the work of the Holy Spirit to that of liberating persons from "various determinisms which derive mainly from the materialistic bases of thought, practice and related modes of action". He noted that in the contemporary world such determinisms have "succeeded in penetrating into man's inmost being, into that sanctuary of the conscience where the

[15] Pope John Paul II, Encyclical Letter *Dominum et vivificantem*, May 18, 1986, no. 9.

[16] Pope Paul VI, Encyclical Letter *Ecclesiam suam*, August 6, 1964, no. 39.

[17] Ibid.

[18] See Pope John Paul II, *Dominum et vivificantem*, no. 52.

[19] See ibid.

[20] Ibid., no. 53.

Holy Spirit continuously radiates the light and strength of new life in the freedom of the children of God". Without in any sense denying the human capacity for a free exercise of the will he nonetheless observed that the individual person's spiritual maturity can be retarded by "the conditionings and pressures exerted upon him by dominating structures and mechanisms in the various spheres of society." He acknowledged that "in many cases social factors, instead of fostering the development and expansion of the human spirit, ultimately deprive the human spirit of the genuine truth of its being and life—over which the Holy Spirit keeps vigil—in order to subject it to the 'prince of this world.'"[21]

In a speech he delivered to the scholars of the Catholic University of Lublin (KUL) in 1987, John Paul II described the temptations of the "prince of this world" in the following terms:

> The human person must in the name of the truth about himself stave off a double temptation: the temptation to make the truth about himself subordinate to his freedom and the temptation to subordinate himself to the world of objects; he has to refuse to succumb to the temptation of both self-idolatry and of self-subjectification: *Positus est in medio homo: nec bestia—nec deus.*[22]

In other words, a person is neither a beast nor God, but a creature made by God in his own image. The pathos of the moral life is generated by the constant struggle of the person to cooperate with the Holy Spirit and the work of grace and thereby grow in the likeness of Christ, against the double temptation to self-idolatry and self-subjectification. In the twentieth century this struggle became particularly acute in the field of sexuality where new ideas and technologies arose, severing the association of eros to love and fidelity. In the late nineteenth century Friedrich Nietzsche had led the charge against Christian ethics with his claim that Christianity had killed eros. Nietzsche's indictment was then affirmed in the early part of the twentieth century by Sigmund Freud, for whom human behaviour could be explained as a response to sexual drives, the repression of which was a major cause of poor

[21] Ibid., no. 60.

[22] Pope John Paul II, "Address to the Scholars of Lublin University", *Christian Life in Poland*, November 1987, p. 51.

mental health. In the decade of the 1960s ideas drawn from the works of Nietzsche, Freud, and (in some cases) Karl Marx formed the foundations of a new post-Christian worldview. The generation of 1968, labelled by French sociologists as the *soixante-huitards*, was the first to take advantage of the manufacture of the contraceptive pill. When Paul VI published the encyclical *Humanae vitae* in 1968 he was not only fighting a rearguard action against hippies, flower power, and "free love", but in many countries, including the politically powerful United States, he was contending with a new generation of upwardly mobile Catholics for whom the use of the pill offered the possibility of significantly reducing the size of one's family and thereby promoting one's material prosperity. When *Humanae vitae* upheld the Church's centuries-long teaching against the use of contraceptives, there was widespread rebellion within the ranks of clergy and laity alike, but particularly within the ranks of aspirational middle-class laity and their more highly educated confessors. It was within the context of this particular pastoral crisis that John Paul II set about renewing the Church's moral teachings in the area of sexuality with reference to a couple's participation in the life of the Holy Trinity.

The young Karol Wojtyła (Pope Saint John Paul II) had spoken of love as a gift of the self, of spousal love as the paradigmatic gift of the self, and of the Trinity as the archetype of such a gift. In a paper presented on the eleventh of April in 1969 to celebrate the fiftieth anniversary of the establishment of the Catholic University of Lublin, Cardinal Wojtyła was critical of the way in which various persons had sought to defend *Humanae vitae* by reference to notions of natural law which were in no way consistent with the ecclesial understanding of natural law. He emphasised that in the ecclesial understanding, natural law is the "participation of the eternal law in a rational creature"; it is not merely "the biological regularity we find in people in the area of sexual actualisation".[23] A year earlier at a theological conference in Kraków he had drawn attention to *Humanae vitae*. It holds that conjugal love most fully reveals its true nature and dignity when we consider that it takes its origin from God, who "is love", and the Father from whom all fatherhood in heaven and on earth gets its

[23] Karol Wojtyła, "The Human Person and the Natural Law", in *Person and Community: Selected Essays*, trans. Theresa Sandok (New York: Peter Lang, 1993), 183.

name.[24] As a consequence, one finds the statement that to make use of "the gift of married love while respecting the laws of conception is to acknowledge that one is not the master of the sources of life but rather the minister of the design established by the Creator."[25]

As pope, Karol Wojtyła followed through the logic of his earlier essays in the defence of *Humanae vitae* with his *Catechesis on Human Love*, based on the two accounts of creation in Genesis, and on the theological anthropology of no. 22 of the conciliar document *Gaudium et spes*. Significantly, the account of the *imago Dei* offered in this paragraph was explicitly trinitarian, not merely "theistically coloured". Therefore in his *Catechesis on Human Love*, delivered as a series of Wednesday audience addresses in the early years of his pontificate, anthropology was linked to trinitarian theology and sexuality was situated within this framework of God's offer of divine filiation. Within this *katalogical* framework (working downward from the Trinity to the person), the married couple is raised to the exalted position of being a "radiant icon of Trinitarian love", and the seal of their marital holiness is viewed as nothing less than a "supernatural work of art". To quote Marc Cardinal Ouellet, a former professor of the John Paul II Institute at the Lateran University:

> The hour of conjugal and family spirituality is therefore the hour of the transcendence of the self into the image of the Trinity, the hour of becoming a house of God, a home of the Most High, an icon of the Trinity, memory and prophecy of the wonders of salvation history.[26]

In *Divine Likeness: Toward a Trinitarian Anthropology of the Family*, Cardinal Ouellet explains that this means that the sacramental mission of the couple and their family is not primarily a job or list of social responsibilities. Rather, more fundamentally, the mission is inscribed in the very being of the couple as a *communio personarum* sealed by the Holy Spirit. As a consequence,

> the doctrine of the *imago Dei* should be reconsidered in a radically Trinitarian perspective.... The gifts of creation, the gift of life, the

[24] Pope Paul VI, Encyclical *Humanae vitae*, July 25, 1968, no. 8.

[25] Ibid., no. 13.

[26] Marc Ouellet, *Divine Likeness: Toward a Trinitarian Anthropology of the Family* (Grand Rapids, Mich.: Eerdmans, 2006), 100.

> gift of *fides* and of the sacrament signify, in the final analysis, the gifts of the Father to the Son and of the Son to the Father in the Holy Spirit. Created gifts express and signify the uncreated love between the divine persons. Thus human love in its beauty and fragility allows us to see, like a living icon, the Glory within God. The Holy Spirit prolongs in marriage what he does in the relationship of Christ and the Church, he makes of it the nuptial incarnation of the "Nuptial Mystery" par excellence.[27]

Cardinal Ouellet also noted that this perspective is "not simply intended to overcome a certain classical formulation that overlooked the particular gift the divine Persons make to the couple". Rather, "its aim is to understand the sacrament of marriage and therefore the exchange of love between man and woman within the horizon of the *imago Dei*, as the couple's participation in the exchange of 'gifts' between the divine Persons." Thus he concludes:

> Assumed within the kenotic paschal drama of Trinitarian Love, conjugal love is therefore inserted into the missionary dynamism of the Church, sacrament and salvation. Natural *eros* and the personal love of the spouses, blessed by God the Creator and sanctified by Christ the Redeemer, belong to the sacramental order of the Incarnation.[28]

Ecclesial Movements and Postconciliar Theology

The papacy of John Paul II, and in particular, his *Catechesis on Human Love*, was supported by a wide variety of new ecclesial movements. The most significant of these in Italy was *Comunione e liberazione*, or

[27] Ibid., 234. This section (on recent magisterial teachings on human love) was originally delivered by the author in a paper titled "John Paul II and the Civilisation of Love", an occasional address delivered at the Catholic University of Lublin on April 2, 2012, to mark the seventh anniversary of the death of Pope Saint John Paul II. A version has been published in Polish in the journal *Ethos*. The exposition of Cardinal Ouellet's contribution to this field can also be found in Italian in the author's article "Una Fragile Icona: L'Amore Tra Uoma e Donna", in *Il logos dell' agape: Amore e ragione come principi dell'agire*, a cura di Juan José Pérez-Soba e Luis Granados (Roma: Cantagalli, 2008). Some material from these foreign-language papers also appears in English in the author's chapter "The Culture Wars: Saint John Paul II—Pope of the Civilisation of Love" in *God and Eros: The Ethos of the Nuptial Mystery*, eds. Colin Patterson and Conor Sweeney (Eugene, Ore.: Cascade Books/Wipf and Stock, 2015), 19–38.

[28] Ouellet, *Divine Likeness*, 171.

"CL", founded by Father Luigi Giussani in 1969. Giussani was a graduate of the Venegono seminary on the outskirts of Milan. Archbishop Javier Martínez Fernandéz has described the theology of Venegono when Giusanni was a student (before the Second Vatican Council) in the following terms:

> That school was characterized by the intellectual effort to recover, for Christian theological thought, the centrality of the figure of Christ in history and in the cosmos and, therefore, at the same time to recover the substantive connection between Christ and the created order, between Christ and human existence. In this way, it would be manifested again in the thought and life of the Church that the whole of creation, the whole of existence, is constitutively oriented to Christ.[29]

One of those who joined Giussani's movement was the young Angelo Scola, a son of a truck driver. After graduating from the University of Milan, he was for a time a seminarian for the Archdiocese of Milan. However at this moment in history members of the seminary's ultraliberal establishment were not very hospitable to students from Guissani's stable. Scola was ultimately ordained for the much less prestigious southern Italian Diocese of Teramo. In one of those historical ironies often found in salvation history, in 2011 Scola was appointed as the cardinal archbishop of Milan (from his position as the patriarch of Venice) by Benedict XVI. Scola is known as a leading proponent of nuptial mystery theology and of John Paul II's *Catechesis on Human Love*. In *The Nuptial Mystery*, Scola observed that the true content of Satan's offer to Adam—"You will be as God" (see Gen 3:5)—is given to Christians by grace:

> We will be as God, but not because we will somehow be able to transform our human nature into divine nature; rather, as Thomas reminds us, the grace of the Spirit will make us capable in paradise of standing before the full glory of Christ. This will be the beginning of our unity with the Father. The action of the Spirit is therefore the progressive divinization of the person. This divinization is produced

[29]Javier Martínez Fernandéz, "The Harmful Division That Invades Us", *Humanitas* 2 (2012): 144.

> precisely through an incorporation.... The dynamism of divinization and incorporation points to the way in which the Spirit works in the church of God, showing himself to be the heart of the world.[30]

Scola also observed that John Paul II's major encyclical on moral theology, *Veritatis splendor*, makes a reference to John 1:17—"the law was given through Moses; grace and truth came through Jesus Christ."[31] It is something of an understatement to say that the moral theology of John Paul II had a strong Christocentric orientation. According to Scola the prime cause of the contemporary rejection of the possibility of a natural moral law is to be located in an inability to recognise Jesus Christ as the universal and concrete norm, and this "means the continuation of the Enlightenment challenge rigorously formulated by Kant, which claimed that a historical event (Jesus Christ) could not be the formulation and proof of universal, necessary truths".[32] Indeed, Scola speaks of a problem of a double extrinsicism—the reduction of ethics to a pure norm on the one side, and the idea of *sola scriptura* on the other.

In an article on the renewal of moral theology in the light of Vatican II and *Veritatis splendor*, Joseph Ratzinger concluded (in implicit concord with Scola) that "no ethics can be constructed without God."[33] He argued that even the Decalogue is not to be interpreted first of all as law, but rather as a gift. It begins with the words "I am Yahweh, your Lord", and having noted this, Ratzinger argues that without the first tablet of the commandments and this preamble the second tablet "would not work".[34] Somewhat emphatically Ratzinger stated, "We cannot yield on this point: without God, all the rest would no longer have logical coherence."[35] This was also the assessment of Ratzinger's fellow *Communio* journal founder, Hans Urs von Balthasar. In his *Nine Propositions for a Christian Ethic*, von Balthasar concluded:

[30] Angelo Scola, *The Nuptial Mystery* (Grand Rapids, Mich.: Eerdmans, 2005), 282.

[31] Pope John Paul II, Encyclical Letter *Veritatis splendor*, August 6, 1993.

[32] Angelo Scola, "Following Christ: On John Paul II's encyclical *Veritatis Splendor*", *Communio* 20 (Winter 1993): 724–25.

[33] Joseph Ratzinger, "The Renewal of Moral Theology: Vatican II and *Veritatis splendor*", *Communio* 32, no. 2 (Summer 2005): 367.

[34] Ibid.

[35] Ibid.

> Where Christ's divinity is not recognised, he necessarily appears as a human exemplar, and Christian ethics becomes either heteronomous, where Christ becomes simply an obligatory norm for my conduct, or autonomous, to the extent that his actions are interpreted merely as the achieved self-perfection of the human ethical subject.[36]

Livio Melina has summarised von Balthasar's moral theology in the following paragraph:

> We have here a powerful theological synthesis of moral theology anchored in the following elements: (1) the main axis is a Christocentric theological anthropology of a filial nature: in Christ we are predestined to be "sons of the Son"; (2) the moral bond is placed within the personal relationship of sons in the Son with regard to the Father; (3) the Law of the Old Testament is summed up in the link of obedience of the Son to the Father; and thus the natural law too becomes a fragment of the Christological whole; (4) the exterior aspect is retained, but it becomes polarized in the Spirit with interiority.[37]

There is thus in the pro-magisterial moral theology of the pontificate of John Paul II a strong anti-Kantian trajectory (of which von Balthasar's work is a prime example) and a corresponding negative attitude toward the preconciliar manuals of theology which were highly propositional, rationalistic, and casuistic. The Trinity was surprisingly absent. Indeed, Peter Henrici has argued that a specifically modern (in the sense of rationalist) moral theology existed between Trent and Vatican II.[38] The following paragraph by Henrici encapsulates the spirit of much of the moral theology of this period:

> The practice of Christian life was unduly burdened by the idea of "making." Asceticism drowned out and marginalised mysticism, while appealing all too frequently to ideas that were at least semi-Pelagian.

[36] Hans Urs von Balthasar et al., *Principles of a Christian Morality* (San Francisco: Ignatius Press, 1986), 80.

[37] Livio Melina, *Sharing in Christ's Virtues* (Washington, D.C.: Catholic University of America Press, 2001), 127.

[38] See Peter Henrici, "Modernity and Christianity", *Communio* 17 (Summer 1990): 140–51, esp. 150–51. (Henrici is a member of the Society of Jesus, a cousin of Hans Urs von Balthasar, and a retired auxiliary bishop of the Diocese of Chur in Switzerland.)

> Morality stood, and still stands, in the foreground of Christian self-understanding. Christian life consists largely of a series of duties that are performed because one is obliged to do so. Kant had become a secret father of the Church. For many Christians, perfection is seen as something "do-able"; they then suffer because they are unable to attain that perfection. Moved by a kind of Christian Pharisaism, Christian existence had become viewed as a meritorious achievement that God commands and by virtue of which one is able to please him. Since all this is not so simple, however, people devote themselves to other alternative projects, such as philanthropy or third world development—at any rate, something that can be done and accomplished.[39]

Livio Melina has subsequently described Kantianism as "the extreme consequence of the pharisaical temptation of an autonomous justification of man before the Law".[40] Against an avalanche of scholarship critical of an anthropology that severs the operation of the intellect from the motions of the heart or that cares only about *ratio* and dismisses *intellectus*, Benedict Ashley has declared that "Kant's rationalism has now lost credibility" and that "no one can read the Bible or the Church Fathers without seeing that these sources are not rationalistic, but give full credit to the rôle of the human 'heart' (i.e., human feeling and the images which move it) in moral decision-making."[41] The fact that Catholic ethics is something quite different from anything discernible from the application of what Kant might call "pure reason" is evident in Servais Pinckaers' seminal work *Morality: A Catholic View.* According to Pinckaers,

> The advent of divine revelation has occasioned a profound transformation in the doctrine of virtue. The first source of moral excellence is no longer located in the human person, but in God through Christ. This transformation is evident in the doctrine of the infused moral virtues, which are not acquired by unaided human effort, but implanted in the human person by the Holy Spirit.[42]

[39] Ibid., 150–51.

[40] Melina, *Sharing in Christ's Virtues*, 127.

[41] Benedict Ashley, *Living the Truth in Love: A Biblical Introduction to Moral Theology* (New York: Alba House, 1996), 128–29.

[42] Servais Pinckaers, *Morality: A Catholic View* (South Bend, Ind.: St. Augustine's Press, 2001), 71.

As Melina has explained: "The Christian moral theology that is rooted in Christ and that takes Christ as a model, is open to the Father, [and as such] it is a filial moral theology."[43] Against the Kantian temptation, Melina has also drawn attention to Saint Bonaventure's insight that Christ is "the *medium* of all knowledge". Thus,

> rational creatures receive an impression of the image and are called to express it in a likeness that depends on their free response. The moral life is located between the "*impressio*" of the image and its "*expressio*" in life. It has as its ultimate end the showing forth of the Glory of God.... Through the moral life man is called to *deiformitas*, to take on the very form of God.[44]

The logic of this Christocentric renewal of moral theology is Michael Hanby's insight that "at issue within the culture of modernity is the Trinity itself and specifically whether the meaning of human nature and human agency are understood to occur within Christ's mediation of the love and delight shared as *donum* between the Father and the Son, or beyond it."[45] Hanby observes that what Pelagianism does is to institute a rupture in the christological and trinitarian economy, creating possibilities for human nature "outside" the Trinity and the mediation of Christ. For this reason he defines the Pelagian tendency as "philosophising without a mediator" and "an attempt to smuggle Stoic cosmology into Christian thought".[46] From this perspective Kantianism is a modern kind of Pelagianism. Since, as Hanby stresses, it is Christ who determines what it means to be human and Christ working inseparably with the other trinitarian *personae* who incorporates us fully and finally into our being, it follows that readings of human nature and human agency which are offered without reference to Christ's mediation are destined to end in some form of moralism—that is, a belief in salvation through the performance of good works and obedience that misses the whole dimension of love. Consistent with this understanding is Cardinal Marc Ouellet's judgment that since God's desire is for the integration of all of creation into the beatitude of his

[43] Melina, *Sharing in Christ's Virtues*, 122.

[44] Ibid., 131.

[45] Michael Hanby, *Augustine and Modernity* (London: Routledge, 2003), 73.

[46] Ibid., 106.

trinitarian exchange, "the Trinitarian horizon of human existence is the foundation of ethical decisions."[47]

Accordingly, David L. Schindler argues that the overcoming of moralism presupposes "a distinctive ontology which in turn carries a distinctive view not only of man but of precisely everything: of every aspect of every entity and artefact in cosmos and culture".[48] With reference to the notion of "splendour" in the phrase "splendour of the truth", Schindler further argues that the reality of divine and human communion emphasised by John Paul II is best expressed in the language of beauty and that this aesthetic accent has at least four implications for individual and social morality:

1. The language of beauty implies an overcoming of moralism, insofar as our moral acts are first called forth by the attractiveness of the other. Our moral acts are of course something for which we ourselves are responsible. But the pertinent point indicated by the language of splendour is that it is the beauty of the other (Other) that first evokes my response and in a significant sense bears it—like the rays of the sun or the smile of a mother. The flower itself blooms, but only as its bloom is called forth by the presence of the sun within it.

2. Secondly, morality is never simply a matter of moral or wilful intentions, but it is also a matter of "seeing" as well as of "doing".

3. The primacy of the aesthetic-contemplative dimension implies that truth is never our possession, strictly speaking. On the contrary, it is always a gift to be wondered at. We hold on to the truth not by attempting to grasp it fully and to exhaust its meaning, but by indwelling what always transcends us.

4. John Paul II's emphasis on the person's constitutive relation to God implies a notion of human nature as related first in a "direct" and "positive" as distinct from "indifferent" or "negative" manner to God. And the pope's emphasis on the person's primarily aesthetic-contemplative nature in relation to God and others entails a notion of truth as intrinsically (also) a matter of love.[49]

[47] Marc Ouellet, "The Foundations of Christian Ethics according to von Balthasar", *Communio* 17 (Fall 1990): 395.

[48] David L. Schindler, "Is Truth Ugly? Moralism and the Convertibility of Being and Love", *Communio* 27 (Winter 2000): 704.

[49] See David L. Schindler, "Reorienting the Church on the Eve of the Millennium: John Paul II's 'New Evangelization'", *Communio* 24 (Winter 1997): 767–68. These four points are not direct quotations from the Schindler article but the author's summary of Schindler's more expansive description of the four points.

This fourth point was emphasised by Pope Emeritus Benedict XVI in his statement that "truth and love are the twin pillars of all reality." This theme was strong in his Millennium Address to the Scholars of the Sorbonne University and in his first encyclical *Deus Caritas Est.*[50] As a cardinal, Joseph Ratzinger wrote that seminarians of his generation had been taught by Romano Guardini (1885–1965), a professor at the University of Munich, that "the essence of Christianity is not an idea, not a system of thought, not a plan of action. The essence of Christianity is a Person: Jesus Christ himself."[51] The following statement from Guardini's work on the theological virtues of faith, hope, and love encapsulates what it means to live life from the perspective of eternity, in an intimate communion with the Persons of the Trinity on a path of deification:

> This *Logos*, which is perfectly simple and yet immeasurably rich, is no order of forms and laws, no world of prototypes and arrangements, but *Someone*, He is the living son of the eternal Father. We can stand before Him, face to face. We can speak to Him and He answers, indeed, He Himself gives us the power to stand before Him and He can grant our request. We can love Him and He is able to give us a communion which reflects the intimacy in which He lies upon the bosom of the Father, and which St. John experienced when His Master permitted him to lay his head upon His heart. This fact established a contrast to everything which natural philosophy and piety can experience or invent. This *Logos*, this one and all, steps into history and becomes man.[52]

One may conclude therefore that the overcoming of moralism, especially in its Kantian manifestation, with a renewed emphasis upon the divine invitation to deification as the axis of a moral theology built

[50] Joseph Ratzinger, *Truth and Tolerance: Christian Belief and World Religions*, trans. Henry Taylor (San Francisco: Ignatius Press, 2003), 183. For a penetrating analysis of the relationship between love and reason in the theology of Saint Thomas Aquinas and the theology of Hans Urs von Balthasar, see David C. Schindler; "Towards a Non-Possessive Concept of Knowledge: On the Relation between Reason and Love in Aquinas and Balthasar", *Modern Theology* 22, no. 4 (October 2006): 577–607.

[51] Joseph Ratzinger, "Guardini on Christ in our Century", *Crisis Magazine*, June 1996, 15.

[52] Romano Guardini, *The Word of God: On Faith, Hope and Charity* (Chicago: Henry Regnery, 1963), 28.

upon a richly trinitarian anthropology, has been a major achievement of postconciliar theology and of the pontificate of Pope Saint John Paul II. It is, however, unlikely to appeal to the so-called liberal mind which is neurotically fixated on the notion of equality. A creature who has been called into a relationship of intimacy with the Trinity will image Christ more or less than others depending on his response to that very invitation and the work of grace. Some people will end up more Christlike than others. As Saint Thomas Aquinas noted in his treatment of the *imago Dei* in the Prima Pars of the *Summa theologiae*,[53] the individual person images his Creator in three different ways: first, inasmuch as the person possesses a natural aptitude for understanding and loving God; second, inasmuch as man actually or habitually knows and loves God, though imperfectly, and this image consists in the conformity to grace; and third, inasmuch as man knows and loves God perfectly, and this image consists in the likeness of glory. While the first is found in all persons, the second is only found in the just, and the third only in the blessed.

Conclusion

As the liberal ideology of radical lifestyle equality becomes more and more totalitarian, not only will the culture of Western civilisation become neo-barbaric, but the form of the barbarism is likely to be worse than anything known in the pre-Christian era. This is because the contemporary culture of death, as Pope Saint John Paul II called it, is built on a conscious and militant rejection of the possibility of Saint Thomas' higher ways of imaging God; it is not built on ignorance of the Incarnation. It is not a culture groping its way towards a receptivity to divine revelation, but rather, a culture in rebellion against Christian beliefs and the very ideal of sanctity. As the liberal philosopher John Rawls expressed the proposition, if a person wants to spend his life counting blades of grass, then that is the good life for him and no one else has any basis on which to challenge his judgment. In short, if we live in a democracy, we cannot go about promoting the idea that sanctity is desirable, because the moment

[53] *STh* q. 93.

one speaks of sanctity, one is saying that some people are better than others because some people are more Christlike than others, and such a claim is regarded as an attack on a democratic social order.

As we move from the pontificates of Pope Saint John Paul II and Pope Emeritus Benedict to that of Francis, theologians are becoming focused on the theme of the Church as a field hospital. The accent is now on ecclesiology rather than on anthropology. However, those who find themselves wounded by the practices of the culture of death and in need of mercy, healing, repentance, and forgiveness are very often those who found themselves ensnared in practices that undermined their dignity as children of God without any prior understanding of the possibilities open to them by virtue of their baptism. The idea that life is about the recovery of the divine image within it through a movement of purification is precisely the "medicine" or "antidote" required to be administered by those running the hospital.

Readings for Further Study

Pope John Paul II. *Encyclical Letter,* Dives in misericordia *of the Supreme Pontiff John Paul II: On the Mercy of God.* Boston: St. Paul Editions, 1981.

_____. *Encyclical Letter* Dominum et vivificantem *of the Supreme Pontiff John Paul II on the Holy Spirit in the Life of the Church of the World.* Homebush, N.S.W.: St. Paul Publications, 1986.

_____. *Encyclical Letter of His Holiness Pope John Paul II: The Redeemer of Man,* Redemptor hominis. Boston: Daughters of St. Paul, 1979.

Ouellet, Marc Cardinal. *Divine Likeness: Toward a Trinitarian Anthropology of the Family.* Grand Rapids, Mich.: Eerdmans, 2006.

Chapter Fourteen

DEIFICATION IN THE *CATECHISM OF THE CATHOLIC CHURCH*

Carl E. Olson

Christoph Cardinal Schönborn, coeditor of the *Catechism of the Catholic Church*, has explained that the *Catechism* approaches the principle of "the hierarchy of truth" by focusing mainly on "three criteria for the organization of the whole work", the first of which is the mystery of the Blessed Trinity.[1] "All that needs to be said about Christian faith and life," he stated, "is directed to this center: communion in the blessed life of the Most Holy Trinity." He then quotes from no. 260 of the *Catechism*:

> The ultimate end of the whole divine economy is the entry of God's creatures into the perfect unity of the Blessed Trinity. But even now we are called to be a dwelling for the Most Holy Trinity.

This theme of the ultimate end of the trinitarian work is found throughout the *Catechism*, sometimes expressed with explicit directness and other times in implicit, less obvious ways. This chapter traces this theme of deification[2] in the *Catechism*, beginning with the first sentence of the opening paragraph: "God, infinitely perfect and blessed in himself, in a plan of sheer goodness freely created man to make him share in his own blessed life." Because of this goal, God draws close to, and seeks, man. The Church, the family of God, is the place of authentic and supernatural unity, whereas it is through the redemptive, saving

[1] Joseph Cardinal Ratzinger and Christoph Cardinal Schönborn, *Introduction to the Catechism of the Catholic Church* (San Francisco: Ignatius Press, 1994), 42–43.

[2] The terms "theosis", "divinization", and "deification" do not appear in the *Catechism*, which instead uses a variety of other terms, as this essay will show.

work of Jesus Christ that such sharing in the divine life is realized: "In his Son and through him, he invites men to become, in the Holy Spirit, his adopted children and thus heirs of his blessed life (*CCC* 1).

The triune God—Father, Son, and Holy Spirit—is perfect relationship in himself. Yet, he created all things in order to impart not only physical life but also supernatural life to man. And he has founded a household—the Church—and he offers men the opportunity to join it, not merely as forgiven slaves or blessed servants, but as actual children.

This invitation forms the basis for Catholic anthropology, for man's dignity rests "above all on the fact he is called to communion with God" (*CCC* 27).[3] Man is a spiritual being who possesses a body and a soul, and from creation he "is ordered to a supernatural end", for "his soul can gratuitously be raised beyond all it deserves to communion with God" (*CCC* 367). When man is separated from God's truth and creative action, he loses his dignity and becomes less than truly human (*CCC* 1700, 308). But man, by his natural faculties, can come "to a knowledge of the existence of a personal God" (*CCC* 35); he possesses a God-given desire for the supernatural and an inner longing for grace, even while he lacks the ability to acquire it on his own (*CCC* 35–38).

Trinity and Creation

This truth of divine orientation is known through divine revelation (*CCC* 50). Although man has a certain natural sense of this orientation, it is beyond ordinary comprehension. This orientation to God's life is rooted in God's very nature, for he "is love" (1 Jn 4:8, 16) and his "very being is love" (*CCC* 221). God is not an angry deity, nor a detached being who demands blind servitude, but "is an eternal exchange of love, Father, Son, and Holy Spirit, and he has destined us to share in that exchange" (*CCC* 221). The *Catechism* emphasizes that the Creator's loving plan predates creation itself:

> God freely wills to communicate the glory of his blessed life. Such is the "plan of his loving kindness," conceived by the Father before

[3] Quoting Vatican Council II, Pastoral Constitution on the Church in the Modern World, *Gaudium et spes*, December 7, 1965, no. 19.

> the foundation of the world, in his beloved Son: "He destined us in love to be his sons" and "to be conformed to the image of his Son" through "the spirit of sonship" (Eph 1:4–5, 9; Rom 8:15, 29). This plan is a "grace [which] was given to us in Christ Jesus before the ages began," stemming immediately from Trinitarian love (2 Tim 1:9–10). (*CCC* 257)

To separate God as Creator from God as Love would erase the reason behind creation, pervert the goal of our existence, and destroy the worth of our being. God creates to demonstrate his glory and "communicate it", for his "love and goodness" are the sole reasons for his creating (*CCC* 293). Mankind attempts to obtain power and glory by grasping, clawing, and competing. God, complete in himself, freely gives his life and shares his glory in order to manifest it throughout creation, and especially in us. This is why he makes us "to be his sons through Jesus Christ, according to the purpose of his will, *to the praise of his glorious grace* (Eph 1:5–6)" (*CCC* 294; emphasis in original). Creatures that we are, we must choose between either seeking our own glory, which will only bring us disgrace and damnation, or seeking God's glory, since all that we are is due to him. God's work will be fulfilled; we choose either to reject it or to participate in it: "The ultimate purpose of creation is that God 'who is the creator of all things may at last become "all in all," thus simultaneously assuring his own glory and our beatitude' (*Ad gentes* 2)" (*CCC* 294).

The Fall and the Loss of Divine Life

In the beginning, God created the original man and woman, Adam and Eve, who "were constituted in an original 'state of holiness and justice' (cf. Council of Trent [1546]: DS 1511)", or an actual sharing in divine life (*CCC* 375). But our first parents committed sin and the Fall took place. This original sin was committed when man, entrusted with free will and given specific limits, broke trust and "*preferred* himself to God" (*CCC* 398; see *CCC* 396; emphasis in original). Man was convinced he was capable of giving himself life, existence, and meaning apart from God, which is the oldest and most fundamental of lies. Man was already enjoying divine life and "was destined to be fully 'divinized' by God in glory. Seduced by the devil, he wanted to 'be like God,' but 'without God, before God, and not in accordance with God' (St. Maximus the Confessor, *Ambigua*: PG 91, 1156C; cf. Gen 3:5)" (*CCC* 398). When God's gift was rejected, man separated himself from divine life and human nature was deeply wounded (*CCC* 405).

Law and Covenant

Because man's nature was so seriously wounded—though not entirely depraved as the first Protestant Reformers wrongly taught (*CCC* 406)—God worked through stages of divine revelation in order to "communicate himself to man gradually" (*CCC* 53). He gave the Law so mankind knew what to do, yet the Law did not provide the grace needed to fulfill the Law. But it did point to Christ and the Kingdom, although only dimly and incompletely (*CCC* 1963). God established covenants as indications of his love for mankind and as promises of redemption (*CCC* 55). These covenants were sacred oaths that God swore, binding himself with solemn actions and signs to specific groups of people. He covenanted with Noah (*CCC* 56–58) and his family; with Abraham (CCC 59–61) and his tribe; with Moses and his nation; and finally with King David and his kingdom. He also told the prophets of a coming time when he would form a "new and everlasting Covenant intended for all, to be written on their hearts ... a salvation which will include all the nations" (CCC 64).

The Incarnation

Finally, in the fullness of time, God revealed himself through the incarnate Word, "the son of God made man" (*CCC* 65). He desires that men should come to him, the Father, through the Son, "the Word made flesh, in the Holy Spirit, and thus become sharers in the divine nature" (*CCC* 51).[4] There has been no change in the Father's will for man since before creation—the goal is still intimate,

[4] Quoting Vatican Council II, Dogmatic Constitution on Divine Revelation, *Dei verbum*, November 18, 1965, no. 2. Cf. Eph 1:9; 2:18; 2 Pet 1:4.

supernatural union. This is now a reality because of the work of the "New Adam" (*CCC* 411). As the *Catechism* states directly, God the Father "wants to communicate his own divine life to the men he freely created, in order to adopt them as his sons in his only-begotten Son" (*CCC* 52). The *Catechism* emphasizes that the primary reason for the Incarnation is that we might become adopted sons of God. The key text (noted in several previous chapters) is no. 460, which references 2 Peter 1:4 ("partakers of the divine nature") and then gives quotations from Saint Irenaeus, Saint Athanasius, and Saint Thomas Aquinas:

> "For this is why the Word became man, and the Son of God became the Son of man: so that man, by entering into communion with the Word and thus receiving divine sonship, might become a son of God" (*Adv. haeres.* 3, 19, 1: PG 7/1, 939). "For the Son of God became man so that we might become God" (*De inc.*, 54, 3: PG 25, 192B). "The only-begotten Son of God, wanting to make us sharers in his divinity, assumed our nature, so that he, made man, might make men gods" (*Opusc.* 57: 1–4). (*CCC* 460)

This is the classic language of the *admirabile commercium*, describing God's gracious "exchange" of his divinity for our humanity, so that our humanity can be, by grace, divinized.

Resurrection and Justification

Through the Paschal mystery, divine life is offered to humanity in a manner both unfathomable and deeply intimate. Christ's death first frees mankind from sin and then "his Resurrection ... opens for us the way to a new life" (*CCC* 654). Here the *Catechism* focuses on the controversial and disputed term "justification". While the first Protestant fathers (Luther and Calvin especially) understood justification primarily as a juridical term used in a sort of cosmic courtroom, Catholic doctrine (both at Trent and later) consistently refers to God as Creator and lover of mankind, the maker and giver of life. Certainly justice is demanded, but not merely because God is a judge whose wrath must be satisfied, but because he is also a righteous and holy Father (*CCC* 62) whose divine life cannot be freely shared with those who selfishly seek their own life. All self-seeking rejection of the Father's divine life and love severs one's relationship with God, which means a mediator is required to close the chasm between God and man. The incarnate Son provides the mediation and, consequently, opens the way to supernatural life and justification. "This new life is above all justification that reinstates us in God's grace, 'so that as Christ was raised from the dead by the glory of the Father, we too might walk in newness of life' (Rom 6:4; cf. 4:25)" (*CCC* 654).

The *Catechism*'s description of justification is closely and deeply aligned with many essential aspects of theosis. Justification is "a new participation in grace. It brings about filial adoption so that men become Christ's brethren" (*CCC* 654). This is the heart of the gospel: while the Son has intimate communion and union with the Father by his nature, man may now possess that relationship through grace. This means that our "adoptive filiation gains us a *real share* in the life of the only Son", a truth "fully revealed in the Resurrection" (*CCC* 654; emphasis added; also see *CCC* 1972).

The Holy Spirit, Giver of Grace

The Holy Spirit is the spark and fire of faith and is the active, personal reason we can approach God as Father (*CCC* 683). The third Person of the Trinity is intimately associated with justification, sanctification, and grace. His grace justifies us and puts us in right standing *with* the Father *through* the Son (*CCC* 1987). Through the Holy Spirit we participate in Christ's Resurrection and are "born to a new life" (*CCC* 1988). He is the vehicle of the Father's divine nature and life. This is why Saint Athanasius states that "those in whom the Spirit dwells are divinized (*Ep. Serap.* 1.24: PG 26, 585 and 588)" (*CCC* 1988). In short, justification entails divinization, including sanctification (*CCC* 1989), detachment from sin (*CCC* 1990), the infusion of supernatural virtues (*CCC* 1991), and conformity to God's own righteousness (*CCC* 1992). It also restores the balance, lost in Eden, between God's grace and man's free will (*CCC* 1993). Man's justification comes from the love of God that is demonstrated by Christ Jesus and given by the Holy Spirit; it is a trinitarian invitation (cf. *CCC* 1994).

Being a child of God involves growing in holiness and perfection. The Holy Spirit is at the center of this work of sanctification (*CCC* 1995). Grace is the loving help the Father gives so that man might accept "his call to become children of God, adoptive sons, partakers of the divine nature and eternal life" (*CCC* 1996). But grace is not merely external favor or merciful aid—it is "a *participation in the life of God*" (*CCC* 1997; emphasis in original). Grace brings us *to* the family and *makes* us family; the *Catechism* states boldly, "It introduces us into the intimacy of Trinitarian life" (*CCC* 1997). Sanctifying grace, which heals and cleanses our souls of sin, is also referred to as "*deifying grace*" (*CCC* 1999; emphasis in original).

The Mystery of the Church

The *Catechism*, in no. 1997, summarizes the familial reality of divine life in a couple of wonderful phrases. It teaches that baptism is the entrance—the new birth—into the "grace of Christ, the head of his Body." Our sonship is completely reliant upon the one Sonship of Jesus. And the *Catechism* places the individual squarely within the context of the divine family, stating that the believer "receives the life of the Spirit who breathes charity into him and who forms the Church." A few paragraphs later we read that grace enables us to participate "in the growth of the Body of Christ, the Church" (*CCC* 2003).

Catholic doctrine states that humanity was meant to share in divine life from the start of creation, but then came the Fall. After the sin in the Garden, the Father still purposed to create a holy family of sons and daughters:

> "The eternal Father ... created the whole universe and chose to raise up men to share in his own divine life," to which he calls all men in his Son. "The Father ... determined to call together in a holy Church those who should believe in Christ." (*CCC* 759)[5]

The Church is the culmination of God's salvific actions, the means by which men are to enter into the divine life: "God created the

[5] Quoting Vatican Council II, Dogmatic Constitution on the Church, *Lumen gentium*, November 21, 1964, no. 2.

world for the sake of communion with his divine life, a communion brought about by the 'convocation' of men in Christ, and this 'convocation' is the Church" (*CCC* 760). The Church is simply and truly God's family (*CCC* 1655). In this light, we can rightly understand the actions and life of the Church's members. These include the sacraments, the spiritual life in Christ, and the life of prayer.

Sacraments: Signs of the Family

Each of us enters the world through physical birth, and we are fed physical food so we can grow and mature. In an analogous, yet real and efficacious, manner the sacraments bring us birth, giving us nourishment and pouring God's divine life into us. We enter into the family of God through a new birth, the sacrament of baptism: "Through Baptism we are freed from sin and reborn as sons of God" (*CCC* 1213). It is a birth of both water and Spirit, which places us into God's Kingdom (*CCC* 1215). It infuses sanctifying grace into the believer and makes him "'a new creature,' an adopted son of God, who has become a 'partaker of the divine nature' (2 Cor 5:17; 2 Pet 1:4; cf. Gal 4:5–7)" (*CCC* 1265). It is the means by which we enter the Church and become members of the Body of Christ (*CCC* 1267). Similar to the natural realm, we can only be born into this new life one time, for it leaves an eternal, "indelible spiritual mark (*character*) of [our] belonging to Christ" (*CCC* 1272; emphasis in original).

God provides his family with nourishment and sustenance in various ways, but the most profound means is the Eucharist, "the source and summit of the Christian life" (*CCC* 1324).[6] It is the unifying principle and reality of the family of God, "the sublime cause of that communion in the divine life and that unity of the People of God by which the Church is kept in being" (*CCC* 1325). The Eucharist is a multitude of varied, yet united, elements and realities. It is sacrifice, communion, banquet, and celebration. It is the sacrifice of Christ made really and truly present (*CCC* 1362–67); it is the offering of ourselves, as sons and daughters of God and as members of Christ's Body, to the Father. As members of Christ's Mystical Body, we unite

[6] Quoting *Lumen gentium*, no. 11.

with him and give ourselves as sacrifice and intercession (*CCC* 1368). In the Eucharist we experience unity with one another and "an intimate union with Christ Jesus" (*CCC* 1391).

This intimate union is both the goal of the sacramental life and the source of divine life. Each of the sacraments is oriented in certain and unified ways toward our salvation. The fruitful result of the sacramental life, states the *Catechism*, "is that the Spirit of adoption makes the faithful partakers in the divine nature by uniting them in a living union with the only Son, the Savior" (*CCC* 1129). Sacraments signify what has already happened (Christ's Passion), show what is accomplished now by God's power and life (grace), and foreshadow what awaits the divine children of God—"future glory" (*CCC* 1130, 1323).[7]

Life in Christ

So, through the sacraments we are made " 'children of God' (Jn 1:12; 1 Jn 3:1), 'partakers of the divine nature' (2 Pet 1:4)" (*CCC* 1692) and now "participate in the life of the Risen Lord" (*CCC* 1694). Christ is the center and focus of the Christian's life, the "first and last point of reference" (*CCC* 1698). He is the reason for living; he has given us everything that we have and is making us everything that we will be. Our lives are to be conformed and patterned to his life, the life of a Son. We are divine sons who follow the One Son: "He who believes in Christ becomes a son of God. This filial adoption transforms him by giving him the ability to follow the example of Christ" (*CCC* 1709). Part of this ordering of our new natures to the example of Christ involves the Beatitudes (see Mt 5:3–12; *CCC* 1716). They are central to Christ's teaching, focused on the Kingdom of heaven (*CCC* 1716); they show us the reason for being and living (*CCC* 1719). This supernatural gift of beatitude " 'makes us partakers of the divine nature' (2 Pet 1:4).... With beatitude, man enters into the glory of Christ (cf. Rom 8:18) and into the joy of the Trinitarian life" (*CCC* 1721).

[7] Quoting *STh* III, q. 60, a. 3, and Vatican Council II, Constitution on the Sacred Liturgy, *Sacrosanctum concilium*, December 4, 1963, no. 47.

The foundation of the moral life, the living out of the Christian calling, is found in the theological virtues: faith, hope, and love. The theological virtues "adapt man's faculties for participation in the divine nature" (*CCC* 1812). They are gifts of the Father infused into our souls to enable us to act "as his children" and to merit eternal life (*CCC* 1813). The greatest of these virtues is charity, "the *new commandment*" (*CCC* 1823; emphasis in original); it is in charity that we most fully imitate the Son. If we are guided and animated by charity, we enjoy "the spiritual freedom of the children of God" (*CCC* 1828).

Prayer to the Father

The fourth and final major section of the *Catechism* is focused on prayer. In prayer, the New Covenant finds expression and is actively realized among God's children, for prayer is "a covenant relationship between God and man in Christ" (*CCC* 2564). Covenant is both a sacred oath and a filial bond that brings about communion between God and man. Within the sacred oath and filial bond of the covenant, "prayer is the living relationship of the children of God with their Father ... with his Son Jesus Christ and with the Holy Spirit" (*CCC* 2565).

Jesus reveals the essence of prayer by showing that we are to approach God with "*filial prayer*, which the Father awaits from his children" (*CCC* 2599; emphasis in original). We are to pray in faith, which is a "filial adherence to God beyond what we feel and understand" (*CCC* 2609). The Lord's Prayer is the perfect expression of this filial prayer and provides a "summary of the whole gospel (Tertullian, *De orat.* 1: PL, 1155)" (*CCC* 2761). Jesus gives both the words of this perfect prayer and the Spirit "by whom these words become in us 'spirit and life' (Jn 6:63)" (*CCC* 2766). The first six words of the Lord's Prayer ("Our Father who art in heaven") display the boldness with which we can approach the Father because of the Son's work. Christ has "brought us into the Father's presence" (*CCC* 2777), revealed the Father to us, and given us divine sonship (*CCC* 2780). Our adoration of the Father is rooted in our new standing with him, because "he has caused us to be reborn to his life by *adopting* us as his children in his only Son" (*CCC* 2782; emphasis in original). Thus, our adoption into God's family should bring about continual conversion. Praying to our "Father" should remind us that we "ought to behave as sons of God (St. Cyprian, *De Dom. orat.* 11: PL 4: 526B)" (*CCC* 2784). It should also humble us, making us as "little children" who trust completely in him (*CCC* 2785).

Conclusion

The *Catechism of the Catholic Church*, wrote Pope Saint John Paul II in his Apostolic Constitution *Fidei depositum* (October 11, 1992), "is a statement of the Church's faith and of Catholic doctrine, attested to or illumined by Sacred Scripture, the Apostolic Tradition and the Church's Magisterium. I declare it to be a valid and legitimate instrument for ecclesial communion and a sure norm for teaching the faith." This authoritative and significant text, as we have seen, repeatedly emphasizes the "center", which is "communion in the blessed life of the Most Holy Trinity", in the words of its co-editor, Cardinal Schönborn, as stated in the introductory paragraph of this essay. It is evident immediately, in the opening paragraph, and continues through the entire *Catechism*, woven into passages concerning creation, the Incarnation, the Church, the sacraments, and other key topics, and presented with perspicuous forthrightness in passages such as nos. 257, 460, 759, and 1997, among others. Its pervading presence throughout the *Catechism* indicates just how integral it is to the Christian faith, without which that faith cannot be rightly understood, deeply appreciated, or fully lived.

Readings for Further Study

Catechism of the Catholic Church. 2nd ed. (Washington, D.C.: Libreria Editrice Vaticana—United States Conference of Catholic Bishops, 2000).

Ratzinger, Joseph Cardinal, and Christoph Cardinal Schönborn. *Introduction to the Catechism of the Catholic Church*. San Francisco: Ignatius Press, 1994.

Chapter Fifteen

LITURGY AND DIVINIZATION

David W. Fagerberg

It is an impressive accomplishment in this book to see the theme of divinization laid out across the broad range of Catholic history: Scripture, the Greek and Latin Fathers, Dominicans and Franciscans, Trent, the embryonic Scheeben and Newman, the French schools, two Vatican Councils, and the current *Catechism*. But the place at which most Catholics will encounter divinization—the fact and the idea—will be at the liturgy, and this essay hopes to make explicit the essential connection between them. The one place where the *Catechism* uses the actual word "divinize" is in no. 2670, where it quotes the following question by Gregory Nazianzen: "If the Spirit should not be worshiped, how can he divinize me through Baptism?" The divinization of the faithful originates in the font of baptism and is nourished by feeding on Christ himself at the Eucharist, and that new life is strengthened and restored and protected and organized (confirmation, penance, anointing of the sick, matrimony, and holy orders) by each of the other sacraments. The divinized life is expressed in a liturgy of adoration and sacrifice. I should like here to explore the connection between these two, seeing liturgy as a necessary context for divinization, and divinization as necessary for an adequate definition of liturgy. In conclusion, I offer an image of what divinization would look like in a person incessantly at liturgy—namely, the Virgin Mary.

What Is Liturgy?

When speaking about liturgy, I initially have in mind something larger than simply the liturgical ceremonies of the Church; I have in mind the liturgical identity that is exercised in those ceremonies. It is as if the ceremonial liturgy is but a hint, something we can see, but is actually connected to something much more spectacular. Man and woman were created as liturgical beings—they are cosmic priests. In Alexander Schmemann's words,

> All rational, spiritual and other qualities of man, distinguishing him from other creatures, have their focus and ultimate fulfillment in this capacity to bless God, to know, so to speak, the meaning of the thirst and hunger that constitutes his life. "*Homo sapiens,*" "*homo faber*"... yes, but, first of all, "*homo adorans.*" The first, the basic definition of man is that he is *the priest*. He stands in the center of the world and unifies it in his act of blessing God, of both receiving the world from God and offering it to God—and by filling the world with this Eucharist, he transforms his life, the one that he receives from the world, into life in God, into communion with Him. The world was created as the "matter," the material of one all-embracing Eucharist, and man was created as the priest of this cosmic sacrament.[1]

Adam and Eve were supposed to rule over creation in royal dominion, as they stood under God in cosmic priesthood. They were to receive the world sacramentally, as a gift and a grace, and transform the raw material of this world into a Eucharistic return of thanks. They were to be the tongue of mute creation, with the capacity to give rational expression to irrational matter's glorification of God. As Aidan Kavanagh used to say repeatedly, "Liturgy is doing the world the way the world was meant to be done."

Hierarchy: Broken and Restored

The descending creativity of God bestows being, which, in its turn, gives ascending praise and thanksgiving to its source. This state of affairs was called *hierarchy* by Dionysius, a term he coined as a neologism, and Louis Bouyer imagines it as a "golden ladder" of being.

> Across this continuous chain of creation, in which the triune fellowship of the divine persons has, as it were, extended and propagated

[1] Alexander Schmemann, *For the Life of the World* (Crestwood, N.Y.: St. Vladimir's Seminary Press, 1973), 15 (emphasis in original).

> itself, moves the ebb and flow of the creating *Agape* and of the created *eucharistia*.... Thus this immense choir of which we have spoken, basing ourselves on the Fathers, finally seems like an infinitely generous heart, beating with an unceasing diastole and systole, first diffusing the divine glory in paternal love, then continually gathering it up again to its immutable source in filial love.[2]

But a dissonance has been introduced into this harmony. Lucifer—the morning star, the prince of this tangible world—broke hierarchy and set himself up as a competing center, taking glory unto himself. Pride, said Augustine, is *incurvatus in se*, a self-centered turning-in on oneself, and this is precisely how Satan seeks to draw Adam and Eve into his enmity for God. "But the serpent said to the woman, 'You will not die. For God knows that when you eat of it your eyes will be opened, and you will be like God, knowing good and evil'" (Gen 3:5). Here we have the first mention of divinization in the Bible, in the Book of Genesis, but it is presented as a false divinization, an ersatz divinization, a divinization that would happen outside the liturgical hierarchy. Satan cannot change the truth; he can only tell a lie about it, so he takes the true promise of divinization and bends it until it becomes a temptation. He twists a promise into a doubt, and then into a provocation to sin. It appears, then, that our human nature was made for divinization, but our nature is not Satan's to fulfill. The Fall is thus the forfeiture of our liturgical career. Reaching out to take from the tree of knowledge prematurely was an attempt at self-accomplished divinization, and it produced a fraudulent version. Hereafter, the sons of Adam and daughters of Eve will require a healing before they can be returned to their liturgical rung on the golden ladder.

Pope Emeritus Benedict XVI affirmed this in his description of liturgy, cosmos, and history in *The Spirit of the Liturgy*.

> *Exitus* is first and foremost something thoroughly positive. It is the Creator's free act of creation. It is his positive will that the created order should exist as something good in relation to himself, from which a response of freedom and love can be given back to him.... The *exitus*, or rather God's free act of creation, is indeed ordered

[2] Louis Bouyer, *The Meaning of the Monastic Life* (London: Burns and Oates, 1955), 28–29.

> toward the *reditus*, but that does not now mean the rescinding of a created being, but rather ... the creature, existing in its own right, comes home to itself, and this act is an answer in freedom to God's love. It accepts creation from God as his offer of love, and thus ensues a dialogue of love, that wholly new kind of unity that love alone can create.[3]

However, the Fall is the rupture of this response. It is saying no to the *reditus*. Sin means that "the arch from *exitus* to *reditus* is broken. The return is no longer desired."[4] Therefore, man's worship now requires something new and additional: "If 'sacrifice' in its essence is simply returning to love and therefore divinization, worship now has a new aspect: the healing of wounded freedom, atonement, purification, deliverance from estrangement."[5] The essence of worship remains unchanged, but it must now assume therapeutic dimensions of purification and healing, which are conveyed in liturgical sacrament.

God has taken all this into account. His design for his creatures, man and woman, has always been to raise them up to a divinized state, and even if he has had to adjust his economy to take the Fall into account, he has not reneged on the original promise. This point is well made by Gregory Palamas when he says,

> The world was founded with this in view from the beginning. The heavenly, pre-eternal Counsel of the Father, according to which the angel of the Father's Great Counsel made man (Is 9:6) as a living creature in His own likeness as well as His image, was for this end: to enable man at some time to contain the greatness of God's kingdom, the blessedness of God's inheritance and the perfection of the heavenly Father's blessing.... Even the indescribable divine self-emptying, the theandric way of life, the saving passion, all the sacraments were planned beforehand in God's providence and wisdom for this end, that everyone who is shown to be faithful in the present shall hear the savior say, "Well done, thou good servant."[6]

[3] Joseph Ratzinger, *The Spirit of the Liturgy* (Ignatius Press: San Francisco, 2000), 32–33.

[4] Ibid., 33.

[5] Ibid.

[6] Gregory Palamas, Homily Four, "On the Gospel Passage Describing Christ's Second Coming", in *Saint Gregory Palamas: The Homilies* (Waymart, Pa.: Mount Thabor Publishing, 2009), 28–29.

It is as if before the big bang, God thought to himself, "What sacraments are they going to need?" The end of a watch is to tell time, the end of a knife is to cut, and the end of a human being is to be a liturgist. God has not forgotten this, and everything in the divine economy (Christ's kenosis, his theandric way of life, his saving Passion, the Church and all her sacraments) was planned beforehand for this end. The Father had Christ before his eyes as he shaped Adam from the clay, and the hypostatic God-Man is the prototype for each divinized man-God. We become by grace what Christ is by nature. That is the purpose of sacramental liturgy.

Asceticism

For us, the journey to divinization now lies at the end of a path called asceticism—from *askein*, which means "a training, or discipline, or exercise". Our path to divinization must follow the route of healing the vices and passions until our love is properly ordered. In the Western tradition, these healing steps were identified as purgation, illumination, and union; the Eastern tradition used the vocabulary of Evagrius: *praktike* (discipline), *physike* (natural contemplation), and *theologia* (contemplation of God). Only when the cataracts of sin have been removed (*praktike*) will we be able to see the created world properly as hierophany (*physike*), and finally come to know God himself (*theologia*). At the summit, we no longer contemplate the creature but the Creator, not the handiwork but the Maker, so Evagrius summarizes this final stage by saying, "If you are a theologian you truly pray. If you truly pray you are a theologian."[7] The person schooled by the liturgical life of prayer becomes a theologian, capacitated for a new vision gained from union with God; union with God is divinization; divinization is personal communion with the Father through the Logos and the Holy Spirit. This means that liturgy is theological, in the sense that *theologia* is communion with the Trinity (liturgical theology); and this is why liturgy is ascetical, capacitating a person for this communion (liturgical asceticism). Adam and

[7] Evagrius, *The Pratikos and Chapters on Prayer* (Kalamazoo, Mich.: Cistercian Publications, 1981), 60.

Eve's journey to divinization was interrupted by their disobedience, so it had to be restarted by the New Adam and New Eve, and our resumed journey to divinization can appropriately be called liturgical asceticism, in my opinion.[8]

If liturgy means sharing the life of Christ (being washed in his Resurrection, eating his Body), and if *askesis* means "discipline" (in the sense of forming), then liturgical asceticism is the discipline required to become an icon of Christ and make his image visible in our faces. The early stages of asceticism might seem negative, in the same way that an antidote to a poison might taste unpleasantly medicinal, but the ultimate purpose of liturgical asceticism is something overwhelmingly positive. Divinization stands at its climax. To be divinized is to enter into the life of the Trinity, to be swept up into the energies that flow between the three Persons. To drive this point home, I use this definition of liturgy: it is the Trinity's perichoresis kenotically extended to invite our synergistic ascent into deification. In other words, the Trinity's circulation of love turns itself outward, and in humility the Son and Spirit work the Father's good pleasure for all creation, which is to cause our ascent to participate in the very life of God; however, this cannot be forced—it must be done with our cooperation. In order to be pure, our worship must be purified by God. Christian liturgy must be vitalized by Christ.

Liturgy as Deifying

We must therefore approach liturgy under theological terms. With what other categories could we define liturgy if not theology? Sociology? Ritual studies? Political cadres? How could these categories do justice to the supernatural liturgy, with its sacraments and sacrifice? Christian liturgy, pouring forth from the empty tomb, is the cult of the New Adam, Christ's stance before the Father, into which we are invited by the Holy Spirit. Liturgists therefore take their place before the altar because they are being divinized by the Holy Spirit and initiated as members of the Mystical Body of Christ. We only grasp

[8] Fagerberg, *On Liturgical Asceticism* (Washington, D.C.: Catholic University of America Press, 2013).

the scope and purpose of liturgy if we remain aware of this divinizing power. Liturgy is the life of Christ soaking into the members of the Mystical Body. The liturgist is born from the baptismal font, which moistens his dry, mortal bones for resurrection; he is empowered by the Eucharistic transfusion of Christ's life into his veins, like an intravenous drip, so that the Holy Spirit will animate his hands for the Kingdom's work. Neglect divinization, and both Church and liturgy are wronged: the former is looked upon as a humanly manufactured item, instead of a divine artifact, and the latter is looked upon as a human worship ritual, instead of the perichoresis of the Trinity inviting our ascent into deification.

An instinct to worship is written into the nature of man and woman, and it cannot be erased, because the Fall did not destroy our *imago Dei.*[9] The human race therefore knows numerous cults that belong to natural mankind, and Saint Thomas treats worship within the four natural virtues in the *Summa theologiae*, specifically the virtue of justice, because justice consists of giving another being his due. "Since then it belongs to religion to pay due honor to someone, namely, to God, it is evident that religion is a virtue."[10] Therefore, wherever consciences are well formed, we will not be surprised to find temples and ziggurats, altars and priesthoods, sacrifices and rites. Since these instincts are written into humanity's *imago Dei*, they cannot be extirpated—but they can be raised! Grace perfects nature! The law of worship belongs to our nature, but as Christ fulfilled the law, he also fulfilled the law of worship. This makes liturgy different from worship, in the way that the Church is different from a Jesus club. Thomas makes the point decisively by saying that religion is a moral virtue, and not an infused theological virtue.[11] Religious worship is

[9] However, as we noted above, this instinct to worship can be twisted and operate improperly, and if it does not find the true God, it will create idols to worship. Man can be religious or irreligious; he cannot be nonreligious. He will worship something. The Church Fathers saw Satan's mischief behind this, and that is why they considered pagan idolatry to be the result of the demons' work.

[10] *STh* II–II, q. 81, a. 2.

[11] "Now due worship is paid to God, in so far as certain acts whereby God is worshiped, such as the offering of sacrifices and so forth, are done out of reverence for God. Hence it is evident that God is related to religion not as matter or object, but as end: and consequently religion is not a theological virtue whose object is the last end, but a moral virtue which is properly about things referred to the end" (ibid., a. 5).

a moral duty, but liturgical sacrifice is faith, hope, and charity fructified. Religion brings one *before* God, but liturgy brings one *into* God, into the perichoresis. The liturgy of the Church is the activity of the divinized. The Christian liturgy is the cult of the New Adam, and in order to participate in this liturgy, the New Adam must dwell in the worshipper, which is why only the baptized participate in the Eucharistic sacrifice (and at one point in the Church's history, the unbaptized left the building before the Eucharist began).

Even the prelapsarian worship of Adam and Eve was not on par with liturgy—another way to understand *O Felix Culpa* at the Easter Exsultet. Created in the image of God, man is called to grow into the likeness of God. The "image of God" refers to this potential—that is, free will, reason, our sense of moral responsibility, everything that marks us out from the animal creation and makes us a person. The "likeness of God" refers to actualizing that potential—that is, being conformed to God. The orthodox theologian Vladimir Lossky writes, "After the Fall, human history is a long shipwreck awaiting rescue: but the port of salvation is not the goal; it is the possibility for the shipwrecked to resume his journey whose sole goal is union with God."[12] Our growth from image into likeness is liturgical asceticism at work, and it does not bring us back to the state of humanity before the Fall; it brings us further up and further into a divinized state. The saint is divinized portraiture, an icon of the image of God, a reflection of Christ, which makes the least member born by the Spirit in the Kingdom of grace greater than John, of whom no one born of woman in the kingdom of nature was greater. The liturgical stature given to Adam and Eve in the old creation is as nothing compared to the liturgical stature of the baptized liturgist who stands in the new aeon.

Mary, Liturgical Person

This eschatological aeon is established by the work of Christ alone, but as regards its effects upon humanity, we have a witness: the

[12] Vladimir Lossky, *Orthodox Theology, An Introduction* (New York: St. Vladimir's Seminary Press, 1978), 84.

Virgin Mary. Benedict XVI said that sin is saying no to the *reditus*—that is, no longer desiring the return. Yet, Mary did just the opposite when she offered her *fiat* to God. Mary said yes wholeheartedly to the *reditus*, and an untainted appetite was preserved in the New Eve, unspoiled by the fruit that the first Eve had eaten. Mary is the first—she is prototype; she is Mother: *Mater Christi* and *Mater Ecclesia*. Salvation is Christ's accomplishment, but had it not been communicated to another person, what good would it have been? Mary is witness that divinization is no longer out of reach. Christ is a divine hypostasis incarnated; Mary is a human hypostasis divinized.

> "To have by grace what God has by nature": that is the supreme vocation of created beings. . . . This destiny is already reached in the divine person of Christ, the Head of the Church, risen and ascended. If the Mother of God could truly realize, in her human and created person, the sanctity which corresponds to her unique role, then she cannot have failed to attain here below by grace all that her Son had by his divine nature. But, if it be so, then the destiny of the Church and the world has already been reached, not only in the uncreated person of the Son of God but also in the created person of his Mother. That is why St Gregory Palamas calls the Mother of God "the boundary between the created and the uncreated". Beside the incarnate divine hypostasis there is a deified human hypostasis.[13]

Jean Corbon says, "The Virgin Mary is the Church as it dawns in a single person."[14] We adopt Mary's posture in the Church's liturgy, as Paul VI has said in *Marialis cultis*. Mary is the "model of the spiritual attitude with which the Church celebrates and lives the divine mysteries."[15] First, Mary is the *attentive Virgin*, who receives the Word of God with faith; "the Church also acts in this way, especially in the liturgy, when with faith she listens, accepts, proclaims and venerates the word of God".[16] Second, Mary is the *Virgin in prayer*; "the title . . . also fits the Church, which day by day presents to the Father the needs of her children".[17] Third, Mary is the *Virgin Mother*; "the Church

[13] Vladimir Lossky, "Panagia", in *The Mother of God: A Symposium*, ed. E. L. Mascall (London: Dacre Press, 1959), 34.

[14] Jean Corbon, *The Wellspring of Worship* (New York: Paulist Press, 1988), 173.

[15] Paul VI, Apostolic Exhortation *Marialis cultis*, February 2, 1974, no. 16.

[16] Ibid., no. 17.

[17] Ibid., no. 18.

prolongs in the sacrament of Baptism the virginal motherhood of Mary."[18] Fourth, Mary is the *Virgin presenting offerings*—of her Son in the Temple, and of her Son on the Cross; "this the Church does in union with the saints in heaven and in particular with the Blessed Virgin, whose burning charity and unshakeable faith she imitates."[19]

Divine grace and the human race kiss in a liturgical embrace cultivated by the people of Israel and personified in the Virgin Mary. This Daughter of Zion's *fiat* is our highest liturgical moment. She is our race's response to the Trinity's kenosis extending itself to invite us into the synergistic ascent into deification. Mary is the prototype of liturgical person, for the true end of liturgy is to arrive where Mary did. She gave birth to Christ in body; we must give birth to Christ spiritually, which, Olivier Clement reminds us, is just another expression for union with God—that is, divinization: "The Word is continually being born in the stable of our heart.... To ensure this birth of Christ in us is the true function of liturgical times and seasons, interpreted inwardly by ascesis, prayer and contemplation."[20]

Readings for Further Study

Evagrius. *The Pratikos and Chapters on Prayer.* Kalamazoo, Mich.: Cistercian Publications, 1981.

Fagerberg, David W. *On Liturgical Asceticism.* Washington, D.C.: Catholic University of America Press, 2013.

Ratzinger, Joseph. *The Spirit of the Liturgy.* Ignatius Press: San Francisco, 2000.

Schmemann, Alexander. *For the Life of the World.* Crestwood, N.Y.: St. Vladimir's Seminary Press, 1973.

[18] Ibid., no. 19.

[19] Ibid., no. 20.

[20] Olivier Clement, *The Roots of Christian Mysticism* (New York: New York City Press, 1996), 251.

CONTRIBUTORS

Chris Burgwald has been the director of Adult Discipleship and Evangelization for the Diocese of Sioux Falls in South Dakota since 2002. He holds both a licentiate and a doctorate in sacred theology from the Pontifical University of Saint Thomas Aquinas in Rome. He and his wife have five children.

Adam G. Cooper is a senior lecturer at the John Paul II Institute for Marriage and Family, Melbourne, Australia. His research interests are in Greek patristics and the theology of the body. His books include *The Body in St. Maximus the Confessor: Holy Flesh, Wholly Deified* (Oxford University Press, 2005), *Life in the Flesh: An Anti-Gnostic Spiritual Philosophy* (Oxford University Press, 2008), and *Naturally Human, Supernaturally God: Deification in Pre-Conciliar Catholicism* (Fortess, 2014).

David W. Fagerberg is Professor in the Department of Theology at the University of Notre Dame where he teaches liturgical theology. He is the author of *Theologia Prima* (Hillenbrand Books, LTP, 1992) and *On Liturgical Asceticism* (Catholic University Press, 2013).

Andrew Hofer, O.P. (Ph.D., University of Notre Dame) is Assistant Professor on the Pontifical Faculty of the Immaculate Conception and Master of Students at the Dominican House of Studies in Washington, D.C. He has authored *Christ in the Life and Teaching of Gregory of Nazianzus* (Oxford University Press, 2013) and articles in such journals as *Augustinianum, Vigiliae Christianae, International Journal of Systematic Theology, Pro Ecclesia, Nova et Vetera, Angelicum*, and *The Thomist.*

Daniel A. Keating (D.Phil., Oxford University) is professor of theology at Sacred Heart Major Seminary in Detroit, Michigan, where he teaches on Scripture, theology, the Church Fathers, and ecumenism and evangelization. He is the author of *The Appropriation of Divine Life in Cyril of Alexandria* (Oxford University Press, 2004); *Deification and Grace* (Sapientia Press, 2007); and *First and Second Peter, Jude* (Baker Academic, 2011).

Timothy Kelly is a native of Great Britain and is currently director of the master's program in Sacred Theology and professor of dogmatic theology at the International Theological Institute, Vienna, Austria. Timothy completed his doctoral studies at the University of Fribourg, Switzerland, undertaking research on the union of Christ and the Church as "one flesh". He also holds undergraduate and graduate degrees in English literature, history of art, and Romantic literature. He is married with five children.

Daniel J. Lattier (Ph.D. in systematic theology from Duquesne University) is the Vice President of International Takeout. He has published articles in *Pro Ecclesia*, *Fides Quaerens Intellectum*, and the *Newman Studies Journal*.

Michon M. Matthiesen, S.T.L., Ph.D. is a systematic theologian who teaches theology and the development of Western civilization at University of Mary. Her scholarly interests include Eucharistic theology, Christian spirituality, and the history of theology from 1900 to the Second Vatican Council. Her work on Maurice de la Taille, S.J., was published last year: *Sacrifice as Gift: Eucharist, Grace, and Contemplation in Maurice de Taille* (Catholic University of America Press, 2012).

David Vincent Meconi, S.J. is a professor of theology at Saint Louis University and the editor of *Homiletic and Pastoral Review*. He holds the pontifical license in patristics from the University of Innsbruck in Austria as well as the D.Phil. in ecclesiastical history from Oxford. He is the author of *The One Christ: St. Augustine's Theology of Deification* (Catholic University of America Press, 2013), the editor of the Ignatius Critical Edition of Saint Augustine's *Confessions* (Ignatius Press, 2012), as well as the coeditor of the *Cambridge Companion to Augustine* (Cambridge University Press, 2014).

Carl E. Olson is the editor of *Catholic World Report* and Ignatius Insight.com. He is the best-selling author of *Will Catholics Be "Left Behind"?: A Catholic Critique of the Rapture and Today's Prophecy Preachers* (Ignatius Press, 2003) and coauthor, with Sandra Miesel, of *The Da Vinci Hoax: Exposing the Errors in the* Da Vinci Code (Ignatius Press, 2004). He has written hundreds of articles, columns, and reviews for numerous periodicals and newspapers. He holds a master's in theological studies from the University of Dallas.

Jared Ortiz is assistant professor of religion at Hope College in Holland, Michigan. He earned his doctorate in theology from the Catholic University of America. He is author of *You Made It for Yourself: Creation in St. Augustine's Confessions* (Fortress, 2016). He also contributed an essay on creation to the Ignatius Critical Edition of Saint Augustine's *Confessions* (Ignatius Press, 2012).

Tracey Rowland is the dean of the John Paul II Institute for Marriage and Family, Melbourne, adjunct professor of the Centre for Faith, Ethics and Society of the University of Notre Dame, Sydney, and honorary fellow of Campion Liberal Arts College, Sydney, Australia. She is also a member of the International Theological Commission.

John Saward is a priest of the Archdiocese of Birmingham, England, fellow of Blackfriars Hall in the University of Oxford, and priest-in-charge of SS. Gregory and Augustine Church, Oxford. He is the author of eight books, several of them published by Ignatius Press. His most recent work is an anthology of English Catholic writing, which he edited with John Morrill and Michael Tomko: *Firmly I Believe and Truly: The Spiritual Tradition of Catholic England* (Oxford University Press, 2011).

Sister M. Regina van den Berg is a member of the Sisters of Saint Francis of the Martyr Saint George, living presently in Rome, Italy. She made her perpetual profession of vows in the year 2000, and in the same year obtained her Ph.D. in philosophy from The Catholic University of America. Since that time, she has served in various apostolates of her community.

INDEX